Nothing's Worst Than a Clown Gone Bad

By: Ponk Vonsydow

Copyright © Ponk Vonsydow 2010

Ponk Vonsydow asserts the moral right to be identified as the author of this work.

This is a work of fiction. The names, characters, and incidents portrayed are based solely on the author's imagination.

All rights reserved. No part of this publication may be reproduced, stored in a retrieval system, or transmitted in any form or by any means, electronic, mechanical, photocopied, recorded or otherwise, without the prior permission of the author.

Cover art courtesy of Ponk Vonsydow, © 2010.

Dedication

For R.K. Sloane

Table of Contents

Title Page
Copyright
Dedication
Chapter 1 An Orphan and a Filth Merchant
Chapter 2 And With a Wonkle Wonkle
Chapter 3 A Puddle of Poobla
Chapter 4 It's Damn Fun
Chapter 5 Extinction of the Human Species
Chapter 6 The Silent Minority
Chapter 7 From Sally to Soap
Chapter 8 Clown Reformation
Chapter 9 Elvis is Thy Neighbor
Chapter 10 World Circus Chronicles
Chapter 11 Four Eyeballs and Three Miguels
Chapter 12 Oh No, It's the Weirdoes!
Chapter 13 Clownboys and Indians
Chapter 14 Roach Thoughts
Chapter 15 Draconian Mindwarp
Chapter 16 Down on the Funny Farm
Chapter 17 Suzie Floosies
Chapter 18 Ruminations on Like Everything
Chapter 19 Boogus Maximus
Chapter 20 Death on the Double
Chapter 21 Suicide Birthday Cake
Chapter 22 Ding-A-Ling Supreme
Chapter 23 Patooty and Petunias
Chapter 24 Where's My Dentist
Chapter 25 Pizza, Pizza
Chapter 26 Carnival Despair
Chapter 27 What's the Haps?
Chapter 28 Blinko Eats KahKah
Chapter 29 Coincidences
Chapter 30 Sicko Messiah

Chapter 1
An Orphan and a Filth Merchant

The quacktitioner held up the squirming new-born clown for inspection. Quickly, a plump candy-striper swatted the clown child on the patooty with the seal of approval, leaving a red ink mark there stating just that.

"Grade-A folks!" said the quack, handing the infant to its mother, who eagerly reached for the fruit of her labor.

"What kind is it?" The proud father beamed as he fumbled with the swaddling clothes. He found a wee-wee-willy-wonker and grew even more excited knowing then that his wife had given him a son. They stood and felt all goo-goo-ga-ga. That is also what the baby clown was saying, "GOO-GOO-GA-GA," over and over as it drooled.

It was obvious that the infant had his father's ears…big, round, twin cauliflower, rubber flappies…the kind of ears that strike fear in the hearts of monkeys. His parents could just make out the triangular birthmarks above his arching eye-brows. He also had his father's feet. Why, they must have been half a foot long, with the second toe longer than the big toe. The baby already had one of its big toes in his mouth as most new-born clowns will do. The child's skin was clown white with just a shade of pink on its cheeks and he had taken after his mother in the nose department. He had a crimson red bulb, which she gave a gentle squeeze to see if the child had been blessed with a honker or a squeeker. "HONK"

This baby was truly a sight to behold, which they did as one, this small group of clowns in the Buffoonville General Hospital.

"So…" said the quack, "whutcha gonna name 'em?"

The father of the boy *turnt* red in the face…bashful like...did a nervous dance.

"Shucks, I kinda wanna name 'em afta muhself."

"Well, then, Blinko, Jr. it tiz" replied the quack.

"Blinko, Jr.!" exclaimed Honey, his mother, as she burst into the traditional fit of laughter. Everyone joined in on the joke as the child was taken down to the infant clown nursery. There Blinko, Jr. was placed into the capable hands of another plump candy-striper. There he would be washed and dried and fed a healthy meal of pancake syrup, then laid to sleep in a crib among a dozen or so new-borns from that week's crop. It was much like a farm too, for *Lord knows dem clowns shore love to make whoopie and all clowns know that be how dem babies be made.*

Now, if Jr. had been old enough to focus his eyes, he would have seen his father mashing his honker against the glass that was the nursery observation window. He would also have seen a fat and rather raggedly looking clown standing next to his old man. He would have noticed the dry and cracked lips, the cankers and sores, the pimples and boils, the bruised bags beneath the jaundiced eyes, the freaky green hair and the soiled ball cap. This was Sicko the Clown. Sicko was Blinko's next door neighbor, and was at the hospital due to the birth of his own son, only his was a MIME!

"Oh, boy, oh, boy! I'ma Daaaady!" Blinko was practically jumping out of his oversize pantaloons.

"Why don't you shut your mouth!" barked Sicko, in a fit of jealous rage. Words like these do not fall easily from mouths of clowns.

"Why can't I ever have a clown? Three mimes, that's what I get!" thought Sicko.

"Hey, Sicko…. whuts the madda?"

"I thought I told you to shut-up! What's the problem…don't you understand *Foolish?*"

"C'mon, Sicko, try to lighten up. Wheez childhood friends afta all. You gotta know I feel bad for you."

Sicko got into Blinkos' face. "Yeah and I suppose next you're gonna tell me you know how I feel…that you understand!!"

Blinko took a step back and wiped some spit off his face.

"But I do, Sicko, honest I do." Blinko was trying against all hope, after all it's natural for a clown to try and be sympathetic. Sicko did something Blinko had never seen a clown do in all his life; he exploded in anger.

"YOU DON'T UNDERSTAND! And if you don't leave me alone, I'm gonna get serious!" Sicko opened his coat to reveal a shiny black tail-feather.

Blinko's face went a shade whiter than normal clown-white.

"Now, hold on there, Sicko…no need for that …as a matter-of-fact I was just about to book!" Blinko's huge booted feet were already running, and then he was gone.

Sicko stood grinning as he watched Blinko high-tail it out the door. He was proud of himself over what a good job he had done frightening the stupid clown half to death. Turning once more to face the curse, the tiny mime baby in its crib, he began to think.

"After all I been through, ain't no kid of mine gonna be no mime!"

Quietly then, he snuck his way into the nursery where his silent child lay. He came up behind the candy-striper that was filling up the baby bottles. She did not notice because she was particularly stupid and it took all of her brains to manage the task at hand. Behind her, Sicko removed the black tail-feather he had purchased for 250 smack-a-rues down in the lower east-side of Buffoonville. This particular model was as lethal as it was illegal, seeing as to how it had been plucked rudely from the arse of the rare Umbrella Bird, a fowl found only in a remote section of South American rain forest.

Anyway, Sicko pounced…gagged the candy-striper with a gloved hand…squeezed her butt for fun…and listened to her giggle despite of herself for the feather was on her neck. Sicko was a master of the art of tickling. He had been trained in this most deadly martial art prior to his four tours of duty in the Great War of Morons over in Nam. But he was home ten years now. He had been diagnosed with a host of fancy sounding disorders but that was all a bunch of bozokahkah. Sicko had merely gone bad, simple and plain and for a clown, that's the worst kinda disorder there be. That, and the fact his no good wife had cursed him with not one…not two…but three mimes for cripes sake. It was more than he could take. He'd snapped, which was why in less than thirty seconds, the candy-striper was in a heap at his feet having been tickled to death. Sicko's technique was so efficient that nobody even heard her laugh.

The tiny mime looked up at the ceiling while suckling its imaginary baby bottle. A smile came across its little mime-face as the odd collection of colors and shapes that was its father's noggin came within its unfocused field of vision.

Sicko stood staring down onto the face of the curse. He was filled with feelings of disgust and rage. He had reverted back to the state of mind he had *learnt on dem killing fields*. He recounted briefly the death of his other two mimes and that of their mother, all of whom he had killed with the feather that same morning. It had all taken place in less than an hour and had given him a profound sense of relief. Now, only this one fresh mime stood in the way of his new life. There the curse lay before him... innocent of everything but its father's contempt.

Sicko stuck his hand deep into the pocket of his pantaloons and then produced nothing more than his gloved hand. His thumb was cocked back pointed towards the ceiling, index finger straight out above the other two curled inwards…the proverbial imaginary gun. This was a weapon harmless to clowns…but to MIMES…placing the barrel of the pretentious gun to the forehead of the silent child, Sicko clenched his rancid, rotting teeth, then quickly tapped the knuckle of his index finger with his thumb….

"BANG!!" he said "YOU'RE DEAD!!" That's all there was to it.

Jealousy is one of the most basic forms of evil. Sicko, of course was full of that particular brand. That's how the new-born Blinko, Jr. virtually came to be an orphan on the very day he was born. Just after killing his own, Sicko had almost decided to kill Blinko, Jr. as well but…NO! In his warped rationalizations, it was freakers like his neighbors, hoggin' up all the normal kinderclowns, that oughta be punished. Never mind the fact that Blinko, Jr. was the Cakes family's first child! That's paranoia for ya. Anyway, he easily found both the baby hoggers in the mom's assigned hospital room and before there was even half a hootenanny, he had fixed them both with the feather. Of course, in due time, all the bodies would be discovered and a routine investigation would be begun with Sicko as the suspect, but he didn't give a crap because he had an angle. Sicko had gotten serious and that meant he was essentially a singular genius in a world of clowns. Escape was the easiest part. He just walked out onto the streets, due east.

"I need some tutti-fruity and a candy cigarette."

*&%$#@

Patty Cakes, Blinko, Jr.'s grandma, was looking out her kitchen window next door at the dilapidated home of Sicko the Clown. The playground in front was swarming with Keystones in their bright blue coats…double rows of brass buttons down the front. The Keystones' jalopy was parked on the curb next to a fire hydrant which had been knocked off its main in one of their many attempts to park. A geyser of water was spewing into the air and making a huge muddy mess of things. Two Keystones were attempting to plug the main. One actually tried to sit on it causing him to become suspended in the air…riding the surge like a brahma bull. Not surprisingly, the 'Stoner landed on top of his partner once the water bull threw him. The smitten one retaliated by hitting the rider over the head with his billy club. This proved ineffective for as the clown was brought down by the force of the blow, his giant feet were kicked high and mighty into the other's testicles.

OUCH!

"Dear, dear, I wonder whut's gone down over at the Sicko's?"

Grandma Patty Cakes grabbed her cane and left the family home to console Granny Sicko who was standing on the porch wearing a sad face. She was forced to navigate her way past several fast moving rivers created by the busted main but eventually made it over okay to take poor Granny Sicko into her arms. However, due to a complete miscalculation of momentum, the aging clownettes bounced off one another and wound up butt down in the muck. Both sat up totally unphased by the accident, for this type of nonsense is normal for the average clown. Both being from the elder generation, they spoke in *Foolish* rhyme:

"Granny Sicko! You poor dear! Whut is goin' on 'round here?"
"Poor, poor pitiful me, Sicko's gone and killed all three!"
"Killed all three of your sweet mimes? Are you sure he did the crimes?"
"It's true, it's true, whut shall I do? For Sicko's kilt their Mama too!"
"You mean to say your son's gone bad?"
"HE HAS, HE HAS, HE HAS, HE HAS!"
"But Cakes, it breaks my heart to say, he killed three others on this day.
A candy-striper on the ward, who watched over our third new-born
And tickled pink your poor son's wife and then took your son, Blinko's life."
"Say it ain't so, how can this be, Oh, agony! Oh, agony!
My heart! My heart! I think I'm croaking! Dizzy, Dizzy, say your joking!"
"I wish I were, tis true when said, there's nothing worse than a clown gone bad!"

?&*°%$#

"Well, who ever did this sure knew what he was doing" said the quacktitioner gesturing towards the two motionless bodies. "As you can see, fellow humorists, they are in a type of catatonic state. Notice the lack of muscular response."
The quack poked them all over with a giant hat pin. Next, he lifted the woman's eyelids and began swinging a silver wristwatch on its chain in front of her eyeballs.
"Her gaze is completely fixed, any normal clown could not resist following this watch as we all know, right?"
No one answered. This was because the two detectives, being normal clowns themselves, had failed to resist watching the watch and as one might suspect they had both become hypnotized. This forced the slightly annoyed quack to go through the typical de-hypnotizing routine and then repeat what had been said all over again only this time skipping the pocket watch routine.
"But the most important indicator of their condition is the color of their skin. Notice the bright pink discoloration over their entire bodies. Only a master of the feathered arts could tickle two clowns pink!"
"E-GADS!" e-gadded one of the detectives. "Is there a cure?"
"I'ma 'fraid not. These two will stay like this and wither away into skeletons, urinating and soiling themselves, laying upon their bed sores like slabs of oyster, with an array of tubes and catheters and breathing machines and so on and so forth until ultimately DEATH comes for them which we can only hope is sooner than later…a fate worse than death in my opinion!"
Being sensitive as any other set of clowns, the two detectives were now crying. The situation was truly sad. One managed a question between sobs.
"What about the poor little boy? Is he okay?"
The quack led them out of the examination room and shut the door behind him.
"You mean besides the fact that he's an orphan? Well, he's physically fine."
One of the detectives cut in.

"Doc, I gotta tell ya, that kids luck ain't worth two rue. He's got a grandma but she's so old it's doubtful that she'll last another week especially now that her only son and his wife are in such a pitiful state. Think you can hold on to him 'til we sort this mess out?"

"He's too young to leave anyway." The quacks beeper went off.

"Well, folks gotta haul patooty" he said, looking at its face. The two detectives watched him turn and walk off down the hall. Then the detectives themselves turned to head out the other direction.

After being hopelessly lost for thirty minutes trying to leave the hospital, they finally made it outside only to hunt for their squad-jalopy for another half-hour. They paused beside it to rest.

"Say, Hoppy."

"Yeah, Smiley?"

"All this stuff is bumming me out, clown. Whut say we head over to Yuckys' Greasy Spoon for some jelly-beans and chocolate milk?"

"You read my mind, pal!"

And with that the two idiots were off on another classic demonstration of their total lack of navigational skill.

%&$@#?

The Keystone's chances of tracking down Sicko the Clown were close to zero. The fact that there were over 200 'Stoners in the field searching for him made their chances even less. Their chances were diminished further due to the fact that most clowns fit the description of funny clothes, big shoes, big red nose, big bright colored hair, etc.

Keystones are notoriously ill suited for their jobs. Nothing personal mind you, it's just that the nature of their being dictates their problems with logical thinking, rational decision making, and concentrating on the matter at hand. After all each and every one of them was a stupid clown.

Using detectives Hoppy and Smiley as examples, one could prove this important fact about Keystones. Presently, the two where busy spearheading the investigation and clown-hunt by relaxing and sharing a few chuckles at Yuckys' Greasy Spoon. Coincidentally, in the booth next to them, was Sicko, the clown gone bad they was all 'sposed to be looking for.

Sicko, upon finishing his candied apple, quietly got up and left without leaving a tip. In fact, he also left without paying. This caused Yucky to come over to the detectives' table to complain that he just couldn't believe that some clown could get away with walking out on a bill right in front of a couple of Buffoonvilles' finest. Of course, the detectives response to all this was a typical "Hey, I didn't see nothin'…did you see somethin'…nah, I didn't see nothin'...me either" type deal. Then, they just sat there looking at Yucky with those stupid grins and dreamy eyes.

"Aren't you two clowns gonna do something?" asked Yucky.

"Like whut?" pondered Hoppy.

"For cripes sake! Like howza 'bout askin' me to describe the clown and then you can notify the beat 'Stoners to haul fools in to face the music!"

Hoppy and Smiley were shocked. They gave each other puzzled looks then focused their attentions back on the cook.

"Jeez, Yucky," said Hoppy. "You ever thought of going into law enforcement?"

"Yeah." added Smiley. "We could use a thinker like you."

Both were being serious for a change.

Duly the detectives took a description of the clown who had walked out of Yucky's, who of course was Sicko. They came back the next day with the artist's sketch of the wanted clown and even after tacking it along side a wanted poster with an artist's sketch of Sicko, identical to the new one, they still failed to make the obvious connection. One would expect nothing less from a couple of 'Stoners.

Two weeks later, the detectives arrested a clown who fit the description of the "walk-out". They questioned him as he was seated in a chair directly under the artist's sketch, which he supposedly resembled. That poster was along side a Sicko poster as well. The poor clown. He didn't look anything like the clowns on the posters, but of course Hoppy and Smiley didn't make that connection either. The innocent clown swore up and down that they had the wrong fool but it did him no good and he faced the music anyway. And with that, the terrible injustice was done as the patsy sat strapped into the chair cringing in front of a record player blasting bagpipe music. YIKES!

$#%@&*

Sicko, who had gone bad completely, was beginning to like it that way. He had been on the lam for several weeks and was doing what he usually did which was to hide out from the law in broad daylight. Hiding out in broad daylight was a trick he had picked up over in Nam. In fact, he took great delight teasing the 'Stoners by running up to them and saying "Nanny-nanny-Boo-Boo-I'm Sicko", typical clown kahkah which was sure to get the Keystones to crack-up with him thinking *surely the real Sicko wouldn't be standing there on the street announcing his presence to the world."* Besides most had forgotten they were supposed to be looking for him anyway. All this was why most bad clowns got away with murder. Your chances of getting arrested as an innocent bystander were usually better than being busted as a criminal. For these reasons, the underworld of happy Buffoonville thrived down on the lower east-side of town.

Sicko was anxious to get serious. He had been ticklish all morning. All he had to do was find a candy peddler who would take him seriously. It was a little on the laughable side today he thought…not too many jokers around to score a confection. You could usually tell which clowns were serious from the others because the serious ones didn't go 'round with that retarded grin on their faces. Either that or you could spot them over-reacting and really laughing it up whenever a Keystone came 'round the corner. Clowns in the habit of getting serious usually hung out in public places in small groups. Getting serious wasn't any fun if you did it with clowns who were never serious. Getting serious with yourself was even worse. Anyway, as fate would have it, Sicko finally spotted a small group of what looked like some fairly serious clowns.

He headed their way…they saw him coming…he made no signal…they grew nervous…they began to act a fool. One whipped out the pins…juggled. Another whipped out a unicycle…peddled 'round the group. Two slapped each other in the face… another had the soda bottle soaking passers-by. Still he came. They grew even more nervous…they laughed…they slapsticked…they danced a jig. He was upon them now. He spoke:

"You fools ain't foolin' nobody, not even yourselves! I'm gonna freak out 'iffin I don't hurry up an' get serious! Any of you clowns know where I can cop some lung candy?"

Whammo, an ugly faced clown wearing a party hat, came up into Sicko's own ugly face. Sicko was about a foot shorter. Whammo made an uglier face out of his already ugly face.

"Whose askin', wise aker pumpernickle!" said he.

"Shin-crack-a-booty-ack!" replied Sicko, who was not in the mood for any funny business.

"I likes this clown!" said Whammo to his little gang, the Jokers. Then he clobbered Sicko right in the honker.   HONK!

Being a clown, the only thing such a trifle hurt was Sicko's pride.

"I'm real sorry you did that" said he as he opened up his coat to show them his feather.

"OH, MY GOLLY…he's a Nincompoop!! Back off fools, this clowns BAD!" shouted Whammo.

"I'm bad alright…all the way down to my funny bone which is startin' ta ache. So, I'll ask ya again. Know where I can get me some lung candy?"

Whammo changed his tune right then not so much for the feather but for the sparkle in the clown's eyes, quite unlike the vacant dim witted peepers to be found among the masses.

"Hey, clown, we can all see that you're a pretty determined chap and lordy knows determination is in short supply 'round these here parts. Whut say you put away that feather and take a look at this."

Whammo held out his hand, palm up. In it were two miniature soda bottles filled with a pink fluid. What that fluid WAS…was "Obvious" and Sicko knew it. Sicko immediately reacted.

"Hey, that's Obvious!! Why, I ain't seen that stuff since Nam." Sicko had come up along side Whammo so that they could be as discreet about the Obvious as possible.

"YOU was in Nam? Me as well! Hey, lets boogie off this street. Let's book out to my hide-out and get serious, war hero.

Together the two veterans left the petty gangsters behind and rounded a corner. Whammo intended to drive them to the hide-out. When they got to his jalopy, Sicko was shocked. Before them was a rusted out heap of spare parts and miss matched panels held together with duct tape and bailing wire. The make and model was a Ford Pinto! A miracle in and of itself, for the vehicle was well over two thousand years old and rather large by clown standards…decadent by all means. The Pinto was all the gruesome twosome could talk about as they left a trail of burnt oil all the way to the secret hide-out's location which turned out to be a vacant lot with the exception of an old oak.

"Naww…this is just too perfect, dude… you don't mean...."

Sicko was impressed, as well as under the influence of some sobering confections they smoked on the way over.

"Yup...you won't find a more bodacious tree fort this side of Nam."

Whammo did a peculiar little whistle and shortly a rope saw fit to fall from the recesses of the oak. Sicko was curious about the rope trick.

"Wait 'til you meet my partner, the one that just tossed down the rope. Ya know in this crazy messed up world, he's like the only dude I can totally trust. I met him in Nam as well."

"How come you're so sure, bro?" Sicko didn't trust any freakin'' clown totally.

"'Cause he's a primate! 100% chimpanzee! And wait till you see what ten years of being serious has done to him. Fool's smarter than me!"

Although neither of the clowns were models of health, both easily scaled the knotted rope to gain access to the tree fort. After all, clowns are literally part monkey. They were greeted by Sam Simian, the chimpanzee, who was holding a gnarly cream pie.

"Whoa there, friend. Catch that in the face and you'll be takin' a dirt nap under the Ferris wheel!" said Sicko. Whammo waved Sam off with the sign for 'IT"S COOL'.

Sam signed back with the international sign for 'UP YOURS' and put the pie in its holster, which was a miniature refrigerator. Whammo spoke:

"You're right about that pie, Sicko. I caught one in the noggin in Nam and it durn near dissolved half my brains. Shoot, some say it did." Whammo removed his party hat to reveal a shiny stainless steel plate.

"Ouch! That looks painful." Sicko pretended to care, humoring him as they say. What he really cared about was Obvious. Whammo replied.

"Couldn't say. Hell, back then I was so Obvious that I darn near faced the music." Whammo offered the clown a seat next to Sam Simian. Sicko sat down and was surprised when Sam produced a metal box which, upon being opened, revealed syringes and tourniquets. Not only that, the chimp busted out the syrup and had it cooked up and thinned out to the right viscosity faster that a ten thousand year old Chinese junkie in San Francisco.

"Dude…" said Sicko "I'm impressed." He was commenting on Sam's talented hands.

"Don't tell me. Tell him. Sam here speaks perfect Foolish, don't ya Sam"

"FREAKIN' A." replied the chimp. "Let us cut the small talk and get serious for a while." And that is just what they did.

Two clowns and a chimpanzee sat and commenced to break the fundamental taboos of their clown society with the aid of the Obvious. They also did some nose candy, a powerful powdered confection which, when combined with the effects of the Obvious, produced intense awareness and a hunger for logic. This combination of candies was known as an I.Q. Test.

After finishing their shares of candy, the three of them went into the customary moment of silence as they adjusted themselves to the surge of intelligence forcing its way through the genetic synaptic atrophy of their naturally retarded minds. Purveyors of hard candy would usually break this easy silence with a commentary of their recently advanced capabilities. Saying things like…. "It's all so clear to me now…Why didn't I think of that?…Eureka! I've finally found the solution."

They spoke long of the forbidden…of the many thousands of years that passed when man, not clown, ruled the earth. They discussed the mythology of the Great Clown Reformation and of the fantastic chain of events that led up to it. They openly denounced the ignorant rhetoric of the World Circus and its idiot Pooblas. They formed elaborate theories related to circus conspiracies and its blatant disregard for thought and the individual.

Then the Obvious began to wear off and they found it difficult to pay attention to each other and often forgot what they were talking about. Sam rolled up some lung candy. They smoked. The rush of awareness returned.

Whammo opened a chest and removed some of his secret treasure to show to Sicko. In the chest was various items all banned and illegal or simply taboo. He produced a Dead Kennedy's record, a band banned even in their day two thousand years ago. He brought forth from the box the S- volume of the Encyclopedia Britannica. There were some text books and other educational tools…ancient diplomas from schools…a dictionary of the English language. Lastly, he produced a miniature American flag. Sicko was truly enjoying himself. He felt enlightened surrounded as he was by so many illegal artifacts from a long forgotten age.

Sam Simian then went over to a strange looking box and began to fiddle with some wires coming out from behind it.

"I think you will find this extremely fascinating, Sicko" said he. Sicko couldn't imagine that anything could be more fascinating than listening to that Sam talk.

"A freakin' talking chimpanzee!"

"What is it? What does it do?" he quizzed. Sam answered.

"It's called a television. An electronic device that is able to make moving pictures. But that is only half the story. Neither Whammo nor myself have been able to figure out what the meaning of the pictures is. The pictures themselves are very interesting and do raise many questions, maybe once you have seen them you will have an idea that we have not." Sam got the junky old set to work and inserted a video tape into an equally ancient VCR. Soon the movie began to play and Sicko was puzzled by the opening credits for he knew not how to read English.

"Whut's that say?" said he. Sam took a seat next to him and smoothed the fur on his chest as though he were a stuffy professor dusting off his smoking jacket. "PLANET OF THE APES!"

Anyway that was how the partnership was begun…Sicko, Whammo, and Sam Simian, the original Clown Filth Merchants of Buffoonville.

*&^%$@

By now it had been over a year since Sicko had gone bad and murdered all those people whose names hardly seemed worth remembering now. There was a fortune in smack-a-rues to be made dealing illegal confections and that was really the only thing that Sicko cared about. It was the perfect racket. The Keystones went out of their way to convince clowns they were winning the war on candy, but any clown could tell you that was bozokahkah. One concept that Sicko understood but that the 'Stoners failed to grasp was that you didn't have to be a bad clown to feel like getting serious now and then. Getting serious really had little to do with going bad. Never-the-less the Keystones and the Grand Pooblas of the World Circus condemned the use of all hard candy and this of course allowed the price of the stuff to sky rocket and simultaneously created a black market dealing in a host of illegal goods. Sicko and Whammo had become millionaires keeping the supply up to the demand, and so long as the stuff remained illegal, they would be rolling in rue.

Lung candy, for instance, was a cheap to whip up, smokeable taffy that was not addictive but quite effective in getting one serious, that sold for about forty smacks per portion. The stuff, however, was just too common and easy to make to turn a good profit. The real rue was in nose candy and the Obvious. A clown could get addicted to either of these.

The act of getting serious affects the nervous system of a clown by suppressing its natural tendency towards humor and other clown behavior and to accelerate and amplify the abilities of the user's mind. To do this, the candy attacks the funny bone, located in the right or left elbow of the user. Over time, millions of suppressed laughs, giggles, guffaws, and chuckles build up in the funny bone so that a lack of candy will cause the user to feel ticklish. Depending on the case and level of abuse, the user must get serious to ward off these withdrawal symptoms or else risk having his own funny bone tickle him to death…thus the name for the most potent of all candy; the Obvious. Any clown who has gotten serious enough to become addicted to the Obvious is obviously serious and seriously obvious in his or her addiction.

Both Sicko and Whammo were addicted to the Obvious but neither cared because they had a never ending supply of the stuff, which they kept stashed under the merry-go-round in the play room. Besides being so serious wasn't all that bad once you got used to it. Sicko had a saying…*"There's more to life than going to the circus, ya know!"*

So absorbed was the clown gone bad in his various dastardly deeds that he hardly noticed the events of the world outside his candy cartel. He was reading a paper that was like maybe the third or fourth one he had seen fit to read in the last year. The only reason he even had the newspaper was because he wanted to amuse himself that afternoon by stealing the paper from a six year old newsie and watch him cry.

"Well, I'll be!" he thought at the sight of his mother's name in the obituary. The report stated that she'd gone and died of a broken heart. And what was this? That blind old suzie, Grandma Patty Cakes next door, had up and died on the same day! *"They were best of friends after all."*

The report said she'd died of a heart attack upon finding the corpse of Granny Sicko. In a brief episode of redeeming qualities, Sicko thought of visiting his mother's grave to pay his respects. These thoughts evaporated when he decided it would be an even better idea to rob her grave of the expensive jewelry he knew she'd be wearing in her casket.

"Whammo might be into this!"

He rang. Forty rings later, Whammo answered but declined to go on the grounds that he was so serious that he was afraid to leave the house. Sicko suffered a momentary lapse of his usual indifference as he worried about his partner. Again, he replaced these diseased feelings of kindness with an even better idea.

"I'll kill him and take his half of the racket."

The only problem there would be was Sam Simian. That and replacing a number of Jokers that Whammo carried who Sicko despised. After all, someone had to peddle the sweet stuff on the street and that certainly was no job for him. Besides, he had never learned to ride a unicycle…not that he couldn't if he felt like it. It's just that he had always thought that riding a unicycle like any other clown was beneath his dignity.

Dignity! Sicko was suddenly reminded of the nightmarish years with his wife and those abominations she offered to him as children. A torrent of humiliation coursed its way around the multitude of sinister synapses in Sicko's throbbing tinker. These thoughts sent him into a fit of rage.

The paper crumpled in his hands…he launched it mightily. Being struck by the wad, an inexpensive statuette of unquestionably bad taste struck the floor. It shattered into a million little clownette statuette pieces. Pussycat in hand and with a drop kick sent the squalling feline out the third story window…down to it's next to last life thanks to the clown gone bad. Shouts of anger, the furniture flew. Not a dish survived as the glasses hid themselves in the cabinets. Funhouses are quite indestructible by design in order to counteract the innocent violence of clown beings. This one was having a worse time of it than usual.

Exhausted he lay on the floor mentally calculating how much candy he would need to execute his little plan without getting ticklish. Later, Sicko killed the owner of a west-side hardware store who rudely tried to stop him from stealing the shovel Sicko used to kill him with. Then, he took off in his little one seat jalopy convertible in search of the Buffoonville Eternal Playground. He could not recall its location…lit up a lung candy short...still couldn't recall. He pulled into a service station, knocking down a neatly stacked pyramid of oil cans in the process.

The station's attendant, who was sleeping on the job, was awakened by the calamity of falling cans and screeching tires. He got as upset as any clown would and became very dramatic over the toppled cans which he had spent all afternoon stacking. The attendant went right up to Sicko's jalopy and began to complain, of course.

"Hey, look whutcha dun to muh…" He was cut short by Sicko who had grabbed the poor clown's nose and stretched it as far from the clown's face as its elastic properties would allow. Sicko needed directions.

"Say, weinerhead, know where the cemetery is at?"

"Umpf…umpf..ith juth acroth throm the orthanedge."

Sicko didn't know where the orphanage was either. He mocked the attendant.

"Where ith the orthanedge?"

"Juth make a righth at the lighth." said the attendant pointing at the intersection yonder.

"You ought to do somethin' about that lisp clown" announced Sicko, as he let go of the other's nose. It knocked the attendant off his feet as it recoiled into his face. FWAP!!

*@#$%?

Orphaned by the death of his grandma, his only surviving relative, Blinko, Jr. arrived at the orphanage that very day. Presently the house-mother, Miss Smoochy, was busy feeding the one year old a healthy meal of candied yams, apple sauce and pancake syrup. The orphanage was always full because clowns are extremely accident prone. The infant was essentially oblivious to the fact that his grandma had died and that he would not be leaving there any time soon. He was really making a mess of things, throwing most of what came his way all over the kindly old suzie. Miss Smoochy didn't mind though because she just loved her little babies. She felt sad for him but wasn't really worried because she knew from years of experience that clowns bounce back from tragedy like kick balls shot from cannons. GOO-GOO-GA-GA.

  Miss Smoochy loved kissing. That's how she had come by her nick name. All clowns had one. Back when she was just a youthful clownette, she had earned a reputation among soldiers from the Second War of the Big-Tops. She would stand at the foot of the docks and wait for the war torn sailors to come off the ships and she would kiss every one of them. Once she had even gotten her picture on the cover of Center Ring Magazine kissing a sailor. Incidentally, she and the sailor had a hot and heavy romance after the magazine came out. The two lovers spent hours making whoopi in the back seat of his jalopy where, after pretending to be reluctant, Smoochy would put her famous lips to good uses. That was another reason she was a favorite with the enlisted clowns.

  As all good things come to an end, the sailor left her for another pretty young clownette he had dated before the war. Smoochy never did marry and before she knew it was well past her prime. Her situation wasn't helped by the fact that all the 'free-love' had earned her was a reputation as a bad clownette…a reputation she didn't deserve because she truly did have a heart of gold. No telling what Miss Smoochy would have thought if she knew that right that very moment, the son of her old flame was just across the street commencing to dig up the grave of the clownette who had stolen her sailor clown. Of course, she didn't notice Sicko across the street because she was too busy wiping up all the yams and apple sauce that was all over the place thanks to little bubbly, baby Blinko. She never got mad at her babies. After all it was the never ending supply of orphans that gave her a sense of purpose.

^&%$#@

KUH-SHICK….KUH-PLUNK!
KUH-SHICK….KUH-PLUNK!
KUH-SHICK….KUH-PLUNK!
KUH-SHICK….KUH-PLUNK!
KUH-SHICK….KUH-PLUNK!
  "Just what in tarnation do ya think yer doing there, mister?"
KUH-SHICK….KUH-PLUNK!
KUH-SHICK….KUH-PLUNK!
KUH-SHICK….KUH-PLUNK!
KUH-SHICK….KUH-PLUNK!
KUH-SHICK….KUH-PLUNK!
  "I said just what do ya think yer doing!!"
KUH-SHICK….KUH-PLUNK!
KUH-SHICK….KUH-PLUNK!
  "I heard ya." said Sicko
KUH-SHICK….KUH-PLUNK!
  "Well, whut the Hell are you…"
KUH-SHICK!!
  "Hey, chuckhead…can't you see I'm busy!"
KUH-SHICK….KUH-PLUNK!
KUH-SHICK….KUH-PLUNK!

"Well, that's obvious!"

KUH-SHICK!

"No, it's not, it's a pain in the patooty and so are you, now beat it!"

KUH-SHICK….KUH-PLUNK!

KUH-SHICK….KUH-PLUNK!

"If you don't stop that I'm going to call the Keystones!"

KUH-SHICK….KUH-PLUNK!

Sicko stopped digging.

"You won't be callin' no 'Stoners, that's for gosh darn sure!"

Morty, the undertaker, was a little confused and a lot scared. He stood there all big eyed in his black one-piece, red pom-poms down the front, thinking that the clown with the shovel looked worse than some of his clients. "Why not?" said he.

Sicko leaned on his stolen shovel, pushed his ball cap back with grubby fingers and grinned. "'Cause I'm gonna stop diggin' this here grave."

The mortician seemed relieved. "Well, thank you."

"You're welcome" said Sicko handing the shovel to Morty. "You're gonna dig it for me, see?"

Sicko pulled out a medium sized feather and waved it gently in Morty's face. Morty apparently got the message. He had heard about clowns like this. He went to work.

KUH-SHICK….KUH-PLUNK!

KUH-SHICK….KUH-PLUNK!

Even in fear of his life, Morty took five hours to hit wood. Immediately, Sicko took away the shovel and smacked Morty in the braincase with it knocking him senseless. KER-POW! Jumping into the freshly dug pit, Sicko went to work trying to pry open the casket. Shortly, he changed his tactic deciding it would be a lot easier if he wasn't standing on top of it. Using the shovel as a lever alone just wasn't working out. What he needed was more leverage and for that he needed a fulcrum. He looked around for something handy. *"No rocks…no logs...but there, that would do nicely."*

It was Morty's head. He wondered if he should chop it off or leave it on. He chopped it off with the shovel blade. From there it went smoothly. The seal of the casket broke like a really sour fart. Sicko tried to ignore the vile stench that wafted all up in his honker. Clowns have such sensitive noses. Granny Sicko's mortified body was in the first stages of decomposition. Sicko was unphased by this. Instead, he focused his attention on her jewelry.

First, he went for the thick antique dime store earrings. Old man Sicko had given them to her on a wedding anniversary shortly before he was killed in a bizarre jump rope accident. The plastic Mardi Gras necklace with the wounded goldfish was easy enough to remove. Next, he went for the wedding ring with the engraved plastic Swiss cheese and pipe cleaner band. It wouldn't come so he merely broke her finger off, stuffing it into his pocket. Lastly, he snatched the funny little mouse sword fighting an eyeball broach from her blouse. After searching her pockets for change, he climbed out of the grave.

Sicko was noticing the headless cadaver's leg hanging over the edge. "Looks like you got one foot in the grave there, Morty." He pushed the body into the pit. The force of impact as Morty's body fell onto Granny Sicko's caused her sides to split and her inards to spill. Sicko picked up Morty's head and looked it in the face. "Keep Ma company, would ya?" and tossed it in.

#&*/@#

"I can give you 500 rue for the cheesy ring and 300 for the lame necklace but I ain't interested in the earrings or the broach."

"Why the heck not!" shouted Sicko.

"'Cause my ears ain't pierced and broaches ain't in style this year" replied the seedy, fat, little midget clown who ran the seediest seedy pawn shop in the seedy side of town. Sicko was hoping for more but wasn't complaining since this clown was the most unscrupulous dealer of precious plastics on the east-side. He collected his rue and split to go check out the floosies over at Slammys' Playhouse…the biggest house 'o' hooter and cooter this side of the Pecos. Whammo could usually be found there once it had gotten a little hazy out side and he wasn't so paranoid. That was one of the downsides of getting serious. *"Sometimes when you stumble onto the truth…"*

Anyway, he was there. The two exchanged crusties.

"Hey Sicko…your threads are soiled, clown."

Sicko made no attempt to dust himself off. "Been digging graves."

Whammo pretended to be surprised. "Digging graves…why? Ya BROKE?" he socked Sicko in the shoulder. Typical slapstick. "Whose was it anyways? Get any goodies?"

Sicko was taking a seat next to Whammo. "Yeah, it was my mother's…she kicked the bucket like last week." Sicko grinned. "I wanted to get her jewelry for safe keeping."

"Pawned 'em, right?"

"Yup."

"Cripes, Sicko, ain't ya got no respect for the dead?" A waitress sat down a couple tutti-fruitys on their table.

"Look who's talking about respect. Wasn't it you who said that if a clown wanted to make it in this business he better be ready to crawl over his dying mother to poke his sister?"

"Yeah, but I ain't got no sister!" The two clowns broke into a round of hysterics rare for individuals as hopelessly addicted to the Obvious as they. A floosie came over to pick on Sicko. They knew each other well.

"Hey, Sicko! What's the madda, got ants in your pants?" She always came on to him with an insult and only when she needed something seriously. It was her way of getting over how repulsive he was. "Shoot, if you wasn't so good looking, I'd bust you in the mouth." She winked, then turned away. Whammo gave Sicko a knowing nudge. Later, back at the Funhouse, Sicko and the dancer got serious with each other. Sicko had a saying:

"Some floosies will do anything for a little nose candy!"

Chapter 2
And With a Wonkle Wonkle

When the people of Earth woke up to face the various mornings across the globe, it was just another miserable day. Certain citizens still felt superior to others because their skin was one color or another. Artists starved. Shoe companies made freaky commercials to sell their tasteless sneakers. Publishing houses continued to con old people into renewing their subscriptions with phony sweepstakes contests. Weed was still illegal in the United States and Chet, a sweaty over-weight redneck, in Mobile, Alabama, was complaining that he could never get any gosh darned service, in his favorite truck-stop diner. Things was tough all over and the planet hadn't seen good times since hard times……and times was hard.

Anyway, strolling through a field in Arkansas was a young man named Phillip Pinkerton. He was dressed in velvet bell-bottoms and a baseball jersey, all the rage that year which was 2073. Presently, he was wondering why no matter what century, the 70's was always cheesy. Before he could come to any logical conclusion though, his train of thought was broken. This didn't surprise him because his mother always told him that he had a one-track mind. What did surprise him was the rather spectacular sight of a neat tear in the space/time continuum manifesting itself ten feet in front of him. From Phillip's point of view, it looked like a black rectangle floating roughly six inches off the turf. Phillip also noticed that mid way up this door shaped void was a golden doorknob. The next thing he knew there was a warm squishy feeling in the seat of his pants.

Then the door kinda swung open to reveal, as one might suspect, a dazzling white light. Phillip squinted as he looked into the intense illumination and through his two slits he could make out the silhouette of a humanoid figure. The silhouetted figure was now coming forth from the void. Terrified, Phillip tried to convince his legs to run but they wouldn't co-operate. He was frozen in fear as they say. At that moment the only person more shocked than Phillip Pinkerton was the humanoid, who was now lying face down in the grass due to the fact that the temporal rift materialized half a foot above the surface of the planet, causing him to trip on his way out the door. Getting to his feet he cursed while stretching his arms out to the sides making the letter "T". Peacefully, the being walked over to the petrified boy.

"Allow me to introduce myself" said the man, "My name is Jesus…Jesus of Nazareth. What's yours?" Jesus had his hands out as if to shake. Phillip went to answer but unfortunately he had forgotten to breathe for several minutes and passed out at the Savior's feet.

#$@%&*

Chet the redneck could not believe his bloodshot eyes. Before him, tearful and wrapped tightly in a bed sheet, his wife screamed.

"What are you doing here? You're supposed to be at the diner having breakfast like usual!" A naked milkman desperately searched for a backdoor out. There wasn't one.

"Couldn't get no service down there. Ain't been getting much 'round here neither! Now I know why. Morning Earl." Earl the milkman shrugged. "Chet" he said tipping his Borden cap.

*&%$#@

It is written that the only person more surprised than Chet, his wife, and Earl was Phillip Pinkerton who was coming to in the hands of the Lord.

"Feeling better?" asked Jesus. The angel was massaging the boy's shoulders. Phillip wasn't sure what was going on.

"Did I hear you say that you're Jesus?"

"You did and I am." Christ smiled at the disturbed boy.

"I mean you're the real deal? Not just some hippie named Jesus?"

"The real deal. Son of God, stuff like that."

"WOW!! Wait till my mom hears about this! She's like the biggest Jesus freak in Arkansas!"

Jesus scratched his head. ....*Jesus Freaks…Here? On Earth?*..."Well, why don't you run on home and tell yo' Mama that the second coming is this week."

"Yeah" said Phillip. "That's just what I'll do, but before I go home can I ask of you a favor, Lord?"

"Sure" said Jesus. He was used to doing people favors.

"Could you cure my acne?"

%^$&#@

Gilbert W. Hassenfeffer, President of the United States, placed his seven thousand dollar shoes upon his obnoxiously huge, cherry-wood desk in the Oval Office and admired his reflection in their highly polished uppers. As he leaned forward to wipe an infinitesimal smudge from the toe of the right shoe, he could not have been prepared for what happened next. The shifting weight of his over-fed and over-paid body caused his overly comfortable chair to roll back on its castors. This left the President in an impossible position. In an effort to balance himself as he fell, he pulled the hotline telephone he had grabbed at crashing onto his head. It killed him instantly. This may sound unlikely but it is important to remember that this telephone was government issue and was built to outlast King Tut's tomb. The thing weighed in at well over sixty pounds. It is also important to point out that had a lesser man than the 300-pound Hasenpfeffer done what he did, the phone would not have budged. Never-the-less this is exactly how it happened. The President's last words were recorded by a bug, which had been planted under the desk by the defeated Republicrats. This tape was later played before Congress and was written into the record as…"GAH-MOOGA-WUMP!"

%^$&#@

The only person more surprised than the President, who was just arriving at the gates of Hell, was Vice President, Oatis P. Newberry, who was just being sworn in as President. The only person more surprised than him was Jimbo Wilson. Jimbo was surprised because he had not been charged with planting a bug in the President's office to spy on the Democrocans since he inadvertently got the President's last words on tape and was duly pardoned. The only person, or in this case persons, who were more surprised than Jimbo was the American population at large. Realizing that the death of President Hasenpfeffer meant that Vice President Newberry would be in charge, they did what any sane population would and took to the streets in a full-blown riot. Soon after the riots died down and the dead, wounded, and maimed had been accounted for, even more scandal erupted as the dead President's family fled the country with the bucket loads of money he had been stealing during his terms.

<&@#$%

Jesus of Nazareth sat in Chet's favorite Mobile truck-stop diner with Phillip. Phillip's face was now unblemished. Both were eating Grape-nuts. Jesus was pleased that his favorite breakfast was still in use on Earth after all the years. In his day they called it Gruel. He recalled that he had in fact eaten Grape-nuts at the Last Supper, all those years ago, when he proclaimed that one of the disciples would betray him. Phillip reminded him of Peter. Rednecks were giving Jesus the crusties, being suspicious of anyone wearing robes despite the fact that all their fundamental religious beliefs were focused entirely on people who did wear robes. They had rednecks back in Christ's' day, too, only they were called Romans. Jesus was reading the Washington Post and took interest in some scathing articles concerning the Hasenpfeffer scandals and the fact that most Americans thought that new President Oatis P. Newberry was a complete idiot. Christ was planning to go to Washington that very day to announce, officially, his second coming. He wasn't particularly fond of the United States but he recognized its current domination and influence over the Earth at that time although it was a close draw with the Chinese. Sp he sought to enlist the services of United States government in order to bring his message to the planet's dominant species, mankind, in a language easier to speak. However, he wasn't fooling himself. He knew that with the population of the world upwards into the billions, there would be a thousand skeptics for every one person he encountered the first time around these parts of his father's creation. Yet, he was optimistic for he had an angle, and he could count on the fact that crucifixions were out of style.

$%#@&?

Bob Forsythe never forgave himself…blamed himself for everything too. Of course, there was no way he could have known about the cat curled up on his car's engine block that morning, but he seriously considered suicide as he scraped its steaming remains from the underside of his hood. This was why he found it odd when later that day a gentle looking hippie said, "I'll forgive you Bob, you'll see." The hippie was number seven out of a group of twelve that was touring the White House that afternoon. Bob was the tour guide. Bob was the first in a long line of tour guides in his family to have ever lost a visitor in the White House…visitor number seven. He didn't forgive himself for that either.

"Who in creation are you?" screamed President Newberry as he slammed down one of the four 60-pound phones on the obnoxiously huge, cherry-wood desk in the Oval Office.

"In the whole of creation, like you here, I am the Vice President," replied Christ in a very mellow tone. Jesus was not one easily rattled in the face of hostility.

"Oh, I see" said the President. Oatis was quite used to having odd looking bearded men in flowing robes barge in on him. After all, most of his country's economy depended on such characters. He sat back in the dangerous chair reminding himself to keep his feet off the desk. A moment of measured silence followed. Finally the President took the initiative. "Well, then. I…Er…I didn't catch your name."

"My name is Jesus of Nazareth" replied the bearded one. Despite this rather shocking statement Oatis seemed oblivious, a testament to his lack of religious education or intelligence.

Okay then….Vice President Jesus of Nazareth is it… well… what can the United States do for you today?"

"I just came by for a little chat, Mr. President." Jesus had taken a seat. Oatis leaned forward and folded his hands on the desk in a very disarming way. He had been taught to do this in public relations school.

"No…no, call me Oatis…It just doesn't seem right you calling me Mr. President, what with you being the Vice President of All of Creation Mr. Jesus." Jesus also folded his hands in a very disarming way because he was love.

It was then that the President's mind began to catch on to reality and short circuit. Oatis felt dizzy shortly thereafter. Then he became disoriented and confused because events of the past week were too much for his feeble faculties to handle. Meeting the Son of God wasn't helping. In other words, he was going insane.

It is written that the presence of angels and other supernatural beings tends to affect the human nervous system quite dramatically. The species is frail neurologically speaking. So much so, that it is arguable that we could have evolved from primates at all. Primates tend to be perfectly sane and relaxed around angels. Needless-to-say, Oatis' mind was weaker than most, which was not surprising because he was, of course, a politician. None of this really mattered though because Christ merely restored the man's sanity with a brisk back-rub.

Incidently, it is also written that a few years after the second coming there were a million millionaire massage therapists, and a million out of work psychotherapists.
Twenty-four hours after Oatis' complete mental breakdown and subsequent miraculous recovery and only forty-eight hours after his hurried promotion to Head of State, the President delivered a highly publicized and controversial public address wherein he announced to the world that Jesus Christ was back! It is written that nobody blamed him for the utter chaos, which followed. In less than an hour Congress called an emergency session to impeach the President on the grounds that he was clearly a madman. The population at large, predictably, took to the streets in full blown riot once again. The entire world stood on its collective ear. But Oatis was not worried for he knew that God was his co-pilot.

Jesus then took it upon himself to clear up this total lack of faith and enthusiasm on the part of the American Congress, so he went to the capital building in search of them. He was amazed to see the place in a shambles and covered in dust. He was confused. The congress supposedly met earlier that day to impeach the President. Eventually, he found an old janitor who explained the enigma. It seemed that for the last fifty years, all sessions of Congress had taken place via cell phone on golf courses across the nation. Figure that…

Christ was beginning to feel slightly frustrated. This would mean that he would have to waste valuable time chasing after golfing congressmen at their country clubs. In response to these feelings, Jesus reminded himself that truthfully his time really wasn't all that short seeing as to how he was immortal. It is written that Jesus found most of the congressmen extremely tanned but irritated by his suffering skills as a golf caddy. Christ figured it would be easier to pose as a human being and politely speak to them rather than give each of them a back rub. Instead, he would maneuver them into talking about the current crisis with the President and all the Jesus malarkey and then reveal himself to them. This usually resulted in congressmen saying things like "Great! Now every freakin'' hippie in tarnation is gonna start in for Christ's sake!" leading Christ to reply innocently, "Why would they do that? I don't even know them!" Fortunately, all it took to prove to the g-men he was who he said he was, was to hit a couple holes-in-one with a putter.

Amazingly, even after the congressmen did the unthinkable and assembled themselves in the Capital to retract the call for impeachment, and even after there was a lengthy televised senate hearing where every congressman told of his personal meeting with the Son of God, and even after President Newberry's presidential "I told you so," the citizens of the United States took to the streets in the third full blown riot that week. That's mindless Americans for ya.

*&%^$@

"This is gonna be harder than I thought" thought the Savior as he watched the newsmen report the violence in the streets, all of it on account of the official announcement of his return. Christ adjusted the king-of-kings sized pillows on the bed and returned his attention to the television bolted to the wall of the Watergate Hotel. Picking up the remote, he changed the channel. CLICK.

As the picture fizzled into focus, he saw a sweating man with hair of steel and his eyes tightly closed pointing at the ceiling. In his other hand, he clenched a modern Bible. In 2073, the Bible was a pamphlet. The man stood at an extravagantly decorated pulpit. Across the bottom of the screen there was an 800-number:
1-800-4-PRAYER.

"EVANGELISTS!" exclaimed Jesus as he sat up in his bed launching a pillow at the screen. "I HATE THESE GUYS!" Jesus forced himself to listen to what the man on the television was saying: "That's right people, Judgment Day is upon us…Our gov'ment wants you to believe-uh… that Jesus Christ is back….they want you to believe-uh…that Jesus is here on Earth right now-uh…but I-uh…Reverent D. Righteous…am here-uh…to tell you-wuh…to tell you-wuh that it's all a big lie-uh!...it is a blasphemy people! Because-zuh…I said…because-zuh…iffin Jesus Christ all-mighty, our good Lord in heaven was here on this world…he'd of shown up right here-uh…on my television ministry! Ah by-by-bicky-by-by-by-bicky-by! I got the spirit in me now-wuh…those evil men in Washington are doing the work of the Devil. God is testing you-wuh…God wants to know if you be-leeeeve in him-muh…show your Lord that you believe-uh…pick up that telephone people and give-uh…"

Christ flipped off, then turned off, the television and began to weep. He thought of all the old folks who had been robbed blind at the hands of people like the Reverent Righteous. He thought of all the people who had been murdered in the various religious crusades. In many cases, there had been genocide. Somehow all of this had been done in his name. He hated that! "I don't even know them!" he shouted out loud as he wiped the tears from his eyes. He knew that there were a few people out there still trying to spread his word undistorted. But there were way too few of these good people in comparison to the scores of exploiters, which, of course, was why he was back…to try to get his message across…AGAIN. He knew what he must do as he lay him down to sleep.

&@$#%^

The greatest assembly of world leaders and foreign dignitaries in the history of man was to be called the Greatest Show on Earth. It would be televised and broadcast to every corner of the planet. The event was to occur, of course, in the U.S.A. GOD'S COUNTRY.

Needless-to-say most of the humans on Earth were as skeptical as they were scared about the whole deal. The United States of America, now home of the Son of God, did not sit well with most of the Earth's' humans. Unless the man to be presented really was the Savior, the world would be dealing with an extremely self-righteous super power with a huge nuclear arsenal becoming even more self-righteous than it already was. It would be difficult to explain the type of global chaos this news created. Never-the-less, anyone who was anyone was set to show up at the designated sight for the second coming…Woodstock, New York.

Presently, the President and Christ were inspecting the fair grounds where the Army Corps of Engineers were building the staging area and other facilities that would be needed to accommodate the millions of people who would no doubt be swarming the place. Jesus was especially interested in the fancy new tools being used by the men in the construction side of things. After all, he was once a carpenter. Looking at an air-compressed nail gun, Jesus spoke to Oatis at his side:

"Shoot…I remember when a hammer was high-tech. Sure am glad they didn't have one of these things at my crucifixion!" The President didn't know if he should laugh at that or not. He changed the subject.

"So, why here at Woodstock, Lord?" Jesus made the letter "T" again and spun around like Maria in the *"Sound of Music."*

"Me and my old man saw a really cool concert here once back in the late 1960s." The President was flabbergasted.

"You mean to say that you and God were actually at the original Woodstock?"

"Wasn't everyone?"

The President was starting to get used to having the shock of his life occurring every five minutes.

%^$#&@

In the vicinity of the staging area, dug into the rolling hills, underneath a bush, wearing full-body camouflage, was Morris Coggins, a paid assassin. Morris carefully assembled his high-powered sniper rifle then aimed it at the podium, center stage. Through his scope he could see the ridiculously huge American flag and the banner across it which read "God's Country!"

The Reverent D. Righteous had paid Morris a million up front to assassinate this phony Christ. Righteous didn't believe for a minute that the Son of God had actually come back. Besides, he stood to lose millions, if indeed this man was the Lord. Either way he wanted this man out of the game. He had spent years building the empire that was God, Inc. and he wasn't about to see it go down the toilet just because the second coming finally came., He figured that if the Romans could do it then so could he. Screw it, if it meant going to Hell, so be it. That's where he was going anyway after all the con-jobs he'd pulled on the elderly. He'd off'ted a few people that got in the way, too. Maybe Satan would appreciate his clever and ruthless dealings on Earth and make him his right hand demon or something. The Reverent had Morris convinced that this was his one-way ticket to Heaven and a damn good life on Earth. Morris had been doing the Reverent's dirty work for sometime. After loading his weapon, the assassin hunkered down to wait. *"Won't be long now."*

?$%^&*

While the Corps of Engineers finished building the facilities and assisted the titanic onslaught of the media there, Jesus was back at the Watergate. He decided to watch some more television in the hopes of getting reacquainted with the state of affairs on this particular planet.

"CLICK" went the remote.

Falling to the Earth at great speed, the secret agent reached into the breast pocket of his tuxedo jacket. "Confound it! I wish those jerks would stop sending me out of airplanes without a parachute!" he muttered as he revealed two solid gold knitting needles. Starting with a single thread of one of his socks, the super spy went on to knit himself a serviceable parasail leaving him naked but no longer in immediate danger of his life. The parasail brought him safely to the ground and, as luck would have it, into the backyard of a man's home who had his laundry hung to dry on a clothesline. Even more incredible than the fact that this man's clothes fit the spy perfectly, was the fact that the man was obviously one of impeccably good taste. Within seconds, the spy was getting his bearings straight with a miniature compass which he had hidden in his pinky ring.

Then a commercial came on for Crazy Bob's Luxury Car Sales in which Crazy Bob himself explained that his luxury cars had so much leg room that you could fit Abe Lincoln in the back seat wearing three foot stilts…unlike Whacko Bobs' across the street whose cars didn't even have room for a doubled over double amputee midget. THEN…the secret agent was soon inside the hideout of Plutonium Fingers, a madman set to destroy the Earth. The spy produced the parts to make an automatic pistol and commenced to killing three of Plutonium Fingers henchmen, then blew up an ammunitions dump instantly killing 27 people working for Plutonium Fingers, 32 innocent bystanders and 14 stunt men. After that, he tried to seduce one of Plutonium Fingers girls into having sex with him, twice. Then, he eventually stabbed seven guards to death with a #2 pencil, and finally killed Plutonium Fingers by orchestrating a bizarre jump rope accident in which Plutonium Fingers was the victim. CLICK.

The anchorman of the six o-clock news was delivering it much the same way a priest delivers last rights at a funeral:

"…The death toll in the Hasenpfeffer riots turned into President Newberry announcing the return of Jesus Christ riots, turned into the governmental approval of the return of Christ riots, has been elevated to 6000. This count, of course, does not include the maimed which now stands at 14,000, the seriously wounded which has been tallied at 22,000, nor the minor injuries which is almost too great to total, but the latest estimate is upwards of 50,000. Property damage due to fire and looting has been estimated at 2.5 trillion dollars…" The anchorman switched over to the anchorwoman:

"In a related story….political and religious leaders from across the globe will be assembling in Woodstock, New York, later this evening, to attend what's being called the Greatest Show on Earth where the main event will be the second coming of Jesus Christ. Delegates from every single country on the planet are here and all anxiously await the message for mankind that the Savior no doubt will deliver. The assemblage has already shattered every record of attendance by world leaders as well as that of representatives of the media, not to mention the several million spectators literally creating a multitude on surrounding hills…a real security problem for the Army and secret service. We'll be back with more news after this commercial break…"

"Hey, hey, hey! This is Whacko Bob from Whacko Bob's Luxury Car Sales! I'm askin'…no I'm begging you to come on down here and check out my latest model luxury car! Why, the cars here at Whacko Bobs' have so much leg room that if you stretched out in the back you'd have to climb a ladder to see out…unlike Crazy Bob's across the street. Why, his cars are so small and cramped that you'll have to take a laxative to get behind the wheel!"

"Hello, again. I'm Fred Slow and you're watching the news at six. In Okaloosa County, Florida there has been yet another bowling alley massacre. Our reporter in the field, Rip Slash, is on the scene...over to you and let her Rip!

"Thanks, Fred." Rip Slash was standing before a mass of police vehicles bearing the seal of the Okaloosa Sheriff's Department.

"I'm here in Valparaiso, Florida where local authorities are conducting a massive man-hunt for an unknown butcher who is wanted for yet another bowling alley massacre, which occurred here last night. This is the type of massacre that has exploded into the consciousness of our increasingly violent culture like a stick of dynamite in a rotten tomato. Unfortunately, it was the men's and women's semi-pro finals when the madman came into the alley screaming…"What? No 13-pound blue and white swirled bowling balls? I'll give you chicken roasting fools bones for your bowling pins!"…just before opening fire with an assortment of automatic fire arms, according to eye witnesses who somehow survived the attack. Authorities report 47 men and women dead, 78 seriously wounded, as well as 65 pins, 22 bowling balls and two pinball machines reported destroyed. The Sheriff assures us that he will spare no expense to apprehend this killer but given that this is the eighth bowling alley massacre over the course of 3-months in as many States, it doesn't appear that there will be an end to the carnage anytime soon. Back to you Fred..." CLICK.

Two hillbillies pulled on a thick rope swung over a tree limb to hang down about five foot with a federal agent dangling on its end. CLICK.

A man in a double breasted pin stripe suit pleaded with the other similarly dressed men not to do what they was doing all the way to the bottom of the bay in his cement shoes. CLICK.

A swollen eyed, fat lipped, broken nosed, washed up, and bloodied former heavyweight champion took a ruthless beating from a tight muscled 20-years his junior champion whose sole mission in life at that moment was to prove to the old man that trying to make a comeback during his reign was a really stupid idea. CLICK.

A delicate, invalid five-year-old boy turned his feeble, bald head towards a water bottle taped to his pillow. Maneuvering his tiny toothless mouth around its elbow jointed straw, he took a spiritless draw from the vessel and then collapsed once again upon his mattress to give the cool liquid in his mouth an unconvincing swallow. The child was utterly surrounded by hideous and sadistic looking medical apparatus. The sight of such ominous gear gave testimony to the serious nature of the boy's disease and the cadaverous state to which it had gotten him. The hopeless baby skeleton lay in his hospital bed slipping further into his illness as the doctors tried everything known to medical science to save him, but to no avail. He was softly summoned from an insipid slumber by a nurse who asked if he would like to have a visitor. As the boy croaked a barely audible "Okay" from his inflamed and swollen throat, his nose began to bleed.

"EDWARD!" said the nurse, "look who's here to see you." Edward summoned all of his strength to press the up-button on the motorized bed. As it lifted the child to a semi-upright position, through the dense fog of his half-hearted consciousness, he tried to focus his eyes in order to identify the visitor. And when he finally held them in focus long enough to do so, he did something he had almost forgotten to do and smiled.

Before Edward stood a grinning, red nosed, white-faced clown with a bald head encircled with bright green hair. The clown wore gigantic red shoes over striped sox under plaid pantaloons. The clown danced a little jig while honking a brass horn with the gloved hand that was not holding the balloons. Then the clown reached down inside his over-sized pantaloons and pulled out his ukulele, which he began to play. The riff went like this:

    Ah-juke-juke
    Ah-juke-juke-Ah-jooky!
    Ah-juke-juke
    Ah-juke-juke-Ah-jooky!
    Ah-jooky-jooky-jooky-jooky-juke!
    Ah-jooky-jooky-jooky-jooky-juke!

Then in a funny clown's voice he began to sing:

    Ah-ding-ding
    Ah-ding-ding-Ah-diddle
    I play this instead of a fiddle!
    And would you like to be my friend?

Ah-biddle-biddle-boodle-baddle-blim!
Ah-diddle-diddle-fiddle-faddel bingo
Ya know I think you're really kinda neato!
And would you like to be my friend?
Ah-biddle-biddle-boodle-baddle-blim!

When the clown finished the little tune, he asked the sickly child if he would like a balloon animal. Two tiny, extremely sunken bloodshot eyes lit up like two candles way in the back of two caves separated by a nose shaped rock. He weakly nodded yes. The clown cracked a giant smile and began to dance again saying "Oh boy …oh boy…you want to be my friend. I'm so happy!!" Then the clown furiously went to work making an elaborate balloon animal. Once finished, he went to the boy's bedside and took a bow presenting the child with his creation. He waited for the boy to take it but after a while it became clear that this was not going to happen. The clown got closer to investigate the matter. An alligator tear left a faint streak down the clown's cheek as he put a sad face on and blew his honker into a polka-dot kerchief. Little Edward was dead.

Jesus wept.

Then he changed his clothes. Later that day the news would report that a clown with bright green hair, big red shoes over striped sox under plaid pantaloons had been seen healing all the sick and dying children all over the world.

%^$#@=

Reverent D. Righteous was screaming mad at the news of these worldwide healings. It was hard enough to pull off his own cleverly hoaxed miracles without some clown going around performing real ones. He had caught the latest report on the television in his private jet in route to the Greatest Show on Earth. He had been invited to attend the show by one of his many powerful friends in Washington…President Newberry. The President was under the false impression that the Reverent would be thrilled at the prospect of being seated on the same stage as Jesus Christ. Of course, nothing could have been further from the truth.

"That Morris Coggins better not foul this up!" he shrieked throwing his whiskey glass at his man-servant. The sight of his man-servant also filled him with rage for the fact that he had to pay the man. "…*Never should have done away with slavery…*"

Upon landing, the Reverent was shuffled off the plane then into his limo. There was the short hop to Woodstock, then a tedious series of security checks until finally he found himself seated next to the new President. "Hey, how ya doin', Reverent?" asked the President.

"*…What a sucker…I've been milking this guy for 15 years…*" thought the Reverent. "Fine….fine, Mr. President." he replied. It didn't surprise the Reverent one iota that this phony Jesus had suckered the President, as well. He cracked an evil grin at the thought of how much more money he could squeeze out of poor old Oatis once Morris had blown this con-artists head off…and laughed at the thought of the President realizing his mistake and coming to him, begging for forgiveness for believing in a false profit.

"With all due respect, Mr. President, I'm afraid you're in for one Hell of a let down."

"What makes you say that, Reverent? Jesus Christ is back! It's a glorious day for mankind, and I'll be honored with the greatest task of my life introducing him to the world before the leaders of every country on Earth."

The Reverent could barely contain his contempt for this fool.

"You don't actually believe this man is who he says he is, do you? Come on, man, I thought the President of the United States would be smarter than that!"

"Now hold on there, Reverent. Jesus performed a miracle on me himself!" Oatis seemed satisfied with this rebuttal.

"Hah! And just what was the nature of this so called miracle?"

"Why, he cured me of my insanity."

The Reverent laughed out loud at that remark.

"Cured you of your insanity? I doubt that….this whole stunt you're pulling now proves that's at least one miracle that didn't work!"

Oatis had always been intimidated by the Reverent but he was the President after all.

"What the Hell are you trying to say?"

The reverent went for the kill. "It means, Sir, that as far as I'm concerned you are still quite insane!"

This was the end of the line for the President who had had it with the Reverent's opinions concerning his sanity.

"What! Shut your mouth, Reverent Righteous, I demand that you respect me on this great day for mankind and keep your opinions to yourself!"

The President felt proud of himself for that was the first time he had dared to take such a tone with his spiritual advisor. The Reverent silently chuckled to himself. It felt good to know he could still make men more powerful than himself squirm.

Next to the President and the Reverent, a neatly dressed Chinese man stood up from his duty of translating what the men had been saying for the oriental dictator, Won Hung Lo. The fat, balding Samurai let out a laugh and said two of the five English words he knew…those two words being President and Bozo, in that order. Won Hung Lo was among the privileged few who would be seated on the stage. This privilege had mainly to do with whom or who didn't have nuclear weapons. Every other leader was seated before the stage on the order of global importance in such a way that the chief of a small forgotten South American Indian tribe would be way in back.

Next to Won Hung Low were a Jewish Rabbi, the latest Pope, and a simple looking Buddhist Monk. The Monk was probably the most dangerous man at Woodstock if it wasn't for Morris the assassin in the hills. The only thing more surprising than seeing the entire census of world's leaders in one place at one time was that for the first time in 2000 years, these three religious leaders agreed on something. That something was that the individual they were about to meet was certainly not Jesus Christ but almost certainly an imposter who would be responsible for the downfall of the United States. They figured that after this, the citizens of the good ole U.S.A. would be so embarrassed that the entire population would be forced to get on a spaceship and move to a galaxy far, far away. The three were cut short in mid laugh when a casket draped with an American flag was wheeled out onto the stage by two marines in chrome helmets. A question asked by

Reverent Righteous could be heard in 274 languages including the one in English that was:

"What the Hell's that casket for?"

An explanation was given by President Newberry and it too was duly translated into 274 languages:

"Within that casket is the corpse of President Hasenpfeffer."

A gasp sounded across the stage then rolled out across the other not so important world leaders who wished now more than ever that they had nuclear weapons. In fact, nobody wished his country had nuclear weapons more than Guh-Mooga-Wump the 2nd, Chief of a small forgotten South American indian tribe. He and his son spoke in their native tongue.

"Jah-moo-moo-ibu-deeko-sug! *If only we had nuclear capability!*" said Guh-Mooga-Wump.

"Wiga-Wiga?" replied his son, "*Why is that?*"

"Ricky-jah-ibu-deeko-sug-himey-ibu-nibu-kibu-mon-sons-o-bitchs-gibby-dingweeby-jah-crib! *Because if we had nuclear capability then we could kill them sons-o-beaches for destroying our rain forest!*"

Guh-Mooga-Wump the 2nd pulled out a pocket mirror and fixed his war paint. His son spoke:

"Rippy-jah-ibu-deeko-sug, ibu-nibu-himey-lima-kibu-meen-Boondaby-nu-wiffle-noon-ibby-booty! *Besides if we had nuclear capability, we could also kill the Boondaby who stole your third wife!*"

Just after midnight, the house lights went down. Morris Coggins checked his sights and aimed the cross hairs of his night-vision scope at an imaginary point where he thought his target's head would be. The Chinese dictator, Won Hung Low, shifted his oriental butt on the insultingly uncomfortable seat, complaining to his interpreter that this was not a chair fit for a samurai. The Rabbi elbowed the Monk…the Monk elbowed the Pope…the Pope turned to face them and upon meeting each other's gaze, they all cracked up like children reacting to a well-executed fart in Sunday school. The Reverent felt like he had the whole situation under control and leaned towards the President to whisper, "Hey Oatis…get ready to kiss your career goodbye" causing the President to shoot back with "Reverent, I'm warning you…"

With 2500 camera crews and tens of thousands of individual reporters of every conceivable nationality on the scene, the eyes, ears, and complete attention of the world was focused on the Greatest Show on Earth.

?@#$%^

It began with an ear-splitting, high-pitched squeal, ending in an even more deafening return to silence as the unnecessarily large P.A. system went into a momentary feedback loop. Due to the fact that this feedback was literally transmitted to every electronic receiver on Earth, it was the proverbial shot heard round the world. The loop was stopped by a quick thinking sound-tech who, although he saved the planet from a most unpleasant noise, forgot where he was and screamed "JESUS H. CHRIST!" over the talk back. This was either the greatest coincidence of all time or the best timing ever achieved for at exactly that moment Jesus appeared on stage directly behind the podium.

Needless-to-say the multitudes were shocked. This was because the angel had bright green hair and was wearing big red shoes over striped sox under plaid pantaloons. Altogether the perfect clown.

>&^%$#

A sweaty, fat, and naturally stupid redneck named Chet sat up in his Lazy-Boy and removed his stinking feet from the back of Earl, the milkman, whom he had been using as a foot rest. He pointed at his 24-inch Curtis Mathis color television and turned to his wife who was wearing a chastity belt and a muzzle. He swallowed a combination of beer and peanuts and said, "Hey that's the same clown that's been goin' 'round healin' all them sick kids all over the place." It was the first time in a long time that he was right about something.

*&$%^+

Morris Coggins wondered if anyone had ever put a contract out on a clown before as he put the cross hairs between two high arching eyebrows.

%^$^&@

Reverent Righteous felt some of his control slip as he and 20-billion people world-wide recognized the clown at the podium as the "Miracle Clown" who had been healing all the sick children.

*&^#$?

President Newberry was still about a minute behind the rest of the planet as he tried to figure out why there was a clown on stage instead of that nice hippie in robes.

&*^%$=

The Rabbi, the Pope, and the Monk took one look at the clown and fell out of their seats laughing. How perfectly humiliating…one nation under a clown…

%^$#@?

Won Hung Low joined in the laughter that was spreading through the crowd like acne in a Jr. High. He said two more English words. "Jesus Bozo"

&%^$#*

"WONKLE! WONKLE!!" went the brass horn. The clown danced a little jig to the delight of the sea of humans there, and the billions who watched the event on television. Then, Jesus the Clown reached down his pantaloons and produced a ukulele. He began to play it. It was a deafening sound, the ukulele. It was being picked up by the countless microphones on the stage then amplified by the unnecessarily large P.A. system as well as being broadcast all over the planet…each of these broadcasts themselves being amplified by radios and stereos and hi-fi's and everything else. The clown began to sing:

Ah-ding-ding
Ah-ding-ding-Ah-diddle
I play this instead of a fiddle!
And would ya like to be my friend?
Ah-biddle-biddle-boodle-baddle-blim!

Ah-diddle-diddle-fiddle-faddel bingo
Ya know I think you're really kinda neato!
And would you like to be my friend?
Ah-biddle-biddle-boodle-baddle-blim!

He finished his song with an elaborate dance move that said…TA-DA!...but was greeted with silence. Then a timid clap from way in back sounded. It was Guh-Mooga-Wump the 2nd. Others caught on and soon the sparse applause grew into a standing ovation. It was one of those situations where nobody was really sure how to behave and there was a kind of bandwagon mentality present. Like everyone was waiting for someone else to react, and then someone does, and before long everyone is standing and clapping much longer and louder than needed saying… "Here! Here!"...more impressed with themselves for having gotten past the awkward moment than with the object of their applause.

Jesus the Clown was taking extravagant bows and waved like a prom queen with that weird twisting of the hand that only monarchs and arch-angels can make believable. WONKLE! WONKLE!

The clown took his place behind the podium and began to clear his throat. People began to hush themselves or shush at others. The clown continued his throat clearing sounds loudly. There was silence, but now the clown had gone into a coughing fit, grabbing at his neck. His face turned bright red. He began to gesture dramatically pointing at his throat in the international sign for "I'm choking!" Finally he was madly thrashing on the floor of the stage making all sorts of gagging noises. The humans of Earth were taken by the drama of it all. The politicians left their seats not knowing what to think. They helped the clown to his feet and began to forcefully pound his back hoping to dislodge whatever it was he was choking on. Then the clown opened his mouth and it seemed to keep opening until he looked like a rattlesnake preparing to swallow an ostrich egg. Then…balloons. The clown was belching up fully inflated balloons by the thousands…magic balloons doing things balloons can't do. The multitude went wild for this, cheering and laughing like children playing with the balloons.

As the crowd calmed down from the balloon trick, the master of ceremonies again reached into his pantaloons and pulled out a classic black top hat and magic wand. He put on the hat, then gestured dramatically at the flag draped casket right behind him and began to speak in that mysterious manner that magicians often do when setting up their tricks.

"I'll bet you all would like to know WHY there is a casket on this stage CONTAINING the recently exhumed corpse of President Gilbert T. Hasenpfeffer!"

The gathering of politicos sat silent and mystified. The clown continued:

"You'd like to KNOW why he is here on this stage instead of in Arlington National Cemetery where he belongs!"

An extended silence hung in the air for 36.7 seconds.

"WELL…isn't anyone going to ask why?"

More silence.

"WHY?" said the Reverent Righteous in a caustic tone. He wasn't enjoying any of this foolishness. The clown turned to face the man. It made for an odd scene for, although not dressed in a clown's suit, the Reverent's weird, stiff-as-steel, evangelists hair made him as funny looking as a clown anyway…
DUELING BUFFOONS!

"WHY? It's because President Newberry would like his old job back" said the clown.

"What's that got to do with it?" puzzled the Reverent.

"The answer is simple. I'll just raise Mr. Hasenpfeffer from the dead and then Mr. Newberry can become the Vice President again.

"You'll do what?" screamed Righteous.

"He said he's gonna raise Hasenpfeffer from the dead, you moron." said Oatis "What's the matta, ya deaf or somethin'?"

"If he is, I'll fix that, too" added the clown punctuating his sentence with a WONKLE! WONKLE!

&^&%$*

With his left eye squinted shut and his right focused down the ultra accurate scope of his assassin's rifle, Morris Coggins could see nothing but the 2-inch diameter target area between the painted eyes of the clown. He was concentrating on that spot because a million big ones were riding on the one shot he'd have at his target. He would wait until he had steeled his nerves, calmed his breathing, and turned his body into an efficient death machine. He would wait until the precise moment when he would get that old familiar "killing itch" that he got just before he took the life of whatever creature he played God with. Morris had no concept of what was taking place on the stage. He had tuned out every sound, every non-essential thought. It was just he and the little 2-inch dot now. Nothing else mattered.

$%#@&=

"I am also raising this man from the dead to prove to your planet that I am in fact who I say I am. Ya know, it saddens my heart that I must do something so drastic every time I come here to get you people to believe. For a world that has so many religions waiting for my return, it's really surprising how many of you don't want to accept the fact that I'm back. Actually, I wanted to wait longer because you people really aren't ready but I am a busy life-form and, with all the cut-backs in Heaven, was forced to squeeze you in this century. So…without further delay let's get this show on the road!"

&*@#$+

Like tens of billions of people across the globe, Chet, the redneck, sat with his eyes glued to his Curtis Mathis.

&%^$#*

Likewise did Phillip Pinkerton, who sat in a stuffy old house with his stuffy old mother, the Jesus freak.

&%^$#*

Bob Forsythe sat in his little D.C. apartment not forgiving himself for not getting his television fixed and was forced to listen to the Greatest Show on Earth over his radio like millions of other unfortunates. Even less fortunate people around the world listened to their town crier.

&%^$#*

Won Hung Low shifted his weight in the insulting chair as his interpreter chewed on his already badly bitten nails.

&%^$#*

The Monk, the Rabbi, and the Pope managed to stop laughing and put on an air of seriousness even though none actually believed this clown could raise the dead.

&%^$#*

This was true also of the Reverent Righteous, who was now only thinking about the assassin hidden in the hillsides.

&%^$#*

Morris Coggins was getting that itchy feeling as his finger curled around the trigger.

&%^$#*

"Wait till you see this, Mr. Smarty-Pants!" said President Newberry to the Reverent as two chrome-domed marines opened the casket to reveal the cadaverous Hasenpfeffer. Jesus outstretched his arms like a "T", then came a thunderous sound: WONKLE! WONKLE!

The mind boggled Gilbert T. Hasenpfeffer sat up in his casket. At that moment, it is probable that the statement "He's ALIVE! He's ALIVE!" escaped from the mouths of

34

every human being on Earth. Such was the thundering exclamation of the multitudes that the sound of Morris Coggin's rifle being fired was completely consumed. This was fortunate for him. Unfortunate for him was the fact that his expertly aimed bullet was diverted from its course when it unexpectedly ricocheted off the gleaming ceremonial spear of Guh-Mooga-Wump the 2nd. It seems that in a fit of disbelief at the sight of a dead man coming back to life the chief had jumped out of his seat thrusting his spear into the air shouting...

"UNGA-BUNGA!...UNGA-BUNGA!...." which does not mean "He's Alive!...He's Alive!" but rather "Freakin'A!..Freakin'A!"

After hitting the spear, the round took a slightly altered course to finally rest inside the brain of Reverent Righteous. As the Reverent dropped dead at the oversized feet of the clown, Guh-Mooga-Wump the 2nd could be heard to say: "BOON-LOOGY! BOON-LOOGY! *MY SPEAR! MY SPEAR"*

The ceremonial spear was over a thousand years old after all. The stage was a pandemonium. Oatis looked at the fresh corpse of the Reverent whose brains were clearly spilling out the back of his head.

"OH, MY GOD!" he said.

"OH, ME!" said the clown.

"What the Hell is going on here for Christ's sakes?" said the reanimated Hasenpfeffer. Hearing that Christ was amused for this was one of the few times that what was going on WAS for his sake.

"Happy birthday, Mr. President." said the clown.

"What the Hell are you talking about?" Hasenpfeffer was totally confused.

"Well, I just raised you from the dead, so it's kinda like your birthday." He punctuated again with a WONKLE! WONKLE! And at the sound of the horn, a clearly murdered man sat up, brains still dangling from his skull.

"Sweet Jesus, it's a miracle!" said the Reverent. MIRACLES INDEED!

? ^&%$#

Morris Coggins and the Reverent D. Righteous found themselves in a heap of trouble immediately after the Greatest Show on Earth. Witnesses who had seen the flash from Morris's rifle overwhelmed him so that he could be taken into custody by the authorities, which he was. Police obtained a complete confession from him after a routine questioning which entailed him being beaten within an inch of his life, then tortured with a cattle prod. The confession had interesting consequences for the Reverent Righteous. To begin with, Morris stated that he had not intended to murder the Reverent because it was he who had contracted him to assassinate the "phony Christ". Therefore, the Reverent was charged with conspiracy to commit murder for putting a contract out on Jesus. Secondly, Morris had, in fact, killed the Reverent, even if the man had been brought back from the dead and since the Reverent had contracted Morris as the shooter, he was also charged with being a party to his own murder. FIGURE THAT!

So, Morris was duly charged with murder and attempted murder. However, there was more to the confession. It turned out that Coggins was the much sought after "bowling alley butcher" wanted in eight States. Also, a search of the Reverent's properties (carried out in haste with questionable warrants) turned up a sizable stash of 13-pound bowling balls with blue and white swirls. By the time the investigation ended, the Reverent was charged with conspiracy in the bowling alley massacres as well. He had sought to put these strategically located alleys out of business in order to buy, then develop the real estate into God, Inc. theme-parks. The mystery behind the collection of the bowling balls came out during the trial of Coggins who was using an insanity defense. He claimed he had been brain washed by the Reverent into thinking that bowling alleys with a lack of 13-pound blue and white swirled balls were witch's covens operated by Satanists who barbecue babies and use their bones for bowling pins. This was why he had to massacre them. WEIRD!

^%&%$#

After a brief intermission to allow the authorities to sort things out, as well as to let everyone calm down after the madness on stage, Jesus Clown was ready to bring his message to the humans.

"What a show, huh?" said the Lord. The billions were silent…hanging on to every word. These were the words of God.

THE MESSIAH SPOKE:

1.0

My father, the Lord Almighty in Heaven, is the creator of this Universe of which your world is but an infinitesimal smudge. You must learn to think of yourselves as less than the center of the Universe.

1.1

Our Father's universal creation has gotten so ridiculously huge that it is I who is set to the task of working out all of the little details. Your world is one of those little details.

1.2

It becomes necessary for me to come here when your problems cannot be solved by one of our angels. I was here last when the Romans were in danger of dominating the planet. Needless-to-say, they didn't welcome me, but I accomplished my mission at great personal sacrifice, as you well know.

1.3.

But that is history. There are matters that I wish to deal with now. Way back before my first visit here, primitive humans were not progressing properly. God decided what was needed was diversity. I believe at the time, most of your ancestors were focusing huge amounts of time and resources building a tower in a foolish attempt to reach God. It would never have worked, but everyone was into it. So, my Dad created different languages and away they went confused and babbling among themselves. The project was scrapped.

1.4.

Like all things, what was good then has soured now. It is time for you to speak the same language again for there are so many of you that do not understand each other.

WONKLE! WONKLE!

1.5

Let my presence here on this Earth influence and shed light on your religious differences as well. For I am here to tell you they are obsolete. There is only one God but he is so busy that he does not care if you kill in his name. That is not the point. You misunderstand because you take yourselves too seriously.

1.6

If you want to know what God expects from you, hear me now. In Like Everything, which is the All, of All There Is, Gods creation is itself but an infinitesimal smudge also. And there are bills to pay. There is a currency in Like Everything and there is a currency in the creation of God. We deal in LOVE. Love can be manufactured in many ways but it is never created with WAR or the killing. You must create Love in abundance for God needs to get the bills paid. And in return you receive in your afterlife out of the flesh, paradise.

1.7

It is in the flesh that you produce Love. Out of the flesh you become Love. Therefore, you must take every opportunity to create Love while you live. You must shape this world you have been given into happiness. You must use your technology to end pain and suffering. You must make everyday one where there is much to laugh at and little to cry for, unless you shed tears of joy. There are creatures that set this example. Listen to them. You dress up to play the fool and then go back to a life of misery. Learn to be the fool. Somebody send in the clowns.

1.8

I must warn you of the competition. Evil is real. It is the opposite of Love. It is Debt. There really is a fallen angel called Satan. He has destroyed many worlds and he has almost convinced you to destroy this one. That is why I am here. To remind you of what the purpose of your lives are so that you do not fall prey to evil. There are sins. Most of you know what they are. But Satan has so corrupted your spiritual leaders that they actually teach sin in place of Love. Teaching hatred of another is sin. Forsaking the pleasures and simple Love found in the act of sexual expression with any other of your species is sin. These sins must not continue or else your world shall be doomed.

1.9

If you do not heed my words and be decent to each other, there will be nothing my Father, your God, can do to save you. We simply do not have the resources. You must think of the task before you as a matter of life and death for that is truly what it is.

2.0

Beware of Satan and his lies. Even if you root him out and create a new era for your kind, he will not be beaten and simply go away. He will only renew his efforts with greater resolve. Satan does not like to lose. Now is the time for you to purge, for I happen to know that Satan is currently leading a campaign against a world of vegetable life forms and it is consuming much of his energy. Do you have any idea how hard it is to teach evil to a salad?

2.1

Believe it or not, this is all I have to say to you. My message is still out there and it hasn't changed all that much. All you need do is remove the unnecessary nonsense and live by its principles. Look upon me now as an example for I AM LOVE.

2.2

CHOW!

*&%^$#

It is written that with his final word, Christ the Clown placed his arms out to form the letter "T" and began to rise into the air swathed in white light. He did this to the sound of every human on earth cheering as only humanity could after hearing directly the call of the Messiah. Jesus looked down upon them and hoped with all his super natural heart that they had gotten the message. He knew that nothing would change overnight, that it would take many years for humanity to find the way, but they had a better chance now than if he hadn't shown up at all. Soon, he would be relaxing on a sparsely populated island in the Caribbean letting the sun give him the tan of the Gods.

&*%@#^

It is written that Chet, the redneck, like many other close minded idiots in the deep South, wasn't sure what to think. He ordered his new man-servant, Earl, the milkman, whom he held hostage with a shotgun, to bring him a copy of the Bible. He hoped to find the message that Christ the Clown was talking about. Promptly, Earl delivered the pamphlet. Chet examined the cover. "BIBLE" it said. He opened it.

GOD CREATED HEAVEN AND EARTH

HE NEEDS YOUR MONEY THERE

IF YOU WANT TO GIVE HIM SOME

DIAL 1-800-4-PRAYER.

&*%@#^

It is written that Phillip Pinkerton and his stuffy old mother shut off the television and went into the kitchen for some home-made peach cobbler. Phillip kept looking in a mirror, which hung on the wall, admiring his new complexion. His mother was beside herself with joy because of all the people on Earth who might have been first to meet Jesus, it had been her only son…not to mention the fact that he wasn't a pizza face no more.

&*%@#

It is written that President Newberry did not get his old job back as Vice President. The fresh back-from-the-dead Gilbert T. Hasenpfeffer was immediately impeached and brought up on charges for all the money he had stolen during his terms. His family was still at large.

?&*%@#

Bob Forsythe received a post card in the mail. This is what it said:

Dear Bob,

I FORGIVE YOU.

    Love,
    Jesus H. Christ

^&%$#@

Guh-Mooga-Wump the 2nd was overwhelmed with grief. The thousand year old ceremonial spear was broken, and Christ was gone. But he was a proud warrior and shed no tears because that was his son's job. Guh-Mooga-Wump the 3rd was crying for his father with his head in his hands. He was crying harder than he did when the Boondaby stole his father's third wife. The only time he remembered crying harder than this was when his father's 13-pound bowling ball with blue and white swirls disappeared after some missionaries had come to tell his tribe about Jesus. They had said that Jesus could do anything and would answer their prayers if they showed faith in him. This was why they were at Woodstock. Guh-Mooga-Wump the 2nd planned to offer the spear as an act of faith, then ask Jesus if he knew what happened to the bowling ball. Now the spear was ruined, Jesus was gone, and no bowling ball…so it was back to the rain forest. They were screwed and out of luck.

AND SO IT WAS WRITTEN AND SO IT WAS DONE

Chapter 3
A Puddle of Poobla

In a funny little town called Buffoonville, most mimes of the 43rd century lived in Mime Manor, a great invisible house on the hills just outside of the lower-east part of town. The mansion was three stories high, not counting the basement. It had 23 small apartments all occupied by mimes, single or married. Recently there had been two things on the minds of the tenants there. One was the very bad clown who had moved into the house next door and the other the silent couple on the 2nd floor who had just had a child. The birth would normally not have been too big-a-deal except for the fact that the couple had given birth to a "clown" baby. The silent couple were feeling very blue for they knew they wouldn't be able to take care of the infant. Clowns simply cannot live on imaginary food. They would have to take the baby to the orphanage. There was no other way. This made them feel sick for they knew there would be a good chance the little clownette would be taught to hate mimes. This was an almost unbearable thought to her parents. Never-the-less, she was left on the door step of the Buffoonville Orphanage that very evening, less than 12 hours old. There she was found by kind hearted Miss Smoochy and was taken in. Others at the orphanage would see to it she was fed and clothed properly because today Miss Smoochy had big plans for another of her brood.

"Where are we going, Miss Smoochy?" said the four year old, as she dressed him in his best little clown suit. Clipping together his ruffled collar she answered:

"Today is a very special day for you, Blinko, because we're going to the World Circus!"

"World Circus?" The kinderclown's eyes went dreamy. Smoochy messed up his hair as best she could. Clown hair doesn't get weird naturally until puberty.

"All clowns go to the circus, baby. That's where we go to give thanks to Jesus Clown. Remember I told you about him. He's the clown who brought our people out of the evil old-timey days."

"Will Jesus be at the World Circus?"

"Oh, I don't think he will be there in person, sweetie-pie, but he's always up in Heaven watching us."

"Is it gonna be fun?"

"Oh, yeah, Blinko, the circus is the most fun place a clown can go, and going to the circus helps clowns to be happy and funny until the World Circus comes back to town."

"How come we can't go to the World Circus all of the time?"

"I guess you could, Blinko, but that would mean you'd have to join the circus, and only the funniest and most foolish clowns get to do that. Maybe if you try really hard, when you grow up you will be stupid enough to join the World Circus."

"I'd like that, Miss Smoochy!"

Blinko, Jr. was growing into a wonderful little clown at the Buffoonville Orphanage. His foster parent, Miss Smoochy, was so proud of him. That's why she had decided to take him to his first circus a year early.

Blinko had learned to speak foolish quickly for a tot and this demonstrated that his tinker was gifted. He was a real smarty-pants. This could be a good thing or a bad thing. Smart clowns either joined the circus because they were smart enough to understand the principles of Grand Lunacy, or they went bad. Thankfully 99% of clowns born into the world were mindless numbskulls.

Grand Lunacy…Miss Smoochy barely had the brains to understand the idea. It had to do with being able to give up your intelligence in order to become a total idiot, and through this idiocy cleanse oneself until the smallest shred of rationality and logic departs from one's soul so that no one can take you seriously, not even yourself.

A clown that takes himself seriously is not funny.
A clown who is not funny is not happy.
An unhappy clown is a clown guilty of sin.

That much most clowns understood, yet it was sometimes hard to live that way. This was why it was important for clowns to read the Holy Comic and go to the World Circus when it rolled in to town. These things served to remind clowns what their job in life was: To have fun, be happy and make love.

Through the pictures in the Holy Comic and the hilarious rituals of the circus, clowns found strength and renewed their faith to carry on serving that Great Jester in the sky.

%$#@*&

Boo-Boo, a Grand Poobla of the World Circus, was looking out the rear window of his shiny red caboose. The ornately decorated circus choo-choo was on its way to hallowed ground in Buffoonville. The grounds, on the west-side of town, were maintained by the city and were only supposed to be used by the Circus, although kinderclowns often played kick ball there. Keystones would catch them at it but usually failed to run them off, having joined the game. No clown could resist a game of kick ball.

Dressing himself, Boo-Boo thought of all the souls he would be saving on that warm spring day. The Poobla wore a triangular shaped hat, three feet tall. The hat was decorated with fringe of tiny white pom-poms and it had a tiny statuette of Jesus the Clown on a unicycle attached to its front. His clown smock was festooned with three large pom-poms which were the same off white as the smock's striped pattern. The smock was topped with a 250-fold, ruffled collar which was needed to support his four chins. His pantaloons were cut off at the knee to show off his sox, which complimented his impressive white shoes…size 37. In contrast to this all-white ensemble was a wide gold belt with a rubber squirt bulb as its buckle. It was a menacing strap, for it had to encompass the Poobla's girth, which was such that he couldn't see his feet despite they're incredible length.

Like all Pooblas, he maintained a large sack full of goodies. The sack was called the "Bundle of Holy Stuff" and was handed down from Poobla to Poobla through the centuries. Its contents included:

1. Brass horn with rubber squeeze bulb.
2. Exploding cigars.
3. King size rubber mallet.

4. A giant boxing glove.
5. Roller-skates.
6. Confetti
7. A kazoo
8. Three bowling pins
9. Party hats
10. The all important Joy Buzzer

Boo-Boo lifted his well-worn circus size Holy Comic book from its place on the desk. He wanted to read his favorite passage. The comic told the 2000-year-old story of Jesus the Clown and his second coming to Earth. No one knew much about his first coming. That was taboo. The comic also held, within its lovingly hand-drawn frames, the many interpretations of God's word, formulated first by old world religious icons then countless other additions by the new world Pooblas, including Poobla Boo-Boo. Boo-Boo's addition to the Holy Comic was a page that children could color in with crayons, depicting Jesus the Clown surrounded by kinderclowns and forest animals. The words in the Holy Comic, despite the many translations and interpretations, were pretty close to what Jesus had actually said, unlike 21st century Bibles. If one tried to live one's life by a 21st century Bible, it would be like trying to find one's house on a 2000-year-old map. Yet if one tried to live one's life by the words in the Holy Comic, one would find it to be slappy silly fun.

?^&$%#

After the choo-choo rolled into town, a warped group of complete idiots began work erecting the Big Top. Then the complete idiots assembled the Ferris wheel and the carousel behind it. Circus would begin after dark to allow for all the colored lights to shine as bright as stars. The big top was a green and white striped model with flags on each of its three masts. The flagpoles were topped with statues of Jesus the Clown in various poses. No circus is complete without music and this one had the most unnecessarily large P.A.system in the Western Hemisphere. The thing could blow your hat off at 100 paces and could be heard piping away for miles. This was how the clowns were reminded the circus was in town. This was also what made you feel guilty if you didn't go. Whether you went or not, you were gonna listen to those pipes all through the night.

&*^%$#

To celebrate Blinko's big day, Miss Smoochy had taken him and seven of the older kids to Yucky's Greasy Spoon for dinner. All had chocolate sundies except for Blinko who got to have the traditional first-circus banana split. It had only gotten dark as they were leaving and they piled into Smoochy's moderately tiny jalopy (indicative of her income bracket.)
"Well, Blinko, it's almost time!"
This caused the children to cheer. It was a short ride.

The Big Top was beginning to fill as they arrived. After paying admission for all her children, Miss Smoochy shuffled them inside. The sight of thousands of clowns, all in one place, was exciting for the kinderclowns, but especially for Blinko.

"Look at all the hats!" he said. Blinko loved hats. All clowns loved hats. Many had hats like the one Blinko wore, which was a baseball cap. Some backwards, some forwards, but most wore theirs side-ways. Hundreds of folks wore the traditional circus hats and perched them awkwardly on their noggins because they were too small. Some clowns wore hats so small the flowers in the band were bigger than the hats themselves. Clownettes wore their elaborate hats like it was a competition, which it may very well have been. Some covered in flowers, some veiled, some with giant brims, some with no brim at all, and every one a different shape, size, and color. One suzie was wearing a fruit bowl and clowns were sneaking away items from it. She didn't seem to mind. Another had a birdcage on her head and the parrot inside it wore a tiny derby.

> Top hats with polka dots
> Bottom hats with stripes
> Party hats and beanies
> All of different types
> Big ones and small ones
> Some are in between
> That one is yellow
> But this one is green
> Babies with sun bonnets
> Adults wearing visors
> A hat with a fountain
> That squirts like a geyser
> Some with propellers
> Others came with fans
> Big ones with feathers
> Are worn by the band
> Hats made of felt
> Hats you can eat
> Some towards the ceiling
> And some towards the feet
> Hats for the cowboys
> And hats for the sailors
> Hats for the postman
> And hats for the mailers
> Hats just for fishing
> Hats just for mothers
> Hats for the poppas
> And sisters and brothers
> Chef's hats and helmets
> And hats made of leather
> Hats for the nice days
> And hats for foul weather

Hats for detectives
Hats for police
Hats for your nephew
Hats for your niece
Hats for your grandpa
And hats for his wife
If you tried to count 'em
I'd take all your life.

"Miss Smoochy, look!" bubbled Blinko, tugging her dress. He was pointing at the Poopla.

"That's the Grand Poopla. He's the funniest clown in town!" She took the boy into her lap.

"Will I get to meet him?"

"You sure will, Blinko, he's gonna welcome you to the circus."

%^&%$#

Dropping his holy bowling pins in perfect clown fashion, the juggling Poobla Boo-Boo brought the gathering to its feet in a howl of laughter. After placing the pins inside the Bundle of Holy Stuff, he took his customary place on a circular riser in the center ring. He raised his hands into the air to signal the spectators to be silent. The clamor died down.

"Good clowns of Buffoonville, would you please give a big hand to the World Circus Monks!" proclaimed the Poobla, as 25 midgets scrambled into the ring with him. The monks ran circles around the Poobla, finally coming to a halt in a curved line, 2-deep in front of him. The audience gave a big hand.

"And in ring number one…the Disciples of Grand Lunacy…masters of laughter, to perform for your pleasure. Let's hear IT for them!!" The fans took him literally shouting "IT!", then laughed at themselves. Making a simple joke by taking something literally was a clown favorite.

The disciples made a broad circle in the center of the ring. They were all dressed in the disciple's habit, which was a strangely patterned one-piece coverall with four medium sized pom-poms down the front. Each also had their heads shaved and wore no shoes.

On cue with the music, one of the disciples stepped out of the circle and into its center. There he placed a water glass onto the dirt and sawdust floor. Then, another of the group came over with a pail and ladle and filled the glass with water. Next, the disciple placed his arms out in front of himself as the drum roll began. Drawing his arms to his chest, he assumed the posture of one about to dive. He shook his patooty in time with the drummer who pa-dump-bumped at the apex of each butticular stride. Finally as the drum roll resumed, the disciple leaped into the air, clicked his ankles and dove headfirst into the glass. PHOONT!

He remained upside down, head stuffed completely morphed inside the drinking glass, feet kicking madly. Eventually he collapsed and then sprung to his feet to go running around the ring in a panic, glass still on his head, as another of his brethren chased after him with a mallet. Soon the chase clown batted the diver over the head, breaking the glass. For a moment the diver's noggin stayed compressed in the shape of the glass like a slab of dog food poured fresh from the can. It made loud popping and squishing sounds as it resumed its proper shape. Five canaries promptly flew out of his ears to orbit his cranium. The clowns in the bleachers cheered and stomped, clearly impressed by the performance. The diver took a deep bow, then got in step with the others as they left the ring.

The fun was just beginning. The midget monks had formed a line in the center ring. It looked like the unemployment line in Hollywood just after the Wizard of Oz wrapped. Anyway, the stoutest of the monks stood squarely in the center of the ring. Then the next in line climbed up onto his shoulders, then the next up both onto his and so on. Eventually the 25th monk was on the shoulders of the 24th. With each averaging 3 foot tall, it was a 75-foot tower of monks. The tower began to sway gently, but before long the wavelength of the towers instability had increased so much that it was certain to topple at any moment. The spectators were rustling about feeling uneasy, for they could only imagine that a great accident was about to occur. Some of the suzies screamed when it finally toppled.

The tower bent perfectly in its center and somehow defied the laws of gravity long enough for the shoulders of the 25th monk to meet the bottoms of the first monk's feet! This created a giant hoop that began to roll around the ring faster and faster until it had slipped from the grasp of centrifugal force to sputter out like a coin on a table top. Then suddenly all motion ceased, leaving the audience awestruck to discover all 25 monks evenly spaced in a perfect circle along the perimeter of the ring facing them, arms out, making little letter "T's." TA-DA!

With that, the initial festivities were over and the Grand Poobla entered the ring. A blue and yellow striped pulpit was brought out to the center of the ring, followed by two elephants in pink tutus who sat on either side of the Poobla like mammoth pachyderm sentinels. The clowns grew silent.

"Let us, bozo's and suzies, bow our heads in prayer." Miss Smoochy looked over to be sure that all her children had their hats off, heads down, hands folded. The Poobla began:

Oh, most reverent nitwit
We thy humbled fools offer praise
To thy profound lunacy
Thou art indeed a divine numbskull
How much so we aspire to thy faultless idiocy
How greatly we desire thy utter lack of brains
Thy attic is truly empty and
Thy thinker thinketh not
Oh, sacred towering fathead
Ye possess not common sense and
Thou marbles hath been lost forever
Pious half-wit
Oh, great and innocent buffoon
Our beloved immortal ding-bat

Silly art thou in heaven above we
Thy grateful dummies
Guide us, oh, blockhead
Show us the path to thy crack-brained ignorance
Oh, hallowed moron, absurdity is thy bidding
We worship thy laughable half-baked folly
Untainted ignoramus
King of dullards
Mislead us into dopiness
Senseless art thou, oh, purely illogical savior
We would tickle ourselves pink
In thy adel-headed name
Immaculate simpleton
We gather in thy Big Top to give testimony
To thy muscular mental atrophy
Lead us oh, holy sap
We are thy loving moronic dunces
Sinless baloney brain
Thy judgment is poor.
Thy mind unstable
Have mercy, oh, weirdo, on us
As we praise thy saintly stupidity
We are but weenies compared to thy
Ludicrous stupor
Unintelligent one
Oh, cuckoo
Your oafdom without measure
Thy cockeyed perfection without competition
Unspotted nincompoop
Give us this day a sliver of thy
Madcap retardation
A tid-bit of thy pea brain
We who are created in thy preposterous image
Ask thy share thy foolishness
Thy never ending lack of smarts
Oh, virtuous boob
Immensely goofy screwball
Pity our hopeless attempts at matching
Thy feeble mindedness
In the circus as it is done in Heaven
We practice thy holy moronic wishes
AMEN.

> "AMEN!" went the clowns.
> "Puh-dump-bump!" went the drummer.
> The band started up.

Dunt-dunt…dunna-dunna…dunt-dunt…duna
Dunt-dunt…dunna-dunna…dunt-dunt…duna

The tune was thousands of years old.

    Poobla Boo-Boo opened the Bundle of Holy Stuff and removed the three holy bowling pins. He began to juggle. One of the monks came out with a golden unicycle, and placed it in front of the Poobla as the elephants were led away. He mounted the cycle by doing a front flip without dropping a pin and then rode off in a terror around the track that skirted the perimeter of the bleachers. Eventually he wound up back in the center ring where he crashed into the pulpit. Miraculously, one of the pins landed on the very top of his 3-foot Poobla's hat as the other two crashed beside him. Picking them up, he went in search of the one missing pin. This issued a whooping laugh from the spectators who could see clearly what the Poobla could not.

    The Poobla mounted his unicycle in order to search for the pin more quickly as several monks frantically chased after him, pointing at his hat. It seemed that everyone under the big top knew where the missing pin was except the Poobla.

    The monks finally tired and were replaced by another who was riding a midget sized unicycle. He quickly caught up to the Poobla and began tugging at his smock. "What is it, young monk?"

    "Can't you see I'm searching for my missing bowling pin?" the monk whistled and pointed at the top of the Poobla's hat. The Poobla could not understand what the monk was trying to tell him. None of this mattered for both being distracted from navigational duties by their conversation shortly crashed into the bleachers right in front of Miss Smoochy's excited kinderclowns. The pin flew off the hat to land in the hands of Blinko.

    Coming to his feet, the Poobla spoke:

    "Oh, joy! Oh, joy! The lad has found my missing bowling pin! Won't someone remind me to reward him later!" Blinko cheered. Stepping back from the bleachers, the Poobla was nearly run over by the rest of the monks who blared by in go-carts. The monks went 'round and 'round the big top performing a host of formations and perfectly executed near misses. Little did they know that in the animal pens, a wee mouse had just sent one of the usually somber elephants into hysterics. She came trumpeting out into the arena creating a 24 go-cart pile up as the monks crashed into her. This prompted the poor animal to make 24-monk pancakes as she stomped them one and all. Eventually she was brought under control and the emergency jalopy was dispatched.

    The only thing more amazing to watch than these events was the uncommon feat performed by the quack, who somehow managed to stuff all 24 of the monk pancakes and himself into the absolutely diminutive jalopy, as well as the tremendous spatula he used to scrape them off the turf. He then made a couple revolutions around the arena, only to stop right on the spot he started from. Leaping out of the jalopy, he made short work of removing the monk pancakes, laying them in an ordered row. One by one he revived the flattened monks with a unicycle pump and upon re-inflation all of the monks faced the audience and took a bow.

WHAT A SHOW!

>^%#%

Now, the Poobla was making rounds, making balloon animals for all the kinder-clowns.

"Will I get one, Miss Smoochy?" said Blinko.

"Climb down there with the rest and see, Blinko." Smoochy knew that the boy wouldn't be skipped for this was the portion of the World Circus were first timers got jacked. The Poobla was coming their way.

"One for you......"
SQURK-SQUEEK-POYT-SQUAK-

"One for you...."
POONT-BWEEP-DOINK-SQWELCH

"One for you....."
BWEEP-VOONT-SKORK-PLURP

"Well now, who do we have here? I remember you! You're the lad that found my missing bowling pin! Tell me, Son...is this your first circus?"

Blinko was shy and only nodded yes.

"Okay! So what's your name?"

"Blinko."

"Blinko is it. Well, that's a funny name for a clown. Why don't you ride on me piggy-back and we'll have some fun."

Blinko looked back to Miss Smoochy to see if it was okay. She waved him off. Boo-Boo turned his back and the kinderclown climbed aboard. The two trotted over to the center ring and the Poobla let the lad down on the riser. The Poobla kneeled in front of Blinko and pointed at the little statuette on his hat.

"Tell me boy...do you know who this is?"

"That's Jesus the Clown!"

"That's right, Blinko, and did you know that Jesus loves you?"

"Uh-huh."

"And do you love Jesus, Blinko?"

"Uh-huh!" The Poobla got up to his feet.

"Did you hear that everyone? Blinko loves Jesus!"

"HIP-HIP-Hurray!" shouted the clowns.

"Today is Blinko's first circus and we're going to baptize him!"

"HIP-HIP-Hurray!"

"Alright then...here, boy, wouldn't you like to be baptized in the name of Jesus the Clown?"

"NEATO!" Blinko was nearly jumping out of his pants..

"SO LET IT BE WRITTEN, SO LET IT BE DONE!"

The Poobla seemed perplexed. Something shoulda happened.

"SO LET IT BE WRITTEN, SO LET IT BE DONE!"

A Disciple of Grand Lunacy ran out and threw a bucket of water on the Poobla, to the delight of the clowns.

"NO, NO, NO, NO...you're supposed to throw the water on him, not me! Now get it right next time!"

"SO LET IT BE….SPLASH!!" the disciple soaked him again. The Poobla feigned anger. This was a well-rehearsed act.

"ON HIM! NOT ME! GOT IT?" The disciple nodded.
"SO LET IT BE WRITTEN, SO LET IT BE DONE!"

The disciple stood holding the bucket directly before Blinko. The kinderclown was already cringing in anticipation of being soaked. The disciple swung the bucket back dramatically…ONE…then forward … back … TWO … forward … back … THREE!! Blinko screamed as the disciple launched the contents of the bucket, but was surprised to find himself covered only in confetti! The spectators cheered for the boy's baptism.
"Well, how do you feel now that your soul's been cleansed?" said the sopping Poobla.

"I feel funny!" replied the youngster.

"Did you hear that everyone? The boy says he feels FUNNY! Another soul saved by confetti! Three Cheers!"

The clowns gave three. He sent Blinko back to the bleachers. Miss Smoochy was all teary eyed and dried her cheeks as the tot came running back to the group. And that was that.

^&%#^%

"Confetti….that reminds me, would any clown like to come out to the center ring to make a confession?"

The Poobla eyed the spectators to see if he'd have a sinner that day. A smallish mayhem began near the first ring, as a reluctant clown was pushed out of his seat and onto the turf by his wife. This was one of the things he hated about her.

"*Why must she always be so ridiculous?*" he thought as he made his way over to the Poobla. Boo-Boo greeted him loudly.

"Oh, good, a SINNER and a SINNER who wants to be saved! A SINNER who wants to confess his SINS right here under the big top. Let's have a big hand for the SINNER everyone!"

The crowd clapped as the embarrassed clown stepped up to the riser.

"So sinner, what's your name?" said the Poobla to the increasingly nervous clown.

"Wiggles, your holiness."

"Ah…Wiggles is it…well, it's a good thing you decided to confess before it's to late isn't it…hmmmm"

"S'pose so"

"BEHOLD!"

This was another of many cues that the Poobla employed. The disciples came running out, props in hand, to begin work building a set that was finished almost as soon as they began. There was a 15-foot high and quite imposing judge's box with two lamps on its desk corners. On top of the desk was a giant sized gavel. Next to the judges box was a midget witness stand and in its center was a tiny chair. A stern looking disciple stood next to the jury box that was full of monks. Wiggles was led to the witness seat and upon sitting was forced to bring his knees up to his chest and under his chin to fit himself into the cramped space. The effect was to make the witness feel as small and unimportant as possible. It even looked that way from the perspective of the clowns. The Poobla took a seat in the judge's throne and put on a curly white wig after removing his Pooblas hat. Immediately, he put forth a question to Wiggles.

"Mr. Wiggles! Is it not true that you have been neglecting to act funny?" He didn't give Wiggles time to answer. "And is it not also true that you haven't juggled in over two months?"

"Well…I…UH…."

"And is it not true that you have been mean to your wife simply because she is a devout practitioner of Grand Lunacy and is only trying to make you laugh?"

"Well….UH…I…"

"And is it not true that you have been going down on the east-side to drink tutti-fruity and spend the rent money on floosies?"

Wiggles could only squirm in his seat as the clowns booed him and gasped in disbelief of both the extent of Wiggles sins and of the apparent mind reading skills of the Poobla.

"And is it also not true that you have been making whoopee by yourself?"

"NO!" shouted a red-faced Wiggles.

"And you have been getting serious with some of your bad clown buddies haven't you?"

"NO! NO! It's a lie!"

"And you refuse to take your jelly-beans in the morning don't you?"

"NO! It's not true!"

"And you won't take out the garbage!"

"NO! I mean YES!"

"And you won't do the dishes either…"

"YES! I mean NO! I mean…" Wiggles broke down and began to cry. He confessed.

"Oh, forgive me… holiness… It's all true! I confess!!"

"Did you hear that everyone? He confessed! Good show, Wiggles, by confessing your sins you can be saved." Poobla Boo-Boo smacked the gavel hard on the desk. POW! He pointed at the jury of monks.

"Jury, do you have a verdict for Mr. Wiggles?" A monk on one end stood to say…

"We, oh, most reverent nit-wit have a verdict indeed.

"And what say you?" said the Poobla.

"Let the sinner be healed. Heal the sinner!" The Poobla turned to Wiggles.

"Well, Mr. Wiggles, the jury thinks you deserve to be healed. What do you think of that?" Wiggles stood up leaving the tiny little chair between his legs.

"Healed? Why should I be healed?"

"Because you are not funny, Mr. Wiggles, that's why! But you'll regain your sense of humor once you're healed, I promise."

With that two disciples grabbed Wiggles and held him firmly as he struggled.

"But I don't want to be healed!" he screamed.

"That's what they all say!" The Poobla had come down from his seat. Then he looked up and began to pray.

Oh, backward frothing Ding-a-ling
Grant me the power to restore this pitiful clown who hath lost his will to chuckle

Great and holy retarded guy in the sky
Help me… to help him… help himself!
In the name of the Father, the Son
And the holy bowling pins… BE HEALED!!

Mr. Wiggles grimaced as the bottom of the Grand Poobla's tremendous boot collided with his butt.

"BE HEALED!" shouted the Poobla once again sending his foot to impact upon the backside of the clown.

"BE HEALED!" The third blow sent Wiggles flying into the air. He crashed into the sawdust, face first.

It was not unusual for a recently healed clown to become unhinged after the third salvo and begin to laugh uncontrollably. This was the usual symptom of the spirit of God and all his immaculate comedy filling one's soul. But it was very unusual for a recently healed clown to do what Wiggles was doing.

Wiggles threw his hat down and began to stomp on it violently. His face turned red and steam began to curl off his bald head and spewed out his ears. Flames shot out of his flared nostrils. He began to shimmy and shake. With his shoulders hunched up and his head hunkered down between them, Mr. Wiggles walked with stiff arms and legs like some kinda Frankenstein towards the Poobla.

The Poobla was shocked at the sight of an enraged clown under the Big Top, of all places, and more so at the sight of him coming towards him. Equally shocked were the Disciples of Grand Lunacy and the 25 monks. The thousands of worshipers in the circus were confused as well. But no one there was more shocked than Mr. Wiggles because he had never been possessed by Satano before…an evil supernatural force imprisoned whatever it was, in a clown's head that makes him be who he was. There was no escape. This is because when Satano possesses your body, its very serious business. Mr. Wiggles let out a sinister laugh as Satano toyed with his body like a dime store puppet. "MOO-HOO-HA-HA-HA-HA-HA-HA-HA-HAH!"

"I'll show you what it's like to get healed, you farcical rot for brains! Nobody's gonna kick me in the butt and get away with it!"

The disciples and the monks formed a triangular blockade in front of the Poobla in a desperate attempt to protect him from the demonized Wiggles. It was a futile endeavor, for after vomiting up a 13-pound, blue and white swirled bowling ball, the possessed Wiggles simply mowed them down with one throw. With the disciples and the monks wounded and incapacitated on the turf, the Poobla was helpless.

The clowning crowd stood frozen, doing nothing for there wasn't a solid backbone in the house. Clowns are natural fraidy-cats and cowards. Blinko was crying being more scared than he had ever been in his four short years. Miss Smoochy was gathering up all her babies and huddling with them in the horror of it all.

The Grand Poobla was stiff as a popsicle as well. Something deep down in his undeveloped mind told him that this was not just some ordinary clown gone bad. Madly he searched through the Bundle of Holy Stuff in the hopes of finding anything with which to ward off the attack.

"The joy buzzer! No, that won't do! The giant boxing glove! Nope, that won't work either. Yes! That's it! The rubber mallet!" The Poobla took aim and hurled the massive hammer at Wiggles. It struck him square in the honker. HONK!

"MOO-HOO-HA-HA-HA-HA-HAH!" was Wiggles only response to the blow. He picked up the mallet and began banging himself over the head with it as he continued to close in. BONK! BONK! BONK!

"You'll have to do better than that, mindless bobblehead!" BONK! BONK! BONK!

"Oh, no, what more can I do?" panicked the Poobla, still searching his bundle. He pulled forth the brass horn and was struck with an answer. Clearly this clown was possessed. This called for an exorcism. Suddenly, he felt calm as he regained his sense of lunacy and shortly gave in to the ridiculous absurdity in order to use his faith to combat the demon. Then in a fit of unrestrained retardation, he attempted to drive the demon from the clown. BONK! BONK! BONK!

> Doodly-doodly-squat!
> My thinker thinketh not!
> Be gone from Wiggles, demon!
> And stay shall you not even!
> I cast this demon out!
> Like boogers from my snout!
> For Jesus owns this soul!
> Climb back inside your hole!
> Nanny-nanny-boo-boo!
> Stick your head in poo-poo!
> Be gone from Wiggles, demon!
> Stay shall you not even!

The Poobla punctuated his ravings with a WONKLE! WONKLE! Any ordinary demon would have found the absurdity of all this more than they could bear. It would be impossible for one to stick around in such laughable conditions. However, this was not an ordinary demon, this was Satano, the titanic dark and dismal god of evil and despair. He was well accustomed to absurdity, for nearly every damned soul to enter Hell made grand fools of themselves begging for mercy and what not. The unspeakable one spoke:

"Only a complete idiot would try that bozokahkah on me! But it looks like there's no shortage of idiots around here!!"

The Poobla was horrified to see that his exorcism had failed. "Run for your lives!" he yelled, "This clown's possessed by Satano himself!" Mr. Wiggles let out an ear-splitting laugh as the clowns totally wigged out and tried to split. None managed to escape, however, because the Devil did a magic trick and froze them in numerous panicked poses. Wiggles came up to the petrified Poobla. "I've got a big surprise for you Boo-Boo."

Satano turned Wiggles back to the immobilized Poobla, then stooped over dropping Wiggles drawers. Grasping a cheek in each hand the Devil spread Wiggles kiester wide saying…"Check out this WONKLE WONKLE, pal!"

It would be needlessly obscene to describe what Satano did to Wiggle's intestines or the heinous sound that it made, however, the end results of what he did created an extremely violent gaseous semi-fluid vapor which creeped in agonizing slowness towards the frozen Poobla and his defenseless nostrils.

Upon enveloping the Poobla (who held his breath instinctively) the vapor seemed to throb and pulsate, as if it knew that eventually the clown would be forced to breathe. This is of course exactly what happened and upon doing so the Poobla squirmed, feet glued to the riser, defenseless against the malevolent, animated odor. If Satano had had the slightest shred of compassion, he might have given the Poobla a swifter death, but he didn't, of course. This left the Poobla to be nasally tortured for agonizing minutes only to melt into a puddle in the last ten seconds of them. The disciples and monks melted with him also. The same fate was left to poor Wiggles, as well. The prince of darkness vacated the body immediately after cutting the lethal cheese in order to escape a stink so vile even his stench battered senses would protest.

Released from their invisible bonds, the crowds rushed the exits as the screams of clowns trampled underfoot were drowned out by those fortunate enough to escape unharmed. Shortly, the Big Top was as silent as it was empty. Save for:

    A puddle of Poobla
    A puddle of Wiggles
    A lingering stench
    Makes nothing giggle
    25 puddles consisting of monks
12 loony puddles with tid-bits and chunks
39 victims all killed by Satano
Who now sits in Hell as he
Plays his piano
"Killed me some clowns
Mostly good but one bad
Every one's cryin' but I'm feelin glad
Cut me a fart and
It killed thirty-nine
I should cut farts like that
All of the time."
Sung the old demon
Somewhere in his Hell
The Big Top was empty
Except for that smell

Chapter 4
It's Damn Fun

When the people of Earth woke up to face the various mornings across the globe, it was just another miserable day. Jesus Christ was back but very little had changed because of it yet. Jesus had said a lot of stuff that previous night and most people were pretty confused. But it was okay because they were like that most the time anyway. Under such mind blowing circumstances, most people did what they had always done and waited to see what their governments would do about it. Likewise their governments did what they usually do, under such mind blowing circumstances, and waited to see what the world's religious leaders would do about it. Hiding out in the Vatican, in Rome, the world's religious leaders were doing what they usually do under such mind blowing circumstances…arguing among themselves.

It was weird because thanks to Christ's little miracle, each spoke in their native tongue only to be understood by everyone. This made it really hard to talk behind the others backs like they were used to doing. These discussions could take weeks, months, even years. But the men of various cloth knew the brunt of responsibility fell on their shoulders. Of all the jerks on Earth, it was up to them to interpret Christ's words. Now many of them wished they hadn't gone around acting as though they had all the answers for so long. Some how they would have to make up for all the lies they had been telling for past 2000 years. Thankfully they weren't' totally wrong. At least they had gotten the "Pay for your sins" part right, even if they had fouled up on what the sins were. Needless-to-say the task set before them would be hard.

=?%^$@

The Son of God was sun bathing nude on a towel on a sparsely populated island in the Caribbean. He was not in the least bit shy about his nudity because he was a God and because the locals were also naked. This string of tropical islands had been designated all nude way back in the late 1990's when there had been much controversy about the size of people's bathing suits. It seemed that surgically enhanced females had taken to wearing "butt floss" as a swimsuit. The controversy created by this, in those backward and puritanical times, branched out to such degree that people simply quit going to the beach in fear of either being arrested or ridiculed. These islands solved the problem by making suits of any kind illegal.

As the golden God took in some rays, he was approached by a small, brown, dread-locked boy who was naked except the rubber flip-flops on his feet. The boy was excited because the hippie had promised him ten dollars if he would fetch some mangos and bottled water. The Savior paid the boy as soon as the delivery was made.

"Can I ask you somthin', Mon?" said the youngster.

"You may…" said the Lord, biting into the fruit.

"Are you a clown sometimes? Are you the clown I saw on the television?"

"What makes you think that?"

"It's just the feeling that I get, Mon …It's your energy…"

"Yeah. I'ma clown sometimes."

The boy began to dance tossing his long locks to a beat only he could hear.

"Would you come over to my house din? My mother be a fan of yours. She cook…we eat." The savior was never one to turn down a chance to break bread.

"An ideal idea!" said the hippie who had gotten up taking the child's hand.

"Here boy, follow me…see if you can walk in my foot prints in the sand. I know the way to your mother's house. Maybe she will have me fix the roof. I used to be a carpenter you know."

"Moms say you can do anything…that be so?"

"Well, I'm pretty good at fixing roofs."

And indeed he was. Later that day, after their meal, when the afternoon rains came, the boy and his mother marveled at what a fine job Jesus did. But it was getting late in the cosmic scheme of things. Even the Lord has to go home sometimes. Christ bid the small family farewell but not before giving the boy a box in a plane brown wrapper. He instructed the child to be out on the beach the next day at exactly 12:30 pm. and to wave at a canoe passing by. The child was to present the passengers of the canoe the box then run for his life because the men in the canoe were cannibals and would try to eat him. With that, the angel made his assent into Heaven.

$%$#@#

The Monk, the Rabbi and the Pope, surrounded by the seething group of other God-fearing men, sat in one of the Vatican's many golden chambers. Many of the men were uncomfortable. This was not because of the gross display of wealth but rather the fact that they were actually lost within the untold thousands of corridors, halls, passages, and tunnels forming the floor plan of the immense structure. These pompous and rarely kind pontiffs were slowly getting used to understanding languages that they could not speak. Presently, the Monk was speaking in a nasally Chinese onslaught:

"So what are we to do? We have heard what Christ said. How are we to carry out his plan?"

The Rabbi, reluctantly accepting the return of the Savior his people didn't accept as the Savior the first time around, replied in Yiddish:

"I suggest we first try to interpret what Jesus meant exactly."

A small voodoo witch doctor objected in a bizarre language that consisted of him dancing, throwing bones to the floor, and screaming while spitting blood.

"I think that Christ's words were self explanatory and do not need interpretation."

"Nobody asked you!" said the Pope in Latin "Besides we all know that's not how it works."

"What's that supposed to mean?" demanded the witch doctor by twisting his head around backwards like an owl. His neck popped and cracked loudly, sending chills down the spines of those closest to him. The Pope replied:

"It's an insult to God to suppose we pitiful human beings can understand his word at face value. History shows us that the relevance of God's word depends entirely on how we interpret the hidden deeper meanings within them."

"Here! Here!" shouted a Baptist minister. "The Pope iz rat. I'ds gonna be-up tuh us to figgur out whut Jay-zus Christ meant. I sez we all puts our heads togethuh and commence to inturpritin' his words right quick like, an then we ought to come up with a hole new ruh-lij-un in order tuh best serve duh Lord, an tuh help the less ment'ly capable peoples with getting in tuh Heaven an all."

The Monk took over from there:

"But was it not a mistaken interpretation on all our parts which led us to fail our common God?"

"In a manner of speaking, yes" said a mild looking Amish peasant dressed in simple black.

"But Christ only condemned our mistaken interpretations where we had been tricked by Satano. He did not condemn the idea of interpreting his word as we have always done. Clearly, he meant for us to correct our mistakes and continue as always doing the Lord's work."

This was met with applause and a vote in which it was almost unanimously decided to implement the minister's suggestion of creating a world-wide new religion. Only the witch doctor abstained which he did by defecating on the floor at his turn. All they need do was study the hidden meanings in what Jesus had said and use this as the basis for the new theology. No easy task, but all felt duty bound, and full of themselves for so quickly reaching an agreement…a precedent.

%$^%#@

Guh Mooga Wump the 2nd and his son Guh Mooga Wump the 3rd were kicking back in the rear of their luxury canoe. The canoe moved along at a steady pace, it being powered by slaves taken from their rivals the Boondaby. They were heading back to the small patch of South American rain forest they called home, or at least what was left of it. One of his warriors, the one with the telescope, shouted to their leader:

"Guh Mooga Wump meen-kiby-jah-noon-digguh-hooky-zoom-uh-mooga-hooky-nu-zoom-dooky-kibby-boonsnoby! *Guh Mooga Wump the 2nd, if you're interested, there is a boy there who is waving to us!*" the warrior was pointing at the beach.

"Kibby-boonsnoby?" replied Guh Mooga Wump the 2nd *"To us?"*

"Uh-huh. Meen-mooga-zoom-dooky-kibby-boonsnoby. *Uh-huh. The boy is waving to us.*"

Guh mooga wump the 2nd thought for a moment, then turned to his son and spoke:

"Ibu-nibu-kibu-meen-mooga-himey-chow-peeny-nibu-ibu-hut-stimpy-mooga-nu-zoom-meen-ibby-wump? *We could kill the boy, then eat him could we not, my boy who is the third king.*"

"Ibu-nibu!" said his son. *"We could!"*

Guh Mooga Wump gave the order "Himey-ibu-pigy-chow-meen-mooga! *Then we shall eat the boy!*"

The slaves brought the canoe around and began to paddle to the boy's location on the shore. Many of the men licked their lips in anticipation of the meal.

On the shore was the little boy with his rubber flip-flops. He was sitting on the box that Jesus had left with him. When Guh Mooga Wump the 2nd and company reached him on the shore, it made for an odd scene. Had this band of cannibals shown up almost anywhere else on Earth, they would have been in stark contrast to the average sun-bather, as they wore nothing save for a hollow gourd in which to stuff their penises. Here on this particular beach they were actually over dressed and in violation of the law. The boy of course was nude like everyone else. He immediately said to the cannibals:

"Don't kill me! Don't kill me I have a gift for the chief!"

Guh Mooga Wump the 2nd was amazed to understand this child's foreign tongue. He replied: "Stimpy…stimpy…stimpy..himey-ibu-piggy-hut-kibu-noo-un-chow-noo-mooga, noon-leeky! Looga-zoom-meen-plumy?"

The little rastafarian understood him perfectly.

"My..my..my…then we shall not kill you and eat you boy, you're lucky, I'm freakin' starving! Where is the package?"

"It's right here!" said the boy, getting up and sliding the box out from betwixt his legs. Guh Mooga Wump the 2nd knelt down to inspect the box in its plain brown wrapper. Then he lifted it into the air and shook it. KA-PLUNK! KA-PLUNK! TOUNK! TOUNK!

"What could it be?" thought Guh Mooga Wump who brought the box to the ground, promptly tearing it open, eager to receive his unexpected gift. What he found brought tears to his eyes. It was his beloved missing 13-pound blue and white swirled bowling ball! There was a small note attached:

Poo-Guh-Mooga-Wump,
Chi-tunk-noon-neebu-ooga-kiby-deeko-goomy-yumi.
Leeky-noon,
Jesus Christ

Dear Guh Mooga Wump,
I thought you would like to have this back.
Lucky you,
Jesus Christ

Tossing the note aside, the chief thrust his hands inside the box. Taking hold, he brought the ball up above his head, marveling at it. Behind him stood his son and the rest. The trip had not been in vain after all! Somehow even though he had not been able to give Jesus the ceremonial spear, his prayers had been answered. The chief began to tremble. The chief began to shake. Then for the first time since he cried for his father when his grandfather died, he began to cry for himself.

The only person more shocked than Guh Mooga Wump's son, at the sight of his father shedding his own tears, was the little dread-locked boy, who was shocked at the sight of Guh Mooga Wump the 2nd's head abruptly plopping down upon the sand…cut off by Guh Mooga the 3rd thus making him king.

The chief's body followed its head dropping onto the sand letting blood dribble out of the stump above the shoulders. The little Rastafarian screamed as he turned, running away. The warriors let him flee.

Guh Mooga Wump the 3rd placed his foot on the chest of his freshly executed father and began speaking in a stern voice: "UH-ZOOGIE-HUMPLE-HUT-YOOGY-DUPY! *A WARRIOR DOES NOT SHED TEARS FOR HIMSELF!"*

Now, he was chief. He reminded himself to be sure and have his own son cry for him over his father's death. Cradling the bowling ball in his arms like an infant, he commanded his warriors and slaves to place his father's corpse in the canoe, board it and set off. He was sorry for having to massacre his father but at least now they would have plenty to eat on their long voyage home.

^$#^%$@

Believe it or not the world's religious leaders had finally come up with a solution. Despite the fact that Jesus Christ had meant exactly what he had said, these men had managed to find an enormous amount of additional information through interpretation. They had spent many moons searching for the hidden messages they felt God expected them to find in the words of his son. All were proud of what a good job they done. With these interpretations in the form of a new and improved Bible, they would be the artisans responsible for helping the planet's population conform to God's will.

The whole thing was kept secret as they worked out the gazillion details of what would be the greatest reformation of the world's religions in history. A new dawn in the evolution of man towards being the living embodiment of God's intent was about to unfold in a monumental leap towards Heaven on Earth. At least that's how they had it figured.

It is written that on the day that these men came before their people to share their interpretations of God's word, and to explain how everyone was supposed to conduct themselves, millions of human beings felt that what these men proposed was completely ridiculous.

+^&$@#

In a fabulously decorated 1000 year old chair, fit for the butt of an emperor, the Chinese dictator Won Hung Low sat forward and said to the Monk: "You must be joking!"

#^%$%@

President Newberry leaned across the obnoxiously huge, cherry-wood desk and said to the Baptist minister: "You've got to be kidding!"

^&$#@%

Guh Mooga Wump 3 rd examined the scratchings in the dirt made by the witch doctor and said: "Jan-zoom-tootsie! *It is crazy!*"

@#$^%*

Chet, the redneck, sat up in his lazy-boy and talked to the glowing screen of his Curtis Mathis: "I can't freakin' believe it!"

^%#@$%

From a high balcony in the Vatican, the Pope stood before a crowd of some 250,000 devoted Catholics, non-Catholics, and various others. He was dressed in his usual papal robes and hat. He was also wearing a pair of gigantic white shoes, with his face painted to resemble a perfect clown, a red nose bulb along with all the other clown trappings. "It's damn fun!" he proclaimed to the bewildered masses.

#^%$^%

It is written that it took a while for the announcement to settle in. It also took a massive effort on the part of the human beings to pool together their resources to outfit the entire population properly. Not to mention the complete remodeling of thousands of public buildings and churches. But it was as they say "DAMN FUN!" After a few years the reformation was essentially complete.

ALL THE WORLD A CIRCUS AND ITS PEOPLE THE CLOWNS

Chapter 5
Selected readings from: The All Knowing Owl Speaks
Volume: 970,553,267,849,100,371: Jehovah's Domain
Book: 463,967,885,301 : Earth History
Chapter: 46,783,345 : Extinction of the Human Species
Paragraph: 354,648,512,633

354,648,512,633: SAYETH THE OWL

YEAR 52 S.C. (2125 A.D.) It is written that the Great Clown Reformation was not without its share of unique problems. For many, who dressed up in clown suits and wore the correct make-up according to social stature, still did not get the joke. There were those who were simply born without a sense of humor…humor being the sixth-sense according to the Doctrines of Grand Lunacy. It was considered no less a disability than being born blind or deaf. However, there were many more human beings being born without a sense of humor than either of those and the World Circus was desperate for a solution.

354,648,512,634: SAYETH THE OWL

It came to pass that the World Circus was solicited for funding by a Negro woman scientist named Suzy, who lived on one of the planet's land masses then known as Africa. She herself had been born humorless, which was known to be a disproportionate problem in the people populating her country at that time. One of her theories as to the alarming rate of unfunny people there was that the hundreds of years of oppression these people had endured had all but wiped out their ability to be insincere. Another of her theories was that humor was based upon insincerity or the individual's disposition towards it. She herself served as an example for she was a very serious woman who took her and the other's problem quite seriously. She was dead serious about finding a cure to her seriousness and made a serious solicitation to the World Circus who had a hard time taking her seriously. But eventually they came to realize that this serious woman's sincerity about insincerity was pretty serious and they gave her the serious amounts of rue she needed to get serious about her sincere research. Seriously.

354,648,512,635: SAYETH THE OWL

Suzy began by making a complete study of all known sources of humor, almost all of which she did not find in the least bit amusing. Many of her test subjects were unmoved as well by the general stimuli such as jokes, slapstick, or situational comedy. But it was discovered that there was one type of humor that she and nearly all of her participants laughed at and that was the "unexpected, well executed fart."

354,648,512,636: SAYETH THE OWL

Suzy was excited to have isolated this funniest form of stimuli. This would mean that she could begin an in-depth analysis of the matter and hopefully learn what was at the core of the fart. As it turned out, the fart was discovered to have been funny all the way back to the dawn of man, and was therefore considered a type of genetic memory. What all this proved was that the answer lay in the field of genetics, and that deep in the D. N. A. code of man was a disposition for humor, so she only needed to devise a plan to bring it to the surface. Suzy was also excited because she just happened to be educated in the field of genetics. She also started to eat a lot of beans.

NOTE: By this date in Earth history most forms of science were in sharp decline having little to do with being a clown.

354,648,512,637: SAYETH THE OWL

More research was found to be necessary. There was a complete examination of all the traditionally funny creatures found on the planet. There were also complete examinations of the rapidly growing clown culture. She needed to formulate a combination of traits, from various sources, in order to model her gene codes. It was decided that the importance of looking funny physically could not be underrated. Therefore, she and her colleagues began isolating genes that would give the genetic model the appearance of a grotesque clown.

GENE: [dominant] skin/properties=Albino
GENE: [dominant] nose/properties=bulbous/red
GENE: [dominant] lips/properties=huge
GENE: [dominant] feet/properties=large
GENE: [dominant] ears/properties=large/protruding
GENE: [dominant] hair/properties= unmanageable/bright colors
GENE: [dominant] scalp/properties=baldness
GENE: [dominant] birthmarks/properties=local/brows
GENE: [dominant] birthmarks/properties=local/cheeks
GENE: [dominant] structure/properties=fatness

354,648,512,638: SAYETH THE OWL
The genetic model for the internal functions of the specimen was based on the idea that the specimen would be surviving on a diet of sweets and junk foods only. The genetic model for the body was also necessarily modified to accommodate for clown behavior. Clowns need to be physically tough, yet flexible and limber, so as to avoid serious injury during daily activities. For this she used modified genetic code from cats and gorillas. The real challenge came with the genetic coding for the mind of the specimen, for this was the most essential set of codes in determining the insincerity of the genetic model.

GENESPLICE: [Chimpanzee] brain function
GENESPLICE: [Orangutan] brain function
GENESPLICE: [Spider Monkey] brain function
GENESPLICE: [Laughing Hyena] brain function
GENESPLICE: [Prairie Dog] brain function
GENESPLICE: [Seal] brain function
GENESPLICE: [Sea Otter] brain function

GENESPLICE: [Hamster] brain function
GENESPLICE: [Cuckoo Bird] brain function
GENESPLICE: [3-toed Sloth] brain function
GENE: [dominant] Schizophrenia/brain function
GENE: [dominant] Retardation/ brain function
GENE: [dominant] Non-lethal brain tumors/brain function

354,648,512,639: SAYETH THE OWL

    With the genetic model complete, and all the required genetic codes isolated, the team began combining all the genetic material with a virus, which was to be introduced into a human host. The virus was designed to enter the subject and begin modifying its DNA to be that of the genetic model, then replicate. The team theorized that this would either kill the subject or cause a complete metamorphosis. The next obstacle was finding a willing subject to test the virus on. This problem was solved when Suzy announced that it should be her, for if the experiment was not a success she didn't want to go on living her humorless life anyway.

354,648,512,640: SAYETH THE OWL

    The team injected Suzy in a laboratory and her condition was closely monitored. They were pleased to see that she didn't die right away. Day after day they recorded the minute changes in her physiology. Sure enough, she appeared to be changing into a living, breathing clown. The entire transformation took nine months, which coincidentally was the same amount of time as the gestation period of the human reproductive system.

354,648,512,641: SAYETH THE OWL

    Suzy was nothing like her old self when she was finally released from quarantine. In fact, she may well have been the most insincere being on the planet. She was certainly its first full-blooded clown being. The team was proud to announce to the world that they had found a cure for those born without a sense of humor. What the team was not prepared for was the discovery that the virus in Suzy's body was infectious and could be contracted through the most casual of contacts. The team began to transform in a matter of days after Suzy's release from the sterile environment of the labs and within a year nearly half the world's population had been infected. Two years later, the entire planet was undergoing the metamorphosis and by the third the human species was extinct, having been replaced by clowns completely by the year 55 S.C. (2128 A.D.). However drastic this sounds it is important to keep in mind that….

Chapter 6
Selected readings from: The All Knowing Owl Speaks
Volume: 970,553,267,849,100,371: Jehovah's Domain
Book: 463,967,885,301 : Earth History
Chapter: 46,783,758,345 : The Silent Minority
Paragraph: 354,648,512,433

354,648,512,433: SAYETH THE OWL

Theirs was a silent world and they had always been silent in it. Ages ago when the crazed World Circus Pooblas branded them as the Devil's children, burning them at the stake, not even then did those innocent ancestors, burned alive, speak….nor did they scream.

From: Poems of Nastina

They spoke not at their beatings
They spoke not at their trials
Not when accused of heresy
They stood and mimed denials

354,648,512,434: SAYETH THE OWL

These clown's differences had been the only known birth defect after the extinction of the human race. Honestly, these people weren't really defective, but clowns considered them to be a curse. As the world was acting foolish, only the mimes were forced to struggle through life. That is if they even lived at all. In the old days, horrified mama-suzies often tied their cry-less babies up in a sack, tossing them into a river to their deaths. Or they might turn them over to the World Circus, who would sack and drown them for them.

Occasionally, a clown mother would not have the heart to murder her own and would secretly hide the silent child away in an attic. These clownettes of old hid their curse in shame. The discovery of one kept was the stuff that often tore families apart. Whole towns were known to gather at the doorstep demanding the mime be brought out to be lynched. The frenzied, blood-thirsty, town-clowns would attribute all the misfortunes that had befallen them onto the curse. They demanded swift and ruthless justice.

Some mothers would run away with their mime child in the hopes of finding a place where their children could escape persecution. There was no such place for many, many years. Most were caught and set to the stake as their children were hanged by the devout lunatics.

354,648,512,435: SAYETH THE OWL

During these dark ages of Grand Lunacy, it was in only the remotest corners of the world that a mime could grow into adulthood. Even so, the mime would live in a world that met it with cruelty and alienation. Time brought the clowns out of the Dark Ages and into a Renaissance. Things improved only slightly for the mimes. Now, the silent were given the right to live, but only in sanitariums, surrounded by other condemned clowns with a tendency towards sincerity. As the centuries wore on, the silent would remain locked away despicably in sane asylums for generations. Nothing changed at all for these quiet clowns until the Great War of Morons had come and gone. There was a tremendous revolution of thought after the wars and the silent were given limited rights by law. The World Circus had decided that mimes should be treated as clowns with a fundamental mental illness and that the responsibility of dealing with them should fall upon their parents. So, as the years went by, the mimes were once again being locked away in the attics of the world. Many parents of the quiet clowns secretly wished the practice of sack and drown would come back into fashion. Many did regardless.

354,648,512,436: SAYETH THE OWL

Now, the only clowns found in sane asylums were clowns gone bad. There had never been such a thing as a bad mime. This was the nature of the injustice towards mimes, for not once in 2000 years had a mime intentionally hurt a clown…except maybe clown pride. Truthfully, life in sane asylums had not been so bad for the mimes. They were not isolated and alone like in the attics. There were other mimes there, as well as clowns gone bad who, although far too serious, were more thoughtful and understanding than the average fool. If the tinker-quacks had been more observant, they might have noticed that mimes were quite capable of fitting into clown society if only that society would accept them for what they were…perfect clowns. But they didn't, of course, because they were colossal idiots.

Then, in more recent moments of clown history, the mimes began to organize themselves into small troops. They began to live together in these little silent troops on vacant lots and in remote locations where clowns did not often tread. Being so pure at heart, not one mime harbored hostility towards the clowns who had been so cruel to their kind. No, these gatherings and mini-communes were simply what happened when the mimes were left to their own devices. Somehow, after so many years of persecution, the clowns had forgotten about them but only for the moment, as it turned out.

354,648,512,437: SAYETH THE OWL

The clowns had been so busy doing away with the mimes that none of them knew very much about them really. This was unfortunate because the silent were more that just different; they were special. Had clowns known the true nature of their mime brothers and sisters, their world might have been an all together different place. This was because the mimes were actually the purest representation of the clown being. The silent were love. Love is the product that clowns exist to produce. It is their responsibility to their God and the World Circus, after all. Had clowns known the true nature of the mimes, they would have considered them silent prophets. The reality of the situation was nothing like that. Mimes were and would continue to be the outcasts. Of course, this is just what one might expect from a world full of clowns, for when had clowns gotten anything right? Their very existence represented a major puzzle to begin with.

354,648,512,438: SAYETH THE OWL

Aside from the fact that mimes were the perfect form of clown being, there were many other things which made them unique. The most extraordinary thing about them was their heightened spirituality that caused them to exist in a parallel plane of reality with the clowns. For instance, let's say that the clowns exist in this sentence (yet mimes exist in these parenthesis) which is in the middle of this sentence which stops here. What this means is that mimes could participate in the reality where clowns dwell but had a world of their own within that world which was off limits to the average clown because clowns were not spiritually advanced enough to deal with it. This also means that mimes could do things that clowns could not. It is this that embodies most of what makes mimes different from clowns and specialized in their private reality.

From: Poems of Nastina

The silent live in a silent world
On a ship of love with sails unfurled
The silent need, like all clowns do
They just pretend to make it true
Pretending to eat if they are hungry
Pretentious pizza or ice cream sundies
And if they don't pretend to eat,
They pretend to starve till death they meet
The silent live in fantasy homes
With invisible walls and pretend phones
Fantasy keys to invisible doors
Fantasy mops for invisible floors
Fantasy vacuums for invisible dirt
Fantasy closets for invisible shirts
If they think they're rich, their homes a castle
If they think they're poor, their homes a hassle
In a mimes world, all things seem true
Their imagined homes work like ours do
Rain doesn't pass through a pretend roof
Unless caused by a roofer that goofed
They pretend to call on pretentious phones
To get the leak fixed if the roofer is home
If the roofer notices his not-phone ring
He pretends to hear the invisible thing
He pretends to hear his client's complaint
He pretends to protest with restraint
He knows he has to make it right
He wants his pretend pay that night
The silent pretend to have jobs to do
They're working clowns like me or you
They pretend to get tired at the end of the day
An invisible bath takes the fatigue away

At the end of the week, they pretend to get paid
Alone with their loves, they pretend to get laid
If not protected, the suzies get pregnant
The mister pretends to be distant and vacant
They go and get married by a pretend priest
Then all sit and chow on a pretentious feast
And nine months later when big in her girth
The mom-to-be suzie pretends to give birth…………….….and does!

345,648,512,439: SAYETH THE OWL

The fantastic thing is that in many ways the pretend world of the mimes manifests itself literally in the world they share with the clowns. For the silent, their fantasy is a fact. They see it, hear it, feel it, taste it, smell it, react to it, they just don't talk about it.

345,648,512,440: SAYETH THE OWL

As the mimes became common place in the world of clowns, a new type of attitude was developed in clown society. Where once clowns simply feared the mimes and thought of them as a curse, clowns now had come to loathe and despise them. Hate them even. This was a first. Clowns had never managed to really hate anyone in all their recorded history. Dislike, maybe, but not out right hate. Hate was simply too dark and distasteful for the average clown to stomach. It just wasn't in them. It wasn't in their genes…until now. All the sociological upheaval, in the form of a general rise in sincerity abroad, had created a new attitude among the population; leaving clowns susceptible to rudimentary evil…hatred being one of the most elemental forms of said evil. All the clowns needed was something to hate and the mimes were the perfect scapegoat for that. Here was a group of beings, in the minority, who had always been considered by clowns to be a lower form of life…a group who, until recently, had always been where they belonged, locked up or, better yet, roasting on a stake somewhere. Here was a group any clown could pick on and get away with it, and with a clean conscience.

345,648,512,441: SAYETH THE OWL

There was another interesting phenomenon related to the mimes that caused clowns to hate them, something called "inviso-stuff." A word coined by clowns describing all the invisible stuff that the mimes left all over the place. The inviso-stuff created a real threat to the clowns. It was easy to wreck ones jalopy into an imaginary mime-mobile in what looked like an empty parking spot…or, what about smashing one's honker on the wall of a mime manor in a supposedly vacant lot. One invisible roller skate left on a busy side walk could practically start a panic when a clown slipping on it sends it to trip up the next pedestrian. The list went on and on.

345,648,512,442: SAYETH THE OWL

Dimwitted clowns were simply unable to cope with the problem and soon their frustrations grew ugly. They formed clown supremacy groups. They named their groups after the problem of inviso-stuff. The fact was, they could not see the stuff, and therefore they were called the Not-Sees. These hate-mongers held meetings as often as they wished and being clowns the semi-serious proceedings soon turned ribald and became just like any other assemblage of clowns…a party. In time, the clown supremacists became known as the Not-See Party. The Not-See Party remained relatively small until a rise to power of one clown in particular took place in the later years of….

Chapter 7
From Sally to Soap

The twisted looking chair was empty. The hundreds of needles protruding from its seat and backrest carried no weight. Yesterday's blood was dried in minute globules here and there on the chairs unpleasing surface. Soon, this cruel throne would be filled with an equally cruel being.

Six-hundred and sixty-six chairs of the same description surrounded the disgusting filth-covered conference table. This massive, lop-sided, dripping wet slab was littered with rotting and half-eaten creatures of unknown origin. The carrion seethed with maggots and worms. Bowls of fermented oatmeal generously embellished the table's top, which had been set with ancient china made from the bones of murdered children. The silverware had not been washed in over ten thousand years. Servicing the foul table was a double amputee on his peg-legs who placed soiled napkins at each setting around the hideous piece of furniture in preparation for that evening's meal.

666

Peg-Legs filled 666 crusty goblets full with a concoction of body fluids and sour milk from a humanoid dairy…animals whom, like the amputee, were eternally doomed to reside in Hell. It was ironic that Peg-Legs ended up slaving in Hell's Kitchen. When he was alive on Earth, that was what he had always called his restaurant. Now, he actually WAS in Hell's Kitchen. His luck had always sucked. Peg-Legs thought he would never encounter a being more evil than the mobster he had owed all that money to…the mobster that watched as henchmen sawed off both his legs with a skill saw. Yet all of the 666 beings soon to gather in this unholy hall made that mobster look like Goldilocks.

Once finished with his duties, the waiter hobbled over to a thick chain which hung down from a ceiling so tall it could not be seen. The chain had a giant meat-hook attached to its end and it was the hook that Peg-Legs grasped to give the chain a mighty tug. This rang the dinner bell…a dinner-bell loud enough to wake the dead so they would not be late. Before the bell had finished its deafening resonation, the hall was magically filled with 666 un-dead who were as sinister as they were eternally starved. At the head of the table, sat Satano, Lord of Darkness and Despair, Prince of Evil, the fallen angel, a demon without mercy, the unspeakable Devil, the taker of souls, Mephistopheles, a tyrant of filth, Old Scratch, Archfiend, Monarch of Hell, an oppressor of light, Antichrist, the serpent, Moloch, Beelzebub, Sally.

666

Peg-Legs, being from the 20th century Earth, had always imagined the master of sin to be a red, leather skinned, horned devil. He'd had no idea upon arriving in Hell just how diverse the Universe was. The king of pestilence almost never assumed the form of a devil. In fact, one could never know what form the monster of monsters would take or what sex for that matter. Today's version of his ruler was especially disturbing because the god of doom had taken the form of a teenaged humanoid female and was instructing his servants to call her Sally. This was another problem in an endless torrent of problems for Peg-Legs and the billions of other dammed souls. The rotten one always had different names and it was illegal to call upon him with the wrong one. To do so would mean arrest and an unfair trial, and no one but no one wanted to get tied up in the judicial system in Hell. In fear of this, most of the dammed called the incarnation of absolute evil "what's-his-face."

666

Sally slid her torture chair back and stood at the head of the putrid slab. Fourteen villains down, a kindly looking, balding, human being of the male variety gave her a hard stare. He examined her cute bangs, which complimented her bedroom eyes. Her lips as red and sultry as the finest Chinese silks appeared moist and tasty. The most perfect and gigantic breasts he had ever seen accentuated her exquisite beauty. Nothing was left to his imagination as he worked his eyes down her shapely body…the tiny waist, the flat stomach with a jeweled navel. Finally, there were her fantastic thighs. Indeed, no man could resist this masterpiece in flesh…except this particular villain. This was because he was a child molester and upon finishing his examination he had gauged the girl's age to be about 15, which made her ten years too old for his tastes. The child molester's occupation was what had gotten him a seat so near to the goddess of immorality. In any case, he wasn't the only zombie to admire Sally's sex appeal.

One hundred fifty nine rapists did drool
Sixty-two cannibals savored the sight
Two hundred sinister lesbian ghouls
Wished they could spank her with all of their might
Seventy murderers dreamt of her dying
One hundred sadists dreamt of her pain
Forty molesters of children were crying
For if she were younger she could have been game
Five homosexuals couldn't care less
While twenty bisexuals could not decide
Ten teenage masochists wished to confess
Dreaming of Sally whipping their hides
Nine necrophiliacs dreamt of her rotting
Beneath their disgusting sexual needs
Sally was naked aware of this plotting
These ghouls could serve her purpose indeed

666

"LET THE FEAST BEGIN!" ordered Sally stuffing a worm laden leg belonging to an unidentifiable corpse into her beautiful mouth. The 666 fiends detonated in an orgy of unrestrained gluttony. Peg-Legs cowered in a corner failing to avoid being pelted with various smatterings as the demons filled themselves. Adolph Hitler inquired of Sally why the meeting had been called as an eyeball fell out of his mouth.

"It's not nice to talk with your mouth full, Adolph" said Sally reaching for the slug chowder which steamed in a topless skull before her. She greedily swallowed the wicked slop as it ran down her chin dropping in sickening globs onto her massive mammarian mcgillicutties. Nothing was sacred at dinnertime in Hell. Such was the fate of the dammed.

666

"Maniac persons!" saluted the black-hearted she-devil. "I have asked you here to feast with me at the table of obscenity, and to celebrate my malevolent plan to further corrupt the global circus your world has become!"

Sally shot flames from every orifice as if to punctuate her remarks.

"Those of you seated in the cruel chairs on this never ending and blackest-of-nights are Earth's most infamous villains. But as you know much has changed. It has now been over two thousand years since Jesus Christ went back to Earth and ruined all of the wicked work we did there. His second coming caused 21st century humans to become clowns and that accident has proven to be more damaging to our cause than we could have foreseen. If only you humans weren't so freakin' stupid, this whole thing could have been avoided!"

Sally slammed her tiny fists down on the slab yet they made a thunder clap, cracking the table in several directions, while sending a shock wave through the room. The ghouls hardly reacted for this was routine devil behavior. He/she/it always used dramatic violent force to illustrate her points.

"The clown reformation destroyed 2000 years of corruption! There is no place for evil in a world full of beings whose only aspiration is to act a fool and have a good laugh whenever possible. We all know that the essential ingredient for evil is to take one's self seriously. In doing so, one develops a sense of pride which leads to egotism and vanity; thus forming self-esteem and pretension, and the need to better on's self to feed these feelings. Henceforth, in the pursuit of ego-satisfying experiences, humans are exposed to the greater evils of greed, conceit, self-gratification, and the telling of lies. Thanks to our efforts, before Christ returned to your planet, these negative qualities could be found in almost every human being. It was easy then to manipulate the more egotistical ones of your kind into taking a step up into the ultimate evils of murder, rape, coveting power, and the making of war. You before me serve as an example of these successes. But all was lost in so many odd years after the reformation when 23rd century scientists used genetic engineering to create the living embodiment of their ridiculous religion. Therefore causing the human race to become extinct, replaced with the so called superior clown beings…all that remains of your pitiful species."

The zombies stirred in their seats enjoying the intense pain the chairs delivered as the needles imbedded into flesh. The Lord of Flies continued her oration.

"Fear not, my death angels, we haven't given up on destroying your world. I give you now a chance to reclaim what's been lost, by taking part in the latest development of my plan. You see, butchers of joy and prosperity, our relentless drive to instill the fundamentals of evil into the clowns society has begun to succeed!"

The un-dead delegates cheered the demon as she let out another thunderclap, which caused dust and a million years worth of dead mice and insects to fall from the impossibly high ceiling.

"We gain ground even now. Utilizing fear, hatred, and several drugs that destroy the sense of humor in clowns, we shall spread evil once again into God's cherished creation. And we will not stop until every clown goes bad, every joker gets serious, and nothing is funny enough to laugh at except God's pie in the face!"

Sally's speech was greeted with a sudden out burst of violence as the zombies, heated by her words, began to tear each other apart in a frantic bloodbath. This pleased the Devil.

When the clamor died down, Sally laid out the details of her plan in what seemed like a small eternity. So detailed were her descriptions of the details and of subsequent details that upon more details, it related to lesser detail. To her tired and perpetually cranky hench-persons, this second speech was tedious. Many would have died of boredom had they not already been dead. Finally, Sally closed her speech by committing suicide. The old Devil always had a knack for dramatic endings. The Hellish representatives of Earth devoured her remains and smeared her blood upon themselves in the hopes that some off her evil would rub off on them.

^&%%$#

Meanwhile back on Earth, in the realm of the living, Sicko the Clown had just finished doing something only a serious clown would do. He was reading a book. The book had been a complete failure when it was originally published way back in the 21st century. But now it was considered a classic by serious clowns who dared to read it in the 41st because the principal characters were described as human beings with black skin. Imagine that! There was no such thing as colored skin in the 41st century, and therefore no discrimination on that basis. Clowns discriminated against each other on the basis of the size of ones feet. Besides, there were always the mimes to hate. The book was called "Negro's I Have Met Whilst Yachting." It was all about discrimination. Sicko loved to read forbidden literature written by human beings. Human stories were odd to a clown because their value system was totally different. That's what the clown gone bad liked about them. It seemed to him that he was becoming more like the extinct humans everyday. Sicko cared nothing for the teaching of the World Circus nor the principles of Grand Lunacy. He felt the whole chit-bang-and-she-boodle was bozokahkah. As of late, where the World Circus was concerned, it seemed as though its days of unquestioned global domination were numbered. Clowns were turning to alternative lifestyles like never before, and most of them seemed to involve some type of hard candy.

Sicko was becoming a very wealthy clown now that he had gotten rid of his old partners. It had been easier to do than he thought it would be. It turned out that Sam Simian wasn't nearly as loyal to Whammo as Whammo believed. The genius chimpanzee hardly got his nose out of his accounting when Sicko shoved Whammo out of the tree fort during an argument years ago. Between filth merchants this was the equivalent of a sumo wrestler being shoved out of the circle. Once you were out, you were out. What Sicko didn't know was that Whammo was already sick of the business and had knocked up a floosie from Slammy's Playhouse and had been on the verge of dropping out of the racket anyway to settle down with the suzie. That's why he didn't challenge Sicko after being shoved out of the fort. Whammo figured that Sicko had just done him a favor.

Sam Simian posed no threat either because all he really wanted was a tree to hide out in. The ape could care less about the candy racket so long as he got his fix and all he had to do to get his candy was maintain the books for Sicko who was notoriously bad at math. Math was another one of Sam's talents. In the end, Sicko had moved his entire operation to his funhouse on the outskirts of town leaving the tree fort to Sam Simian and only using the fort on occasion as a place to shoot up the syrup

$@$%#@

Gazing towards a distant hill, Sicko growled to himself at the sight of Mime Manor, which was pretending to exist on a hilltop. Sicko couldn't actually see the house, rather he determined its location by seeing all the mimes inside going about their business. He cursed himself for being so careless as he picked his nose.

"Mimes! I oughta kill my realtor for selling me this house so close to those vermin!"

Sicko began to giggle after realizing that he had in fact already killed his realtor for that very reason. Looking down to the shallow grave where the realtor lay buried, he giggled some more as he picked his nose some more. The years of unbound criminal activity had had a profound effect on this clown. He had been so serious for so long that he could hardly remember his former life as a good clown. Even if he could he wouldn't have cared.

A freshly whoopied clown, Sicko was still lolly gagging in his filthy bed. The sight of her made him giggle again as he watched her stick a syringe between her toes and shoot up the Obvious. That's what was tickling him, making him giggle. He was starting to think up jokes. He needed a fix. Sicko went over to the merry-go-round and searched for a syrup bottle. There wasn't one. That's right. He was supposed to conserve until tomorrow's delivery. But he thought he had. Where was the stuff? Then he remembered the clownette. She must have been doing doubles behind his back!

"You! You banged my last hit!"

Sicko was on her even as he cracked up. His addiction was extremely serious and his funny-bone swollen twice its usual size. He was killing the suzie…enjoying it for all it was worth…she went quickly…he let her drop dead at his feet.

"Now, I'll have to go into town and score. I knew I shoulda held back on that last deal and got a bigger supply for my rue…Guh-huh-huh-ha-ha-ha…Oh no!"

Sicko's eyes popped out as he slapped his hand over his mouth. He had the giggles and was beginning to worry.

"Where are the freakin'' jalopy keys?"

They weren't under the merry-go-round
Or the cushions of the chair
And even though he searched the drawers
Of course, they were not there
He looked beneath the Chinese rug
And good old lazy boy

They weren't inside the vases
Which he one by one destroyed
They were not found to be within
The toilet or the tub
They weren't inside the toy chest
Or giant boxing glove
The keys did not reveal themselves
Inside his old ice box
Nor were they even to be found
In Sicko's dirty sox
He searched in every room there was
Then searched them all once more
He checked in all his pockets
But found lint inside all four
He crawled around to look below
Then leaped to check up high
He checked inside the fruit cakes
Then he checked inside the pies
But Sicko never found the keys
His mind let him forget
That they were in the pocket of
The freshly killed clownette

Had Sicko gotten serious, he would have easily recalled where the keys were. But he was starting to feel goofy and weird and wasn't able to concentrate that well just then. The only other form of transportation in the fun house was his never used unicycle, which, of course, Sicko did not know how to ride. He knew that hitching a lift was unlikely since he and the mimes next door lived out in the sticks. Besides, he wouldn't ride with a mime in one of their inviso-lopies if his life depended on it which right then, it did.

Abruptly the clown was overwhelmed by a titanic urge to laugh. It welled up in his throat like a pumpkin being forced down a rubber hose. He tried to hold back, knowing that once he began to laugh it would only get worse. Getting the giggles was like when something is so funny you just hafta laugh, only you laugh so hard for so long that you hafta laugh about how hard and long you just laughed only to laugh about the fact that you were just laughing about laughing and so on. He exploded into laughter.

WAAAAAAAAAAAAA-HA-HA-HA-HA-
HOOHOO-HA-HA-HA-HAR-HARDY-
HOE-HOE-HA-HA-HAHEE-HEE-roooont-
YACK-YACK-YACK-YACKY-HOE-HOE-
HA-HA-HOO-HOO-roooont-snort-HA-HA…
BLAAAAAAAAAAA-HA-HA-HA-HA-HA-

Sicko fell to the floor in anguish, gasping for breath. The feeling of his funny bone being struck consumed him. Inside he felt the way a gong sounds. He could neither resist it nor wish it away. He lay there rolled up in the fetal position, tears streaming down his face as he tried to suppress the next wave. It broke.

 AHHHHHHHHHHHH-HA-HA-HA-HA-
WAAAAAAAAAA-HA-HA-HA-HA-HA-
WOOOOOOOOOO-HOE-HOE-HOE-
HEEEEEEEEEEEE-HEE-HEE-HEE-
YUUUUUUUCK-YUK-YUK-YUK-
HE-HE-HE-HA-HA-HA-Haroooont-snort
YEEEEEEEEEEE-HAH! HAH!…HAH!

He was going to die laughing and he knew it. He was gonna lay there helpless laughing himself right into the grave. His funny bone was going to release five years worth of hysterics into his nervous system in five minutes and it was gonna kill him. Another wave hit him. It was as if his neck had been broken. It completely paralyzed him and cramped his guts with such force that he pooped his pants. It was the equivalent of a shotgun being cocked prior to being fired…a tremendous backwards heave in preparation for the forward surge.

 Ack!…Ack!…Huuuuuuuuuuuuuuufffffffftttttt…
 BLAAAAAAAAAAAAAAAAAAAAAAAAAAAAAAAAAAAAAAAAAAAAAA-HA-HA-HA-HA-HA-HA-HAROOONT-
 BLAAAAAAAAAAAAAAAAAAAAAA-HA-HA-HA-HAHA-HAROOOOOONT
 WAAAAAAAAA-HA-HA-HA-HA-WAAAAAAAAA
HA-HA-HA-HAROOOOOOOOOONT
YEEEEEEEEEEE-HOE-HOE-HOE-HOE-
WAAAAAAAAAAAAAAAAAAA-HA-HA-HA-HA

It was starting. He could see that his skin was turning pink. This was it. He began to wonder about the after life. He wondered weather or not he would be going to Hell. He felt pretty sure it would be Hell, but then he didn't believe in that bozokahkah anyway. He thought about the Devil… *"I'd sell my soul for"……*

666

 On Earth, she had appeared to be a very uptight and strict Christian. She had condemned the sinners and championed the righteous. She went to church every day and made sure that everyone there was as devoted to the Lord as she was. She was very narrow-minded and allowed no questions or free-thinking. She never fornicated, she worshiped a dead person and when she died she still went to Hell anyway and became Satano's secretary…a fitting reward for the evil
church lady. On her desk there was a little red light bulb. When this light bulb became illuminated it signaled her to assume the position because in a few moments the Devil would be coming to the office to collect contracts for soul sales. The reason she had to bend over the desk whenever the malevolent monster came round was because Satano

liked to spank her with a giant paddle. This was part of her damnation and her reward for serving him so well when she had lived. Usually, she pretended not to like it but the Devil knew better.

666

Sicko, in his death throes, thought he was seeing things when a bald, goateed clown squatted down and stuck what looked like a squirt gun to his neck. Then he was blasted into a mild state of awareness. He stopped laughing and began gulping air. He was in a great deal of pain. The laughing fit had broken several ribs and his elbows were throbbing. He parted his lips.

"More…." he croaked. The stranger gave him another dose. Sicko moaned as he was taken up into the realm of intelligence he was accustomed to. He sat up and surveyed the odd clown who had literally just saved his life.

Satano was dressed in a flame red jumper with black pom-poms. The material had a shiny look to it. His black clown's shoes were the largest Sicko had ever seen. He wore no party hat. Sicko noticed that he felt very relaxed in the presence of this clown. He felt like he was a joker you could trust. He felt warm and safe. These feelings gave him the creeps.

"Did I hear you say you would sell your soul for some more of the Obvious?" quizzed the demon.

"Did I say that? Can't seem to remember now, thought I was just thinking."

"Oh, you said it all right, at least in your heart, but what difference does it make now that you've gotten what you wanted?"

Sicko stood up grunting with the sharp pains from his broken ribs.

"Say…what's with that nifty squirt gun you dosed me with…pretty cool…I'd like to have me one of those."

"Here, have this one…and it's fully loaded, too."

Satano tossed the gun to Sicko. Then the Devil brought forth some paperwork and a fountain pen from the folds of his jumpsuit and began spreading it all out on Sicko's hot chocolate table.

"Well, it appears that everything's in order. Now all you have to do is sign and we can get down to business." Satano leaned back in the chair he had seated himself in and placed his hands behind his head, yawning and stretching as though this brief meeting had worn him out. Sicko was more than curious just what this clown was talking about.

"What the Hell are you talking about and who the Hell are you supposed to be?" said the clown gone bad.

"WE are talking about the sale of YOUR soul to ME and I am Satano, ultimate clown gone bad, not at your service, only here to cut a great deal for myself and to give you all you could ever desire in this life at your eternal expense."

Sicko stood there looking at the clown. He scratched at his crotch…farted… spoke.

"You're full of crap!"

Satano was unmoved by the insult. He was used to having to prove to the inhabitants of Earth his powers. What was with this planet anyway? Never a soul on it that would take you at your word, human or clown. He snapped his fingers and instantly the room was chest deep in little translucent, pink soda bottles filled with the Obvious. More bottles than Sicko had sold in the last five years, and more than he could do in his lifetime.

"All yours, Sicko, and not just these. I will give you a never ending supply of the Obvious in the form of a spigot down in your basement. Just turn on the faucet whenever you desire. But that's not all. I have plans for you. If you sell your soul to me and become my servant, I promise that one-day you will be the most powerful clown that's ever lived. You'd like that, wouldn't you?"

Sicko looked around at all the syrup and began to play with the bottles, showering himself with them…grinning the ear-to-ear grin that only a clowns rubber face allows.

"DEAL! Where do I sign?"

It is written that Sicko never once had second thoughts over selling his soul. It seemed like the logical thing to do at the time. He was stoked! After the Devil left, he was forced to spend several days moving all the little bottles into the garage using a shovel. Then he used the shovel to bury the dead suzie out in the backyard next to the realtor's shallow grave. In the process, he accidentally unearthed one of the realtor's arms. On the end of that rotting arm was a balled up, decomposing, clenched fist. Sicko became curious about it and forced the hand open by breaking off the fingers. He was thrilled to find another set of keys to the jalopy in the hand of the dead clown. Sicko had been using it ever since he killed the realtor. It is written that Sicko would attribute any and all of his good fortunes to his allegiance to Satano.

666

Meanwhile…in the lowest of the lowliest low points of the lower, lower depths of Hell, Satano, who had now taken the form of an ugly little six-eyed spider, began to spin a web between the wall and a skull attached to a skeleton that leaned there. Once finished he sat in its center waiting for one of the poop-eating flies to come along and get trapped. In Hell, no creature was too small or unintelligent not to deserve being tortured now and again.

His name was Uglor. Uglor was one of the poop-eating flies hovering over the stinky logs of dukey. Uglor noticed something shimmer over there. Being helplessly attracted to shiny things he aimed his flight in that direction. As Uglor wondered why he had this uncontrollable urge to fly towards shiny things, he was caught by the wings in Satano's web. Had the small collection of cells, which served Uglor as a brain, been hundreds of times larger, he might have been afraid. But Uglors germ sized brain was limited to two tasks at a time and presently it was occupied with why he liked shiny things so much and trying to fly again. It was because of this that he also didn't notice the ugly little six-eyed spider coming to bear on him. Everything on Uglor's mind was replaced in an instant as a fang cracked through his exoskeleton and into his tiny brain.

Satano treated 20 or so of Uglors buddies to the same fate. Soon he grew bored with this and transformed himself into an unhealthy looking rat, leaving the fly-catching game to a real spider building its own web. Besides, Satano was already full of fly juice. The real spider did not last long though as the rat got its attention by jiggling the web. The spider tried to spot an escape route while running away and feeling terrified because ITS brain COULD handle three tasks at a given moment. None of that mattered. In the end, it was eaten by Satano, the rat. Satano was surprised just then to be attacked by a dungeon-sized cat. The scroungie, flea ridden feline had snuck up on the rat as it was occupied chasing the spider. Satano let himself be caught, then subsequently be ripped to pieces and devoured by the cat so that he might enjoy pain from a rodent's point of view. Satano grew tired of this as well and decided to give the kitty something to think about by turning himself into a blasting cap and detonating.   KER-POW!

666

The only person more surprised than the poor old pussy was poor old Peg-Legs whom at the moment of detonation had just stooped over to pet the animal. He was instantly smattered in gore and found that the explosion had blown off his outstretched arm and a sizable portion of his face. Leaving a trail of blood and cat guts, he set off on his original quest to find Satano. The amputee had just spent 200 years waiting for the Devil's mail to be found in the post office of Hell. Now that it had been located, he was hoping to be given a couple of mercy points for delivering it. Satano had sent a letter up to Heaven to complain about what he always complained about which was everything. Now, two lifetimes later, there was a reply to Satano's complaints.

Peg-Legs had been hobbling around Satano's estate forever and was beginning to wonder if he would ever find the prince of darkness. He wished to call out but scratched the idea for he knew not what name the demon was presently using. This led him to wonder if he hadn't already found his master but failed to recognize him because there was no way to know what form the Devil was in at any given moment. Quickly he abandoned this train of thought for it could only lead to madness.

666

Meanwhile Satano, in the form of a blind maggot, was inching his way across the slime covered path back towards the pile of poop. Satano's favorite dirty trick was to eat an elaborately complicated network of labyrinth like tunnels in poop. In this manner, newly hatched maggots would find their way in but not their way out. Later, the maggots would mature into buzzing flies yet would still remain trapped inside the stinky maze. The result would be a loaded turd, which in Hell was considered a party favorite. These turds would be presented as gifts during infernally dammed ceremonies of unholy matrimony. The bride and groom would grab ends and snap it open releasing a cloud of angry flies to symbolize the stenchful rotting putrescence of the married undead.

Peg-Legs unknowingly stepped in the pile of poop and on Satano, the maggot, smashing him into paste. In a rare moment of nostalgia for Satano and a monumental shock for Peg-Legs, Satano assumed the form of a red, leather skinned, horn headed, winged, pointy tailed Devil. Peg-Legs was astounded to see his master take the form of his long forgotten vision of evil incarnate. Thrusting out Satano's mail he screamed through flapping, bloody folds of his messed up face.

"Master, look! The mail! The mail!"

Satano forgot about torturing Peg-Legs instantly.

"Mail? Did you say MAIL?"

"Yes master…the mail!"

Satano scratched his chin and raised an eyebrow.

"Why, I haven't gotten any mail in over two hundred years! What a pleasant surprise! I wonder what it might be…maybe a birthday card…or my tax returns from the Infernal Revenue Disservice!" Satano eagerly went through the small pile.

BILL.
BILL.
BILL.
BILL.
BILL.
BILL.

"What's this? A letter from Heaven?" He tore it open. Upon reading the letter, an upside-down, crucifix-shaped vein bulged out on his forehead:

From the Offices of Jesus Christ
Vice President, Jehovah's Domain

As if containing tiny lungs, Satano's temples noticeably throbbed. He read further….

Dearest Satan,

Thank you for your constructive criticism of Jehovah's Domain. We will, of course, give consideration to your countless derogatory suggestions, excluding only the most vehemently destructive ones, such as suggestion #1: Why don't you shove the entire freakin' Universe up your holy….

Satano's head caught fire as steam shot out of his ears. He read on…..

…..However, we do not plan to pay you restitution for lost income after your business was greatly damaged by the clown reformation on Earth. Also, for the 200 millionth time the answer is NO, you cannot have your old job back.

Love
J.C.

Satano screamed as he spontaneously combusted. Within seconds, he was but a pile of gray ash on the path. Then a finger seemed to grow from the pile. Peg-Legs took a backstep as he watched. Then up with it came a hand until an entire arm stuck out from the cobblestones. With the bright sound of a cooking bell, a teapot materialized in the hand and it began to poor steaming hot tea upon the ash. With a scream, a red skinned baby Devil came up from the ashes skeleton first, muscles second, skin third. The baby grew into a fully-grown gargoyle in less than a minute. Peg-Legs ran for his own good, but to no avail.

"YOUUUUUUUUUUU!" said the Devil. "YOUUUUUU BROUGHT ME THE MAIL!"

A bolt of lightening shot out of the gargoyles fingers and struck Peg-Legs frying him like a frog in an electric chair. He evaporated in a cloud of smoke.

After the big let down, Satano found that he desired some privacy. But where to get it? There was no such thing in Hell as privacy. He thought about it and realized that a good disguise might do well. It is written that he materialized in a condemned commune for faux hippies as a clean bar of soap.

PEACE AT LAST

Chapter 8
Selected readings from: The All Knowing Owl Speaks
Volume: 970,553,267,849,100,371: Jehovah's Domain
Book: 463,967,885,301 : Earth History
Chapter: 46,783,345 : Clown Reformation
Paragraph: 354,648,512,378

354,648,512,378: SAYETH THE OWL

In another not so unusual coincidence, the humans managed to execute Christ's directives while all together missing his point. In the great Clown Reformation, religious leaders of the 21st century interpreted the words of Jesus Christ literally and with associations to his appearance. They decided that the path to righteousness lay in presenting oneself as a clown and to participate in a circus as a religion. These clowns were very thorough and provided in great detail how this should be carried out across the globe. Not that difficult to do considering the meager size of the planet Earth and its small population at that time of only ten billion.

354,648,512,379: SAYETH THE OWL

The doctrines of Grand Lunacy, as they were known, took the world by storm. These holy papers spread humor and insincerity to the masses and were eagerly accepted as a new lifestyle by so many lost souls. The doctrines had detailed illustrations painstakingly drawn on their parchments, printed as a full color comic, bound in a glossy cover bearing a portrait of Jesus Christ dressed as a clown as he appeared at Woodstock. Jesus Christ was thereafter referred to as Jesus the Clown or Jesus Clown and Holy Buffoon. Within 50 years (EARTH TIME = 1year = 1orbit/SOL) of the second coming of Christ (2073 A.D.), the reformation of all of Earth's major religions, bureaucracies, industries, and infrastructures was complete. World Circus Pooblas declared the year of the second coming, year 0001 S.C. Now, united as clowns under God's Big Top the humans felt they had successfully executed their Savior's plan. In many respects they had.

1. With the advent of the communications miracle all major political differences were settled.
2. War went out of fashion for it was not conducive to a clown based economy.
3. War resources were diverted to medical and agricultural science. This resulted in cures for almost every major disease and an end to hunger world wide.
4. Marked increase in productivity by clown/humans due to humor in the work place and relative leisure due to economic boom result in food, housing, and clown suits for all.
5. Love energy (converts=positrons/inter-dimensional) was being produced in great quantity, fulfilling mankind's obligation to its creator.

354,648,512,380: SAYETH THE OWL:

The reformation effects on industries on Earth were duly retooled to produce the many things the average clown needed. There was great demand for items such as:

Bowling pins, balloons, ukuleles, little red wagons, giant shoes, party hats, soda pop, pogo sticks, whistles, Pom-poms, scooters, joke books, giant boxing gloves, rubber mallets, ruffled collars, ice cream, suspenders, pop corn, bells, oversized pantaloons, roller skates, striped sox and stockings, do-hickeys, silly putty, propeller beanies, bananas, pin-wheels, rubber chickens, smocks, marbles, velcro, banjos, go-carts, pancake syrup, rubber bands, kick balls, tutti-fruity, punch bowls, kazoos, hobby horses, candied apples, polka dots and plaids, Ferris wheels, hot dogs, kites, merry-go-rounds, lollipops, hula hoops, jelly beans, collapsible furniture, skate boards, seltzer bottles, harmonicas, Jews harps, unicycles, cotton candy, jump ropes, cap guns, confetti, brass horns, squirt bulbs, noise makers, big wheels, magic wands, carnations, exploding cigars, poodles, tutus, bathrobes, stink bombs and the all important joy buzzer.

354,648,512,381: SAYETH THE OWL

The automotive industry was retooled as well for clowns demanded smaller and smaller vehicles called jalopies. Jalopies, although much smaller than the smallest Pre-Reformation automobile, were designed to hold 12 to 18 passengers. These junky looking cars were also known to be quite indestructible, as was required due to the complete lack of driving skill on the part of the clowns operating them.

354,648,512,382: SAYETH THE OWL

However, nothing changed the planet or its inhabitants more than the genetic engineering of a "clown virus" in the year 52 S.C. (2125 A.D.) after which all pretension was literally genetically removed from the species. The years after that saw the planet's civilization being completely fashioned around the clowns and their specialized habits and behaviors. Clowns were often known to…….

Chapter 9
Elvis is thy Neighbor

Blinko, Jr's new foster family was composed of a garbage clown and his wife, who worked down at Slammy's as a stripper. The garbage clown's name was Laymo. Laymo was a barrel chested, strapping clown with a fantastically small brain. He was handsome by clown's standards, which meant that he was rather funny looking, and that was why he had been able to marry such a beautiful clownette as Chesty. Chesty was the type of suzie that looked like she was all made up ready to hit the town 24-hours a day. She had a pair of mammarian mcgillicutties that would put a smile on the face of an old impotent orangutan. Her face was warped and designed with a total disregard for elegance or symmetry. Her teeth were crooked. Her eyes were crossed. Her nose was misshapen. All and all she looked like the sort of clownette that was carved out of wood and put on the front of a ship. Prom queen material; the funniest looking suzie you ever saw.

Alas, this clownette was barren. Chesty figured that she was infertile because God felt it necessary to equalize the Universe. After all she had been given five suzies worth of good looks. The truth was that Laymo was the sterile one. Both were too dim-witted to think of that. This was why they sought to adopt a child and that was how Blinko had come to live with them on about his sixth birthday. The garbage clown and his wife were quiet, as they looked upon the child entranced. It seemed as though the child's entire consciousness was being absorbed. Miss Smoochy had warned them about the tot's trances and the erratic blinking that accompanied them. Was it fate or some strange coincidence that the physical manifestation of the child's trances was that of his very name? The world would never know.

The two recalled what Miss Smoochy had said about the lad's past, before they had taken him into their home. She had told them of the murder of the kinderclowns parents and of the time he witnessed the killing of the World Circus Poobla and the other circus clowns at his very first circus. She told them how it was after that first horrible circus that he had begun to demonstrate these relatively regular trances where he would be still and silent, blinking rapidly. She told them that although weird, the trances did not seem to affect the lad in any negative way and that it was best to just ignore it. The child had no recollection of what he experienced during the trances, so asking him about it was futile. None of this surprised the two eager foster parents because they had both been informed of the regularity of emotional problems in orphans. What did surprise them was that five minutes after they had signed the papers to take the boy home, and as they were getting into their jalopy with the kinderclown, Miss Smoochy was run over right in front of them by a deliverlopy.

Miss Smoochy had evidently been returning from the fruit stand next to the cemetery when she dropped some of her bananas. Bending down to pick them up revealed her bulls-eye brand bloomers. Bulls-eye brand undergarments get their name from the big red and white bulls-eye printed on their seat. Unfortunately, clowns are compelled to try and hit the bulls-eye, as was the driver of the deliverlopy who had banged the old clownette up pretty bad before he realized what he was doing. They all stood there looking at her as she died, seconds after coming to rest upside-down in a rose bush planted at the base of the stairs leading into the orphanage. There was little they could do or say but to quickly hustle themselves and Blinko back inside and wait for the Keystoners to arrive.

?%$@%$

Duna bandon dun dun
Duna bandon dun dun
Duna bandon dun dun dun
Duna bandon dun dun
Happy birthday to you
Happy birthday to you
Happy birthday, dear Blinko
Happy birthday to you…..

    There was a small gathering of clowns around a beat up kitchen table.
    "Go ahead, Son, and blow out yer candles!" popped off a deep clowns voice as little Blinko leaned over his sixth birthday cake. The kinderclown blew as hard as he could, spittle flying out of his tot-sized mouth and onto the cake. This made the sound of a beach ball going flat.
    "Don't forget to make a wish!" said his twenty-seven year-old foster suzie. Blinko blew out all but one of the six candles planted crudely in the green and yellow cake. The candle shined before the subdued clown child who sat blinking as it burned. He had gone into the trance.
"Wow, Chesty, check that out," whispered Laymo to his wife. "He's doing it just like that old clownette said." The two clowns were paying attention to Blinko's trance like state.
    "It's like weird. You think we should try to snap him out of it?" said Chesty pushing her bra strap back up on her shoulder.
    "Don't see why not." SNAP! SNAP!
    Laymo was snapping his fingers in Blinko's face. It had zero effect. The lad just continued to blink and stare at the rapidly shortening candle.
    "Wow, Laymo, he's really out there isn't he?" said the suzie as she blew out the candles flame. Blinko came around at that very instant. The two seemed pleased by the coincidence. Laymo came to kneel by the youngster's side.
    "Hey, kid you okay? You gonna wig?"
    Blinko yawned and stretched like a cat after a nap.
    "No, I'm fine. I do that, don't know why, and I can't remember nothing about it when I come out of it."
    "Well, you was acting kinda weird there for a minute, had me and your mom here worried."
    Blinko looked at this suzie that Laymo was calling his mom. She flicked a piece of fuzz from her sweater off one of the impressive cleaves of her cleavage then stuck a fresh piece of gum into her mouth.
    "Yeah, kid…SMACK….SMACK…you ever like need to talk, you just come right on out with whatever's bugging ya and we'll have us a little family meeting…SMACK … SMACK."

Laymo stood and went over to the fridge for a tutti-fruity. It made a popping and fizzing sound as he opened it. He pulled a long draw from it.

"Yeah, dude, like we're gonna be hanging with each other for a long time I reckon, so lets not have no secrets, okay?" Laymo took another pull of the fruity. BURP!

The kinderclown sat there all quiet like, then out of no where he began to pitch a fit and cry.

"DON'T LOVE ME! DON"T LOVE ME!" he said as he went running out of the room. The adults gave each other looks signifying that what their boy had just done was not expected. Then they followed him and found him freakin'g out on the bed in the room they had arranged for him. Chesty patted him on the back.

"Now, why would you go and say something like that, Blinko?"

Between sobs the kinderclown managed a reply "Because anyone who loves me DIES! Both of my parents, my grandmother, Miss Smoochy, and even Poobla Boo Boo! And if you try to love me, you'll die too!"

Blinko again got up and ran out of the room leaving the two clowns puzzled. This time though they were surprised to hear the door slamming.

"Did he just do what I think he did?" quizzed Laymo.

"I don't know…we better go look for him" replied his teary eyed wife. It was hard for her to see this young clown in pain.

They found him easily for Blinko had not run off. He was merely sitting on the front porch. Laymo sat down next to him.

"Hey, clown, you need some company?"

"No."

"You just wanna sit here on this porch for a while?"

"YES."

"Okay…look we we'll be inside if you need us, we're pretty laid back 'round here so don't get all uptight with us, we're cool."

Laymo and Chesty left the youngster on the porch.

%#$@$#

As his new parents went inside Blinko wondered what his new life with them was gonna be like. He had never had two parents before. Miss Smoochy was all he'd ever known like that. It made him cry to think of her. He thought of how much easier it would be to adjust to all of this if she was around, but he knew that would never happen. She was dead. He wondered how long it would be until these clowns were dead as well. Nobody lasted long where he was concerned. His eyelids felt heavy from crying and his honker was sore. He decided to go back inside. His foster folks watched as he plodded his way across the playroom and onto a white couch with red polka-dots. He lay there and soon was fast asleep.

Meanwhile, Laymo was eating a big bowl full of sugar coated corn flakes with bananas and milk. His long purple hair was spilling off his forehead and into the bowl. He didn't care. Personal hygiene was a myth for clowns. He looked across the table to admire his hot wife. She was filing her nails and chewing gum.

YUMPF…YUMPF…GULP. "Ya know somethin' babe?"

"No what?" FILE…FILE.

YUMPF…GULP. "I'm worried about the kid ya know?"

"ME, too." FILE..FILE…SMACK…SMACK.

YUMPF…GULP.

"Yep, I bet all that weird stuff with the circus totally messed him up, I mean he was only like four years old then, and now his nanny goes and gets herself killed right in front of the kid. For cripes sake, bulls-eye brand bloomers was banned forty years ago! What the Hell was she doin' in a pair of them things for anyhow?"

Then there was a smallish commotion coming from the playroom. It appeared that Blinko was having a bad dream. The foster parents got up from the kitchen table and took off for the playroom, overreacting to the trouble. Laymo tripped over his own feet and Chesty tripped over Laymo. When the two stopped tumbling, Laymo found his honker stuffed up Chesty's patooty. But there was no time for that sort of funny business. Their boy was crying in the playroom. When they got there he was wiping tears out of his eyes. Chesty sat next to the child and scooped him up into her arms. Blinko's head became nested in her massive mammarian mcgillicutties and he seemed to calm down immediately. This made Laymo feel proud. Like father like son. Chesty carried the boy back to his bedroom and tucked him in. Once he had fallen asleep, the two left him, hoping he would sleep with out disturbance through the night.

During the course of the night, pint sized Blinko would continue to have gallon sized night terrors. Eventually it was morning and he woke up feeling alone. He was used to being awakened early by Miss Smoochy in a room full of orphans. Rubbing his eyes, he moped over to his dresser to find a clown suit to wear. Opening his pants drawer, he selected a pair of baggy overalls with short legs. He then got out a red and white striped shirt with matching sox. He was still green when it came to dressing himself and so by the time he got it all on, he looked out of order and all together the perfect clown. This was good because today would be Blinko's first day at school.

*&@#$%

He remembered what Miss Smoochy had told him about clown school. This was where all clowns went in order to learn all the stupid things a stupid clown should know. She had told him he would be taught to read so that he could one day know for himself the wonders contained inside the Holy Comic book…a book bringing unenlightenment and farcical lunacy to all…not to mention all the other clown favorites which were mostly pop-up books and silly poems about silly things. Arithmetic would be explained so that he could count his jellybeans or know how many of his marbles had been lost. The perpetually joking teachers would help him to understand the basic principles of humor, sarcasm, and facetiousness. They would teach him the history of the World Circus, which had been spreading disorder and constant goofiness for the past 2000 years. He would learn the sacred juggling act, the importance of the rubber mallet and the giant boxing glove.

Later, Disciples of Grand Lunacy would visit the clown schools to teach the kinderclowns the essential mannerisms of clowndom. Physical education would play a vital role. Coaches would teach the children to fall down repeatedly without injury. They would be taught how to react to slapstick properly. The coach would also teach them how to ride a unicycle and perform gymnastics as well. All of this knowledge was necessary if

Blinko expected to grow into an unproductive idiot like everyone else in Buffoonville, or the world for that matter.

One thing that Blinko had going for him was that he had a lot of experience dealing with strange children, due to constant exposure to new orphans arriving at the orphanage. He was not what one would call shy. After all the changes he had been through recently, the idea of going someplace filled with kinderclowns his age was something he was looking forward to.

Like every pair of giant clown shoes ever clownufactured, Blinko's child sized pair squeaked horribly as he attempted to sneak down the hall to peek in on his new parents. His shoes became silent when he reached their door, which was cracked open. He stuck his head inside.

"Peek-a-boo!" he said.

As usual Laymo and Chesty were heavily crashed after a night of hardcore whoopie and didn't budge. The tot's phrase was far too weak to damage the wall of slumber these clowns had built. He tried again a little louder…

"PEEK-A-BOO!"

The phrase launched itself out of the child's mouth. It hurled itself across millions of molecules in the direction of Laymo and Chesty's ear drums. Reaching its destinations the message was directed to the two clown's brains. Here the phrase met its doom as the concept of responding to it was obliterated by the concept of not waking up even if the funhouse was on fire. Both clowns stirred and shifted positions like two soldiers digging into a foxhole. They weren't gonna wake up. Poor Blinko. Now he would have to make his own breakfast.

In the kitchen he felt small. The place just wasn't built for someone his size. It took great effort just to pull the gallon of chocolate milk out of the fridge. Yet he managed to make a bowl of cereal and felt proud of himself for making do without a mommy. He figured he better get used to it. He had been there for two weeks and not once had anyone gotten up to fix his breakfast for him. Then he heard the school bus honking its horn. It was time for him to leave for school. And so he did with no lunch or school supplies.

Laymo, the garbage clown, was scheduled to work that fine Monday as well as the rest of the week. This was precisely why he wasn't about to drag his sorry self out of bed. Buffoonville County collected the trash supposedly every weekday but the garbage clowns never picked up the refuse when they were supposed to and only did the job on Tuesdays and Thursdays. Actually, what the garbage clowns did on those two days was just drive around town and ignore the heaps of garbage as they passed them by on the streets. If any clown happened to complain to them about the garbage piling up they would say:

"I'm sorry but we only collect the trash on this street on Mondays, Wednesdays and Fridays..." and then drive off laughing.

The fact of the matter was that the Buffoonville garbage clowns never picked up any trash at all because for some reason the trash just seemed to disappear on its own on Saturdays. This was a very well kept secret among the garbage clowns who never cared where the trash was actually going because as long as this kept occurring they could goof off all day. In fact, generations of garbage clowns had kept the secret, handing it down to their offspring as the decades passed. This was a feat within itself for keeping a secret was something that almost no clown could manage. The secret had been kept for so long that there wasn't even a city dump. As a result of the disappearing garbage Laymo was probably the laziest clown in Buffoonville. He even had the audacity to complain at the end of the day how he had been busting his butt all day out there to other clowns who really had been busting their butts.

&* ^%$@

Meanwhile in Buffoonville Elementary School, it was lunch time. Blinko was looking longfully at the other kinderclowns as they ate their sack lunches. Soon his teacher, Mrs. Applebeans, noticed that he had nothing to eat and she went over to him.

"What's the matter child?" She looked at his name tag.

"Blinko…right? Didn't your mommy pack you a lunch?" Blinko fidgeted in his seat like most clowns his age do when confronted by a strange adult. He replied so quietly she could hardly hear.

"No…my mommy was asleep when the bus came."

Mrs. Applebeans wrinkled her nose and took a seat by Blinko. She patted his knee.

"Well, let's see if we can do something about that okay?" She stood and walked to the last of the six rows of lunchroom tables assigned to her class that hour. "Class!" she said. The kinderclowns ignored her and continued to munch their sammichs and cut up with each other. Mrs. Applebeans knew that this would call for stronger measures. She spoke out once more this time using her secret weapon.

"Class… ZIP IT!" Suddenly the entire class fell silent as they ran their tiny stubby fingers across their lips zipping their mouths shut. Like a lot of things, this was something no clown could resist doing. Mrs. Applebeans was pleased.

"Thank you, children. Today, we are going to have our first lesson in the theories of Dr. Curtious…his first doctorate is in Acts of Kindness. Does anyone know what kindness is?"

A cute little clownette wearing a dress printed with baby elephants raised the hand that wasn't busy twisting her blue hair.

"Yes, and what is your name, sweety?" asked Mrs. Applebeans.

"Uh-huh." replied the tot.

"I said what is your name, sweetheart?"

"Nope, you were right the first time" whispered the suzie. Mrs. Applebean's tinker clanked and sputtered then she made the connection.

Oh! Your name IS Sweety! Now, I get it. Okay, Sweety, can you tell us what kindness is? Be sure to speak up so everyone can hear."

Mrs. Applebeans sat down and placed her hands in her lap signifying that the suzie had the floor. Sweety stood and spoke right up without hesitation or fright.

"Kindness is loving
Loving because
Loving is what every
Good clown does
Kindness is giving

To others in need
For giving to others
Is kindness indeed."

Mrs. Applebean's clapped as she stood to praise the suzie. "Very good, Sweety, that is exactly right." Sweety had quoted directly from Dr. Curtious. Giving to others is just what I want everyone to think about. Blinko doesn't have a lunch. Can anyone here spare some of their lunch so that Blinko won't have to go hungry?" Almost immediately Blinkos classmates began to come to where he sat offering him small portions of their meals.

"Here, Blinko" said Apache, a small indian clown, as he handed Blinko a candied cob of maize.

"Take my fortune cookie" said a delicate geisha girl.

"Hey, dude, eat this!" said a six-year-old clown sporting a mohawk and a nose ring. "These gummy snakes are killer kahkah, clown!"

The profanity made its way across millions of air molecules and into the hearing organs of Mrs. Applebean's head where they then proceeded directly to the section of her brain tuned to pick up words like that for immediate reaction.

"Who said that!" she exclaimed in her most aggressive voice which wasn't very impressive due to the fact that clowns are too good humored to show much anger. Her colossal old ladies shoe tapped the waxed floor in ever-increasing repetitions, as elapsed time brought forth no confession. TIPPITY-TAP-TIPPITY-TAP. "I said who said that?" She was feigning ignorance.

The old clownette knew it was Elvis that had said the bad word. It was always Elvis that said the bad words. Elvis also happened to live next door to her. Therefore, she had been dealing with him ever since he had managed to toddle his way out of his playpen into her petunia garden to urinate on her pink poodle. Her neighborhood had been going downhill for the past decade. Clown trash like Elvis's folks were just another example of that sad fact. Her funhouse was situated just on the other side of the choo-choo tracks marking the lower east-side of town. When she and her husband had first moved into the place, the neighborhood was considered to be the nicest in Buffoonville. But now it was a slum polluted with hard candy, violence, and other sins. She had been absolutely horrified to learn that Elvis was going to be in her class that year but on the other hand looked at it as an opportunity to try and point the evil little clown in the right direction. Now, she, as the teacher, could officially discipline the youngster, as she could not at home as his neighbor.

"I'm only going to ask once more time and then you'll all be in trouble." Mrs. Applebeans crossed her arms and once more began tapping her foot. TIPPITY-TAP-TIPPITY-TAP. Elvis felt a type of rage building within him. He was emotionally volatile and prone to mighty temper tantrums. Now, he was on the spot. Elvis, like Blinko and the other children, were a new breed of clown in a sense. They were all the offspring of a generation of clowns who in large part had begun to question the all encompassing authority of the World Circus. Because of this, the kinderclowns were growing up in a world of ever declining humor and ribaldry. For centuries the planet had been one big happy circus but the last two decades had brought much social upheaval in the form of long forgotten ideals resurfacing modified to the extent that clown society dictated. Had the literal tonnage of literature from pre-reformation Earth not been banned and locked away in the Vatican, scholars and pundits of clowndom might have noticed the trend for what it was…a marked step back into the past. The clowns of Earth were starting to resemble their ancient ancestors, HUMANS! This would explain why Elvis had the emotional problems he did as well as what he said. "I did, you freakin' blind old suzie!"

Elvis punctuated his remark by throwing a carton of chocolate milk at the teacher. It sailed past her only to collide with the face of another third grader, Apache. Apache jumped out of his seat and began to bow up for the battle to come. Mrs. Applebeans was so shocked that she was unable to react fast enough during the mere seconds it took for the indian to reach Elvis's location and before she regained her composure, Apache had already bloodied Elvis's honker. This caused the angry clown to run out of the lunchroom humiliated in defeat. Apache was also running because he was after Elvis feeling he wasn't finished beating up on him just yet. Fortunately for Elvis, Mrs. Applebeans caught him by the frock of his suede clown suit. Elvis ran out of the lunchroom, down the halls, out the main doors of the school, down the front steps, into the parking lot, onto the sidewalk, all the way across town, across the choo-choo tracks, into his neighborhood, down his street, up his driveway, through the front door of his house, and into the living room where he was greeted by a puzzled clown who was his father.

%$#@%$

Whammo's life had changed a lot ever since he knocked up one of the dancers down a Slammy's Playhouse. Seeing his son come barreling into the living room reminded him for the millionth time that he shoulda used protection all them years ago. Whammo was essentially oblivious to the comings and goings of his son, Elvis, but today was different because the kid had a dried blood on his face and was home in the middle of the day when he ought to be in clown school. He peeled himself up off the couch and spoke.

"Hey, you little half a midget, ain't you 'sposed to be in school?"

Elvis wiped at his tear swollen eyes with his tattered sleeve and tried to act cool in front of his old clown.

"Uh… I'm sick, dad… I gotta nose bleed and stuff."

Whammo wondered momentarily if that was where the last of his nose candy had gone yesterday but replaced the thought with placing the blame rightly on his lying and conniving wife, Dew Drop.

"Whatever you say kid, be sure to let your mom have a look at you later, right?"

"Right." Elvis scrammed into his room and lay on the bed looking up at the yellowed and water stained ceiling.

After Whammo's wife, Dew Drop, came home from an afternoon shift at the strip joint, he found her standing before him as he came out of a deep thought. She dropped her coat to reveal her sexy dancers body clothed in even sexier lingerie. Whammo produced a syringe full of the Obvious and made short work of draining it into one of his weakened veins. As the rush of awareness filled him and the ticklishness subsided, he said began refilling the syringe while telling Dew Drop, "Babe, the kid's home, he's pretending to be sick."

Ouch!" she cried as Whammo jabbed her in the butt with a needle freshly laden with Obvious goo. She took her place next to him on the couch and took in some deep breaths as everything came into focus and her own fidgeting nerves grew quiet.

*&^%$#

Elvis did not know that his emotional problems stemmed from the fact that his mother was a heavy user of the Obvious all through her pregnancy with him. The sweet stuff in her blood was now his physiological constitution. Elvis embodied a clown in conflict with his very being in that his mind had been permanently altered by his mother's addiction. This was why he was such a serious little clown. Elvis at the moment was trying to live down the whipping Apache had given him by getting back to work on a tiny chair he had been building. Elvis was wrapping conductor coils around its backrest, which meant he was almost finished with the little electric chair. Now, it might seem a stretch that a six-year-old clown could be smart enough to build a working electric chair but this kinderclown was smart as heck thanks to all the candy his mother had used as he gestated. His heart swelled as he thought of how much fun he would soon be having frying toads in the seat.

%$#@%$

Elvis had been killing frogs since he was four. It all started one summer two years ago when he had caught a toad in the Mrs. Applebeans garden. At first he was afraid to touch the toad that was desperately hiding among the petunias from all the dangers it might face. Something like Elvis was a toad's worst nightmare. Eventually, Elvis worked up the courage to grab the toad that immediately peed on him being scared to death. After the terrified amphibian peed on him, Elvis got so mad that he just threw the frog as hard as he could straight up into the air. Of course, the frog came down on the driveway with a squishy smack and met its doom a few moments after. Elvis ran over to the frog and found that he liked the feeling he got watching it die. In fact, he liked the feeling so much that he spent the rest of the day searching for toads to kill. The fourth toad lay twitching on the concrete with multiple internal injuries as Elvis's mother called him inside for dinner. Mrs. Applebeans was of course completely baffled to discover four dead frogs on her driveway after returning home from her classes.

In the weeks after the first toad murders, Elvis continued with the behavior. He killed about ten frogs the same as the others until he discovered that it was twice as fun to simply throw them straight down onto the pavement as hard as possible. This way he got to see the effects of the impact up close. From then, on the front of his house was littered with numerous corpses of toads in various stages of decomposition at all times, a phenomenon that puzzled his parents as well as the horrified Mrs. Applebeans. The frog corpses were further ruined as traffic ran over them repeatedly and the sun dried them out. This resulted in perfectly flattened and dried-out frog mummies which Elvis called "toad paper." He began to collect the toad paper, once the process was complete, so he could glue them into a scrapbook, which he hid under the bed.

By and by Elvis grew tired of throwing the frogs onto the pavement and he began to kill them by smashing them to death with a brick. He liked this because it really messed the frogs up and it had such a hands-on feeling to it. Still, after a while, he grew bored of this and of collecting the toad paper and so began experimenting with other ways to kill the frogs.

Paperization of frogs who are falling
Onto the pavement where Elvis is mauling
Toads under bricks in his four year old hands
Smashing and smashing them hard as he can
Soon toads are drowning in old mason jars
Legs weighted down with a stone from not far
Toads under hammers and toads under foot
Toad paper stamps in a toad paper book
Toads getting roasted on small wooden spears
Half a toad there, the other half here
Toads full of needles and toads full of nails
All of whom wish they'd been born as snails
Little clown Elvis, destroyer of frogdom
God gave him victims and Lord knows he hogged 'em
Froggies that suffered from limb amputation
Toads in a blender who died of gyration
Toads left in cages to die all alone
Toads skinned by Elvis right down to the bone
Frogs fed to Fido and frogs fed to kitty
Frogs ground on graters to parts itty-bitty
Elvis is six, building toad seat of doom
Indeed they'll be frying upon it, like soon

^$%#%^

Blinko stopped by Elvis's house after school. The two lived only one door apart. Miss Applebeans lived between them.

"Hi, Blinko" said Dew Drop in a serious voice. "Elvis is in his room, go on back." Blinko ducked under her arm which held the screen door open and he skipped with excitement into the back hall where Elvis's room was located.

The kinderclowns room was different than most. The usual cheerful wallpaper had been torn away to hang in leaflike shreds. There was a noticeable lack of toys. No bowling pins, no little red wagon, no kickball. There was a Jesus on the unicycle hanging upside down on one of the walls. Strange word-filled books lay scattered about. Elvis hadn't made his bed, nor did his room look as though it had ever been cleaned. There were cobwebs in every corner, dirty clothes thrown haphazardly towards an empty hamper on its side. Even the clothes were kind of bizarre. Most of them were black and printed with the logos of bands Miss Smoochy had warned Blinko never to listen to because they played Satano music. Besides all of this, the most disturbing thing in the room was Elvis himself. The child's bulbous nose had a ring in it. He also had a lot of earrings in both ears. His mohawk haircut completed the picture. Blinko knew that the clown presented himself this way because he was just a little punk…a tough guy, a bully.

Blinko chuckled to himself at the thought of how little good Elvis's appearance did him in his fight with Apache.

"Whatcha' makin', Elvis?" said Blinko. Elvis took his eyes from his work to acknowledge Blinko's presence.

"It's a miniature electric chair," replied Elvis who went back to work on the coils.

"An electric chair? What's that?" Blinko came 'round for a better look at Elvis's project.

"An electric chair is for killing things with electricity."

Blinko was puzzled. "You kill things with that?"

Elvis completed the last wrap around the backrest and twisted it tightly off.

"Yes, I kill things with that," he said.

"What kinda things?" asked Blinko. He was feeling weird about the nature of the conversation but was too curious to stop.

"Toads and frogs." Elvis smiled and it made Blinko uncomfortable.

"Why do you like to kill frogs?" Elvis grinned ear-to-ear quickly thinking of the feeling he got every time a frog died at his hands.

"Because it's damn fun, that's why."

"You think killing frogs is fun?"

"I don't think it's fun, Blinko, I KNOW it's fun. I do it all the time."

"Don't your folks get mad?"

"Of course not, stupid."

"Why not?"

"'Cause they don't know about see, and you better not be thinking of telling on me!" Elvis was shaking his fist at Blinko. "Or else…POW! Right in the kisser." Blinko shrugged and wasn't the least bit scared of his friend's threat. Blinko had been in plenty of fisticuffs during his years in the orphanage.

"Don't worry, I'm no tattletale. What I'd like to know is how have you been killing them up to now?"

Elvis pounded his fist in his open hand. "I usually smash 'em to death with a brick. Sometimes though, I cut 'em into pieces with a knife."

Blinko's eyes went wide. "You gotta knife? Can I see?" Elvis said nothing but went to his mattress, which was on the floor without a bed frame and reached under it to eventually produce a meat cleaver which he then tossed to Blinko who nearly caught it blade side but thanks to his juggling skills, he caught it by the handle perfectly. Blinko liked knives.

"So, how come your going to all this trouble? Isn't it easier to just keep smashing 'em the way you have been?" Blinko was flipping the cleaver hand to hand.

"Sure, it would be easier but I'm bored with that. Besides, this way will be more humane."

Blinko didn't understand the word humane. "Humane? What's that mean?"

Elvis looked annoyed. "It means being nice to something."

Blinko got that. "But then wouldn't it be more humane if you didn't kill the frogs in the first place?'

"HELL, NO! Of course, not!" Elvis's face was twisted.

"Why? I don't get it?"

"Because the way I see it, the stupid frogs want to die."

"How do you figure that?" quizzed Blinko.

"Well, I've never heard 'em complaining about it even when I smash'em slow or burn 'em alive."

Blinko's jaw dropped open. "But, Elvis! Frogs can't talk!"

Elvis didn't miss a beat. "Well, neither can mimes but nobody seems to care when they pretend to die."

"Elvis you're not making sense."

"Well, it makes sense to me and that's all I need to know get it? Besides even if it doesn't make sense, it don't matter because clowns aren't supposed to make sense anyway right?" Elvis's weird logic had cornered Blinko.

"Well, yea, I guess so…but"

"Look, clown, why don't you just shut up and give me a hand here. I need to attach this power cord to these screws here to make this thing work."

Blinko was amazed at how smart Elvis was. Little did he know that Elvis was a born genius due to all the Obvious his mother had done while pregnant with him. He gave in and assisted the Mohican as he continued to think about Elvis's irrational rational.

%$#^%$

Meanwhile Elvis and Blinko's folks had gotten together at Whammo and Dew Drop's place for a quiet syrup party. It seemed to help justify their addictions if they called their shooting sessions something like a party or a barbecue or brunch. The four clowns were doing the usual thing clowns on Obvious do, which was to get serious and talk about heavy stuff. Tonight's topic had to do with contradictions in World Circus theology and the Doctrines of Grand Lunacy. Whammo had the floor.

"My personal favorite is the "Jesus the Clown is watching over us" bit. The way I see it, if he is as dimwitted and retarded as the Pooblas say he is, then how could he be smart enough to handle the millions of souls who pray to him and remember what everybody needs of him? Hell, I'm a pretty intelligent clown and I can't even remember what I had for breakfast.

"No doubt!" It was Chesty's turn now. "And, if God is all powerful, can he create a rock so big that he himself can't lift it?"

"Of course, he can" replied Laymo. "Wait, I mean can't. Hell, is that a trick question?"

"The world may never know" offered Dew Drop. "And you know, Whammo's got this picture out of some pre-reformation book called the Bible and it's titled the crucifixion of Jesus of Nazareth and he ain't even a clown. Instead, he is one of those hu- somethings."

"Human beings" interjected Whammo. "Ya know, I think the World Circus is sitting on top of some real heavy baloney, clowns…like they try to deny our genetic roots to humanity and stuff. And that picture kinda tells me something about it ya know?"

"What?" said Laymo, "Tell us, dude." Whammo sat back on the polka dot couch, scratching the plate in his head.

"Well, I've been thinking like what if the picture is for real clown. That would mean that like Jesus was a human being, right? And, in the picture, he's like nailed to the thing. I mean somebody 'hadda do that to him. I can't say why they did it but I bet it killed him!"

"That would mean he's been dead for a long freakin' time." replied Chesty. Whammo continued "Right, but the World Circus says he came to Earth for the second time in pre-reformation days and that's how our ancestors all became clowns or something, because he told us be."

"Well, yeah, but what's your point, clown?" said Laymo as he lit a candy cigarette and passed it to the others.

"The point is that I can't figure out why if he was a human being back then, why he showed up as a clown. If you study the Doctrines of Grand Lunacy, there is a little cartoon there that talks about how right after Jesus came, the humans dressed themselves up to look like clowns until eventually they had turned into real ones. The Pooblas say that Jesus turned us all into clowns because he loved us, but I don't buy it."

"So..." said the group.

"So…what I think is that Jesus was mad at the humans for nailing him on that thing and he turned everyone into clowns as a joke to get back at them."

Laymo was struck with a sudden realization and it forced him to his feet as he let it out.

"Then that would mean that the World Circus and all it stands for is some kinda mistake! The Pooblas are completely full of crap!… and if us being clowns is all a big practical joke on humanity then that means that the only jokers who are for real are clowns that get serious."

The group fell silent for a moment as Laymo's words sank in. All of them could see the logic in his conclusions. It was mind shattering stuff for fools to think about. It was during this momentary break in the conversation that Blinko and Elvis came strolling past the two couples and made way for the door while carrying a small chair fixed to a rectangular wooden plank. The adults said nothing about it being too absorbed in their conversation.

"Maybe one day clowns like us can take over and put an end to this ridiculous malarkey," said Whammo.

&%$#%$

As their parents continued with their Obvious deep thoughts, Elvis and Blinko set up the frog electric chair out in back of the house.

"C'mon" said Elvis nodding to the left. "We gotta truck out of this neighborhood if we want to have any luck finding a frog to zap."

Blinko was curious about that and apprehensive about making a journey into neighborhoods unknown. He still didn't know his way around that well. He spoke:

"How come we gotta' go to a different neighborhood, Elvis?" Elvis answered as though annoyed at Blink's constant stupid questions.

"Because, I killed all the frogs in this one a long time ago."

Blinko's world was changing faster than he could cope with. It seemed like every minute he spent with Elvis he was forced to break some rule that Miss Smoochy had taught him. Now, he was sneaking around strange neighborhoods in search of a frog to kill in the chair Elvis had made.

"Killing?" he thought. *"Clowns aren't supposed to kill."*

The two kinderclowns found good hunting grounds about a quarter mile from their homes. It wasn't long before Elvis had a frog in hand.

"Got one!" cheered Elvis. "C'mon, let's hurry back before our folks start wondering where we are." Running fast as they could, it didn't take them long to make it back. Once at the sight of execution, Elvis handed Blinko the frog.

"Here, hold him for me while I get out the cotton candy bag ties. I use 'em to hold the frog in the seat." Blinko took the frog which terrified out of its pea sized brain urinated in his hands.

"Ooooooh, gross! It peed on me!"

"What? Did that frog pee on you? See that's another reason you gotta kill 'em for peeing on you and stuff."

Blinko still wasn't sure about it but he held the frog in the seat as Elvis secured its little squirming arms and legs to the chair. Then Elvis wrapped another tie around its belly and finally put the metal thimble on its head, like a cap, held in place by a rubber band.

"Okay, Blinko, go over to the socket and get ready to plug it in when I tell ya." Blinko did as he was told and then felt queasy upon realizing that, if he was the one who plugged in the chair, then it would be he that killed the frog. So far, he had only planned to watch.

"You ready over there, Blinko?"

Blinko swallowed hard. He wasn't sure if he could do it.

"NOW!" shouted Elvis. Blinko hesitated then sent the plug home. There was an instant buzzing sound along with a sharp pop and then crackling sounds as sparks shot off the chair.

"Turn it off, turn it off!" exclaimed Elvis. Blinko yanked the cord out of the socket. There was a cloud of smoke obscuring the chair. Elvis fanned at it to clear the air. When he was finished he looked at the seat. It was empty with the exception of a tiny piece of throbbing gristle. Elvis began to laugh like a maniac and Blinko laughed as well, despite of himself. As bad as what he had done was, he had liked all the excitement. Elvis was right. Killing frogs was damn fun. Then, he fell into the trance, blinking erratically.

Chapter 10
Selected readings from: The All Knowing Owl Speaks
Volume: 970,553,267,849,100,371: Jehovah's Domain
Book: 463,967,885,301 : Earth History
Chapter: 46,783,345 : World Circus Chronicles
Paragraph: 354,648,847,362

354,648,847,362: SAYETH THE OWL

After the extinction of the human race, clowns enjoyed several hundred years of prosperity and fortune. During this time, the World Circus was a lavish spectacle as it traveled around the globe on its powerful locomotive. However, this period was to be short lived. Clowns being utter idiots had not thought to teach the next generation of their kind to tend to the articles of their civilization and soon there was a shortage of skilled labor to clown the machines. This labor shortage was followed by the collapse of their industrial complex as the tools and machines themselves fell to ruin with no one to fix them. By the 300th year after the second coming, the clowns were living in the Dark Ages.

354,648,847,643: SAYETH THE OWL

Poobla's of the World Circus were not in the least concerned about these turns of events because:
1. They were privileged and lived in luxury hoarding what was to be had for themselves.
2. They were too stupid to notice that things were not like they used to be.
3. They refused to believe that conditions had ever been better in the first place.

The Pooblas just went about their routines in the World Circus as though all the suffering and hardship around them did not exist. But, obviously, there was a problem and it began to grow worse over time. Toil was taking its toll on the clown masses and some were starting to go bad. For each one of them, there was a dozen who had begun to get serious. The World Circus in those Dark Ages treated these serious clowns as possessed by Satano and his evil minions. Cast down into the tickle chambers, they were tickled until they were once again laughing. Often the results of these tortures were only temporary and the hooded nincompoops would tickle them repeatedly for weeks at a time as the Poobla's stood by juggling and telling jokes in an attempt to drive the demons out. Many ended up Pink. Most were tickled to death.

354,648,847,644: SAYETH THE OWL

As life became increasingly difficult more and more clowns found it hard to put on a happy face. This resulted in the steady increase of clowns being dragged off to the tickle chambers by the Disciples of Grand Lunacy. Also the World Circus Pooblas, in the face of so many clowns gone bad, began to increase the number of World Circus activities, the masses were expected to attend. This left little time for the clowns to tend the fields and bake the cookies and so only made life worse. Eventually, the Pooblas were dragging so many clowns off to be "saved" that the world's population was living in fear of the Circus. Groups of disciples roamed the streets repeating the same old dull jokes in a monotone chant causing any clown who thought he was being watched by them to instantly erupt into a fit of hysterics, singing and dancing, and foaming at the mouth, for fear of being accused of heresy.

354,648,847,645: SAYETH THE OWL

By 550 S.C., there was an ironic turn of events. Years of breeding under harsh conditions had given to the world a fair number clowns who could think. Usually these types were locked away or tickled to death, yet these clowns survived because they proved themselves to be invaluable to the World Circus. These clowns, first of a long line of circus-bred smarty-pants, went about inventing things to improve the world they lived in for the good of all, and to the greater glory of God and the World Circus. For example: food production was aided with the invention of the automatic jellybean picker and the cotton candy gin. Careful examinations of antique joy buzzers led to the discovery of electricity. Electricity led to the eventual powering up of forgotten technology in ruined dust covered factories. And, so it was that the heretics helped the clowns take a step forward out of the Dark Ages and into their own Renaissance.

354,648,847,646: SAYETH THE OWL

By the year 600 S.C., clowns had begun to tire, as the "same as it ever was" world in which they lived in had the same old-line gags and jokes shared among peoples. They were getting tired and lame. Eventually, during the Renaissance, various cultures around the globe began to form their own brands of hysterics. This, in turn, created a sense of nationalism long since gone from the planet's population. It all had to do with the fact that humor from one location was often not appreciated by clowns from another. This was because the new humor was specialized, not generic like that of the World Circus. The theology of the church taught that, that which was without humor was without God and therefore evil. So, eventually, conflict broke out between the nations who considered the others to be evil because they had not found anything humorous in their jokes and rituals. The truth of it was that none of these clowns were all that funny. There was little bodily injury during these little wars. Most clowns on a holy crusade against their neighbors stood on the battlefield with joke book in hand trying to crack up the enemy or convince them to laugh at them which was considered a type of victory.

354,648,847,647: SAYETH THE OWL

Conquered nations usually joined forces with the victors. These greater nations increased their crusades on all boarders until the entire world was at war. This war was called the Great War of Morons. War is generally not funny and so it came to pass that violence erupted on the fronts. Legions of Nincompoops, trained in the deadly art of tickling, made massive assaults upon their enemies, littering the battlefields with pink blithering idiots and the uncounted dead. Smarty-pants were hustled into think tanks full of mysterious pink syrup only to emerge as full blown mad scientists set to create weapons such that the world had never seen. The first of these weapons was corrosive pies that when slapped into a clown's face dissolved the flesh resulting in death. This was known as getting creamed. These pies in the face proved effective for hand-to-hand combat but were otherwise useless and often the result of many accidents as clowns forgot that the pies were deadly and tried to eat them. The smarty-pants then invented the Creampuff of Death. This was a self-contained pie that could be thrown or launched by catapult. Later, the smarty-pants invented a cream machine that was capable of launching hundreds of creampuffs a minute. Innovations in pie sHell technology allowed for megapuffs to be shot from giant cannons borrowed from the circus. These 500 pounders were sheathed in a graham cracker crust and proved devastating when fired into populated areas or the front lines. The discovery of nitrous oxide gas saw the advent of gas warfare. Dense clouds of this "laughing gas" were set adrift. Thousands died laughing, of course. Defensive forces began to fill pails full of pie filling and then placed them strategically on the battlefield. The enemy was left to kick the bucket as they attacked. Espionage was used as clowns disguised themselves as realtors and convinced soldiers to buy the farm. But seriously.

354,648,847,648: SAYETH THE OWL

    It came to pass that the world became divided into its two natural hemispheres, East and West. Superpowers they were called. In order to save the World Circus, the seat of power for the religion was located where it had traditionally always been…in the Vatican…but the influence of the World Circus was limited and overshadowed by war. Smarty-pants had done the unthinkable and dug up the pre-reformation archives there and had begun to use ancient technological information to build weapons of mass destruction. The secrets of these new weapons were instantly known to both sides for the spies were many and no clown could keep a secret anyway. Soon, they had built intercontinental-ballistic-creampuffs-of-death. These mighty pies flew on rocket powered engines and had the pie-power of a million and a half creampuffs. One of these could cream an entire city. The pie race was on. Due to the perishable quality of the weapons they were kept in refrigeration thus this period was termed the Cold War. The Cold War lasted for a period of….

Chapter 11
Four Eyeballs and the Three Miguels

Thirteen black candles burn on flesh
Teenage suzie cadaver their pedestal
She serves as an alter unto Satano
Her life taken in bloody sacrifice
"This soul I give to you black Lord of Flies
This life I take in testimony of my faith
'Tis you I wickedly slave for eternally
I fulfill my Hellbound destiny in blood
My father who art in Hell
Depravity is thy name
Thy kingdom come, thine will be done
On Earth as it is in Hades.
Give me this day my pittance of Obvious
Deliver me into evil as I murder
All those who trespass against us
In the name of Satano, Sally, and the un-used soap
I sin.

666

Hysterical in chains, a sinister clown her tormenter, another sacrificial suzie cannot take her eyes off the sacrificed clownette before her. The clammy hands of the satanic priest came to force her mouth open and deliver the mickey. Soon she will be released from the agony of consciousness with slumber. Now, limp upon his filthy mattress, she is ready. He carries her to the hearth and places her within it.

You hold your soul to keep
As I lay you down to sleep
In a bed of gasoline
Have your death inside a dream
Should you die before you wake
I think that it would just be great
But if you wake before you're dead
It's the wrong side of you're bed

Sicko grinned over his evil little poem as he finished pouring the fuel over the sleeping suzie. Then with a flick a match he ignited her.

666

The sacrifice indeed wakes on the wrong side of the bed as the searing pain of her burning flesh brings her to consciousness. She screams but once, as her lungs are filled with flame.

"This night I give not one but two souls in your name, master…in thanks to my good fortunes in this miserable world." Sicko grinned, being pleased with himself.

666

MEANWHILE IN HELL…

Satano and a recently undead clownette sit watching Sicko the Clown. The disgusting act of desecration viewed in an ancient standard toilet, the toilets water serving as an impossible yet full color high resolution 3D picture screen. Satano was now rather turned on after watching Sicko's little performance as was the undead sacrifice herself. The sacrifice secretly hoped that she could get it on with the demon, it was something she had always dreamed about, a thought Satano knew about instantly. Unfortunately for her, nobody's dream comes true in Hell. Satano thought at first that he might molest the newly arrived zombie but decided he was more hungry than randy and opted to devour the suzie. As his shark-like mouth violently stripped away her flesh, she realized then that Hell was indeed Hell. She also began to realize that once you're dead you're dead and that your body in the ever-after can sustain a lot of damage and then remain that way. Healing was against the law in Hell. As she was cast away horribly maimed for all eternity, she knew then that the damnation clause in her contract with the Devil was not a joke. Now, she would roam with out the equipment to commit her favorite sin. It was the worst thing that could have happened to her, just like all the rest.

666

Satano left the entertainment dungeon and turned off the 3D toilet by flushing it. He knew that the time was right to begin the next stage in his plans to ruin and corrupt planet Earth. He entered then the minds of all 666 delegates from that world and summoned them to his location. Instantly, the soiled ones began to arrive. The 666 despicable creatures stood waiting knee deep in the molten lead and sulfuric acid wading pool which surrounded the "Agony Column", Satano's favorite fountain. Satano arrived there in a little red wagon pulled along by two vicious red eyed Hellhounds. After climbing out of the cart, he released the hounds to sniff at nervous crotches and nip at nervous hands seeking to pet the beasts of the beast.

Satano was now in the form of a small raven haired boy. The child devil hopped up onto the walled edge of the wading poo, then executed a perfect bellyflop into the corrosive liquid. There he began to dissolve and after washing off most of his face, he spoke:

"As you know, we evil delegates to Earth's corruption have been largely successful in getting the clowns there to take themselves seriously."

"Here! Here! chanted the villains. The prince of doom continued:

"Needless-to-say, you can see why I choose to introduce hard candy with serious side effects into the world of clowns. It has proven to be a very effective brand of social corruption. As you know, the World Circus is almost impossible to corrupt directly due to the fact that its pooblas and disciples are too stupid to set into motion any of our brilliant plans. Since clowns only aspire to act silly all the time, they are not apt to desire wealth and power or be greedy, as were the humans of old. So, it was impossible to corrupt them from the top. What we have done instead, thanks to many of you, my wise and timeworn demons, is break down some key elements of the clown's belief system by utilizing basic principles of evil and deceit. Scientists here concocted a candy specifically aimed at clowns to go in concert with the lighter, mind altering candies already found in use. This new hard candy was introduced during the Great War of Morons and was effectively accepted into their society after the war was ended. This candy is called the Obvious.

Now, don't start asking for it down here because it won't do you human beings any good. This is because the Obvious only leads clowns into a serious state of mind, and we all know how serious you human beings take yourselves as it is. However, in the case of the clowns, this candy breaks down the very nature of their being. The Obvious gets them so serious that they just aren't funny anymore. It also tempts them into doing things forbidden in their society such as getting smart, discussing philosophy, thinking in general, and so on. As of now, candy use is commonplace in young clown adults and what's more, the clowns are having children and raising them with a completely new set of morals and ideologies. They are being raised under the new concepts of sincerity as opposed to the original Doctrines of Grand Lunacy. I predict it will be this generation of clowns that will bring on the fall of the Big Tops of the World Circus and allow us to inject more evil into their world."

The Devil was forced to take form in another body, for the acids in the pool had dissolved him to the point that only the top of his skull remained. He was also forced to reanimate all 666 Earth zombies. The mass then assembled along the wall of the fountain. He continued:

"Everyday these clowns are following in the footsteps of the extinct human race. And as evil as humanity was before the clown reformation, I must say how delighted I am to discover just how wicked a clown can become after holding out on sincerity for so long. We have come to learn that it is not that clowns have no natural evil in them, merely that it is still frowned upon by their society and suppressed by their nervous system. There is one clown in particular, among the first to embrace completely his sincerity, that is demonstrating that when it comes to evil, the clowns may very well out do the humans. And, to think he sold his soul to me for one more shot of the Obvious which does nothing more than restore his sanity. After what I saw him doing tonight, it's true there's nothing worse than a clown gone bad."

Satano snapped his fingers and presently there appeared a hulking corpse dripping with unknown slime next to him. The corpse was holding a small wooden case.

"It is time for me to award those of you who were key in my plan to corrupt the clowns using candy" announced the Devil. "Step forward."

Four former Presidents of a country once called the United States came forward. Satano, now in the form of a construction working redneck with a huge butt-crack, complete with hard-hat and tool-belt, removed the President's medals. The medals were sticky eyeballs which one by one he nailed to the foreheads of the heroes. The ghouls behind booed and hissed.

"There now, wear these eyeballs with honor and get out of my face!" The Presidents sank back into line with the others. Satano began to scratch at his butt and commenced to speak in his thick southern drawl.

"Soon, my slaves, the time of judgment will come to pass on Earth. The new generation of humorless clowns will quickly fall from innocence and serve us well. You here this eternal night will be issued new orders I expect carried out in every detail. Now, excuse yourselves from my presence with the exception of the three Miguels who I am ready to hear from concerning the analysis of this month's garbage from Buffoonville."

666

Satano's office was a decaying mass of flesh and gore. All of the things one might expect to find in an office were there, only here they were made from meat. The buzz of millions of flies droned on as the three Miguels entered the office to report their findings. Satano shot them in the kneecaps with a big gun for being tardy even though their arrival was almost instantaneous.

"Master!" said Miguel number two, "You're theory that much could be learned from the study of clown garbage has proven to be a work of genius!"
BANG! A bullet fired from Satano's forty four removed 63% of Miguel number two's mind.

"That's SUPER genius to you. Now, Miguels number one and three, help number two finish his report and stop trying to plug those holes in your knees, I shot you for a reason, pray I don't blow your brains out as well."

Miguel number one stepped over Miguel number two who was still on his painful knees as Miguel number three secretly prayed his brains wouldn't get shot out.

"Well..." said Miguel number one, but his sentence was cut short as another blast from Satano's gun tore through the skull of number three.

"You stupid idiot" screamed the Devil, "You know that praying is illegal in Hell...damn it, number one, you better watch out! Now, what have we learned? Miguel number one straightened his back and continued.

"Well, discarded newspapers have shown outbreaks of candy use and criminal activity, Master...clowns are going bad at an alarming rate."

"I know that" said the Devil dryly. Number One seemed nervous on top of his nervousness.

"Discarded holy comic books suggest clowns have lost faith in the World Circus." Number one took a small step back as the Devil stood up from of his meat seat.

"I know that!"
"Uh...also food wastes have clearly shown that clown diet has begun to change accordingly with the collapse of old belief systems. Foods like vegetables and oatmeal considered to be icky have turned up on discarded menus in the lower east-side of Buffoonville."

"I know that, too, you moron! Can't you tell me something I don't already know? HMMMM...I'm waiting!"

"But Master, how can anyone know that which you do not know for you know everything?"

"True enough slave. Then why are you telling me all these things I already know?"

"Because you told me to, Master."

"I know that."

Chapter 12
Oh No, It's the Weirdoes!

Two hundred forty seven light years from Earth, the red sun rose above the foggy horizon, cracking dawn on a desert planet…a world unbearably hot. Sunbeams fell to awaken a small family of rodent like beings who were sleeping in a pile under a slime tree. Here, water never came in the form of a flowing liquid river or stream. Slime dripping from the bump like nodules on the slime tree served the creatures as the only source of water on the planet.

X-phap, the youngest in the rodentine family, extended its long tube like tongue to lick the crusts of sleep from its single eye. Then it focused its attention on a bubbling nodule to get a much-needed drink. X-phap worked its tongue into the slime trees orifice and began to suck up the thick milky fluid inside. Soon, its entire family would do the same; all would remain there, tongues attached like umbilical cords, lifelines.

Across the desert there were many such families of slime suckers attached to the slime trees and nothing else for at this time in the history of their dry planet, the slime suckers were the only creatures who had managed to adapt after the holocaust which had occurred there. Once, many years ago, the planet had been a thriving metropolis full of these semi-humanoid rat people…people, who had great technologies, great religions, fantastic architecture, splendid works of art, soothing music, and fine poetry, and all the other trappings of a highly advanced culture. These rattish beings were but one of the millions of sentient races across the Universe whose world had served as a top producer of positivite energy within God's ever expanding and diversified creation. But now, their world was lost and buried for eons beneath the sands their once lush world had become, thanks to one ex-employee of the creator.

The red sun had only faced this half of the planet for a few moments, yet the surface temperature had already arisen high enough to have boiled water, had there been any. A human being on this world would be quickly roasted but fortunately for Jesus, dealing with matters a trivial as weather was not a problem. The continuous roar of a large air conditioner levitating one meter above the Savior broke the utter silence of the desert world. A pleasant blast of refrigerated air cooled Jesus as he made way towards the slime tree and X-phap's family. Jesus frequently stopped by planets like these, planets that had been destroyed by Satan. Doing so served as a reminder to him of just how tough the competition could get if not stopped in time.

%^$@##

Back in the really old days before Jesus was born, his Father had always had the resources to rebuild devastated planets such as this one. Back then, Satan's powers were not large enough to counteract God's creation too often. Christ had always thought that his Father's biggest mistake was in underestimating just how determined Satan was to bring down the whole of creation. During those early times, God expanded his work on a magnificent level and for billions of years he bank rolled a huge surplus of positive energy. Jesus recalled that he'd had an uneasy feeling about a century or so after his crucifixion concerning his Father's latest project. God had under taken a huge remodeling job of Heaven. Heaven, being the pinnacle of his creative ladder, did not produce enough positive energy or Positrons of its own to support such endeavors. Unlike the factory planets populated by love producing beings, Heaven was filled with flesh graduates who consumed love. They also expected God to fulfill his promise of eternal paradise, and eternal paradise is expensive as Hell, literally. Therefore, any project in support of Heaven came directly out of God's savings and he had been drawing on his savings steadily as of late.

Anyway, God justified his expenditures on the basis that his creation was now so large that he had run out of room for new souls which arrived in the millions everyday from across the Universe. That was true indeed but he was old, really, really old and Christ felt that the omnipotent one was becoming a fool in his old age…that God was out of touch with the reality of the situation. Christ also felt that God wasn't paying close enough attention to the evil deeds of Satan. If only he could convince his father to take the Devil more seriously. But he knew that would never happen. After all God had already had a billion years to think about it. Still with every conquered planet, Satan grew more powerful and with every new project, God diminished his own. As it was, profits were down to nothing and Jesus feared that the remodel might be just the thing that would tip the scales in favor of the competition. He shuddered at the thought.

*#@%$#

On the other hand, Satan was carefully managing his affairs utilizing or exploiting anything he could to further his dream of destroying God's Universe. Satan created his own business to compete with God's enterprise and had found in his anti-creation venture that there was a profit to be made. Profits in negative energy…hate energy. Satan found that it wasn't that hard to corrupt love-producing worlds into hate producing ones. Where God had the huge overhead of creating the planetary mass and the solar system to support it, Satan's operation, which had no overhead to speak of, was aimed at merely tricking the populations of God's worlds to produce negative energy for him. On a grander scale, Satan was also able to cut into God's profits by way of global Armageddon, milking a planet dry and then convincing its population to destroy themselves, effectively ending the planets positive energy production potential and leaving God with a debt producing lifeless solar system. (God's Universe being unified, each solar system must exist with or without life to maintain the galactic balance.)

Before the birth of Christ, Satan had only managed to do this on rare occasion and only on worlds that didn't reflect well on God's creative vision, and were, therefore, sitting ducks. But now, God's creation was so huge that there were millions of planets he had forgotten about which fell into the hands of the Devil. Satan had become a very powerful being primarily due to God's neglect and lack of judgment concerning his own creations.

*%$@#$

It was here, on X-phap's world, that Christ felt once more the familiar feeling of impending doom. He wondered if it wasn't already too late to stop Satan from destroying the Universe. Standing at the foot of the slime tree now in the shadow of his floating air conditioner, Jesus looked down at the little nest of slime suckers. He recalled what the world of their ancestors had been like. How this world had been so full of life and love. With his mind, he reached into the heart of X-phap to see if there was still room for love within his kind after so many generations forced to eke out an existence in this hostile environment. Indeed there was love in X-phap's heart but it was not directed upon its family but rather upon the life giving slime tree. The tree was all the little rodent could afford to care about. This broke Christ's heart and he began to weep. His tears evaporated instantly, but not quick enough to escape arousing the sharp noses of several slime suckers who momentarily lifted their snouts to sniff the air at the long forgotten scent…the smell of tears.

Jesus left the slime suckers with their precious slime tree and wandered aimlessly into the wastelands. The desert dunes were littered with remnants of a civilization gone totally to ruin. He looked up at the blazing red giant, felt it burn his face. It was then that his air conditioner gave a final blast of cool air then fell apart under the strain of the desert heat. He let the poor thing fall into the blazing hot sand. Now without it, Jesus felt as though he was roasting like a weenie over a campfire.

Jesus was not one to lose his temper but here, surrounded by the evidence of Satan's work, he could not control himself, especially after his air conditioner broke. He simply couldn't take it anymore. Since the crucifixion, it had been his job to rush around the Universe to warn entire civilizations of the competition and to occasionally save the worlds from themselves. How many planets had he saved just in the nick of time? How many had he not been able to save? He knew that lately the Devil was winning. *"Look at it now"* he thought. *"An entire planet lain to waste at the hands of a demon. The only survivors left to a miserable fate sucking the slime out of a tree as twisted as the heart of the Devil which destroyed them."* Christ could not bear it. He did have a little savings of Pozi saved up. Would his life savings be enough? This was the work of a God. Did he dare to spend all his Pozi when his father was so broke? Still he had to try.

"What good is it to be wealthy if I cannot help those less fortunate than I?" He spoke out loud in the silent desert. He then sat down upon the blistering surface of the air conditioner and began to summon his resources.

With his arms outstretched as though crucified, he closed his eyes and began to imagine a world all together unlike this one. And as he thought these things, they were done...a world transformed, lush with vegetation, boundless seas, mighty rivers, and an abundance of life. Rains suddenly poured onto the desert soil and consequently the desert teemed with new growth…a world anew. Then, with the remainder of his resources, he continued the miracle by bringing the slime suckers back to the proud creatures they had once been. He filled each of them with as much love as they could hold in their hearts.

X-phap stood erect for the first time in its life. It looked at the new bodies of its family and for the first time felt love for something other than the twisted slime tree. It gazed upon the slime tree to see that its trunk had straightened and it had grown a hundred feet tall, branches hung low, heavy with fruit. X-phap extended his tongue to taste the silvery water at his feet. It drank from the puddle until its front butt was full. X-phap and its people had been given a second chance and Christ had spared them the memory of the past thousand years when their world was barren and dry. In this way, they could begin life fresh without even the negativity of bad memories.

Already Jesus could feel them producing raw Positrons and this was good. It meant once again that the concept of sacrifice worked. He had sacrificed all the Positrons he had for them and now it was coming back ten fold. Christ wept again but this time tears of joy. His miraculous ears could hear the rejoicing of an entire planet. He decided then that it was time to go back to Heaven and have a serious talk with God. Unseating himself from the air conditioner, he imagined himself home and it was done.

777

Christ stood at the Pearly Gates searching for his keys. He could not simply wish the gate to open. God had put in a Pozi/Nega energy absorption unit in the gate as well as the walls that surrounded Heaven, in order to ward off Satan's spies. Only three angels had the key, God, Jesus, and St. Peter who was at the moment nowhere to be seen. Christ abruptly realized that he had left his key back at the office so he gave up searching for it. He nearly cursed. He had been feeling cranky after blowing such a huge wad on the slime suckers planet and he needed a shower after sweating it out in that desert. It wasn't that he was dirty, it was just that he needed the soothing water to calm his nerves.

"Peter?" called the Savior. No one answered.

"Peter? What's the deal?" Christ called out again. He stuck his head between the bars for a look around and noticed an angel's smock lying on the clouds. As Jesus wondered what the smock was doing there, his attention was caught by something red that was fluttering down out of the sky. When it landed in front of him, it turned out to be a red lace bra. Christ stepped away from the gate and looked upward. There he saw St. Peter and a female angel both of whom were naked. Christ smiled.

"Hey, Peter! Aren't you supposed to be on duty?" Peter launched himself off the cloud, wings beating rapidly.

"Hey, you're right! What was I thinking?" He landed on the path leading to the gate where Christ was waiting.

"Let me in, I forgot my keys." The saint removed his key and handed it to the Savior through the pearly bars of the Pearly Gates. Christ let himself in, then the two embraced.

"Good to have you back, Lord" said Peter. "Care to join me? You'll never believe the things this girl learned to do to make it in show business as the say."

"I'm sure, Peter, but I have no time for that right now. There is trouble brewing and I must speak with God."

Peter could see that Jesus was not kidding around. "That bad out there, huh?"

"That bad!" And off went the Messiah down the yellow brick road.

777

Christ could see the hulking mass of the offices of God in the distance. He always enjoyed going to the office. Once Jesus had entered the long hallway, the first thing he noticed was that it was lit with candlelight. One might expect things to be lit with candle light in heaven but this was, in fact, unusual in the office, which had perfectly normal light fixtures. Christ wondered about the candles until he began to wonder about the sign on the monorail, which said the rail was out of order. This was a real bummer because it meant hiking through the endless corridors and going up a lot of stairs to reach the penthouse office floor. Nevertheless, it looked as though he had little choice, for after ignoring the sign and calling for the monorail, it did not respond.

He set off on foot then, winding his way up and through the various rooms until he was inside the vaulted foyer where the stairs to the penthouse office were. After climbing what seemed like an eternity, he finally reached the office and was again puzzled by the candlelight. Upon seeing his Father and his Father's secretary, Marilyn Monroe, he used an old joke in an attempt to discover the answer behind all the candles.

"Who died?" he said. A pun in heaven for everyone there HAD died, of course. God was not amused.

"Inter-Dimensional Utility Services cut off the power about 60 years ago, been doing everything by candlelight ever since" said God.

"Why? What, are they working on the power grid or something?" Jesus took a seat resting himself after his arduous journey to the office. Marilyn supplied the answer.

"I wish that were true, boss, but the reason is because you and your very old man are flat broke. We didn't have enough Pozi to pay the bill."

"You're joking!" cried Jesus.

"Nope, it's all true, Son. Say? What about your life savings? That should get us by for a century or two." Christ was suddenly regretful for spending all his Pozi back on the slime suckers world. He should have known something like this would happen.

"You're gonna kill me. I spent it all revitalizing a planet Satan had destroyed during one of my emotional moments."

"Well, that settles it then, we're doomed" replied God.

"Doomed?" said Jesus. What's happened?" Marilyn brought him up to date.

"What's happened is the Inter-Dimensional Bank is foreclosing God's domain. We're bankrupt and four payments behind on the mortgage God took out to do that last remodel." God came and sat next to his son putting a hand on Jesus' knee.

"I'm thinking about selling out to the Weirdoes from over in the Fifth Dimension. They offered to buy my creation at liquidation price which would give us enough Pozi to live on for eternity…but there's a catch."

"So, what's the catch?"

"The catch is that the Weirdoes plan to hire someone to manage the creation and you'll never believe who."

"Who?" asked Jesus, but God just gave him that all-knowing look.

"Satan?" shouted Christ, leaping from his chair. "You can't let the Weirdoes buy you out and let Satan take over! He will destroy it all!"

"That's just what the Weirdoes want, Son. They want to clear out everything in the time/space continuum my Universe dwells in to make room for an expansion of their warped existences." The two Gods fell silent for a moment letting it all sink in. Then Christ pondered.

"So, what are our options here, Dad?" God replied.

"As far as I can figure it, we have three. One is to sell out to the Weirdoes but we already know we can't do that because of Satan and their plans to destroy it all. The second is to let the Inter-Dimensional Bank foreclose in which case they will most likely sell the creation to the Weirdoes as well. The third option is a long shot." Christ seemed glad to hear that there actually was another option.

"So, what is it?"

God took a deep breath, held it then exhaled slowly. He spoke calml:

"We could go to the Greatest Extreme to save the Universe."

"And what extreme would that be?"

"No. You misunderstand me, Son, the Greatest Extreme is a place."

"Oh. So then, why would we go to the Greatest Extreme?"

"You're kidding me! Exclaimed Jesus. "You mean the All Knowing Owl that... "

"That's right, Son, the one that knows how many licks it takes to get to the center of a tootsie pop."

Christ quit pacing the floor and plopped back into his seat as though relieved.

"Yeah...yeah, that's the ticket! The Owl knows everything there is to know about Like Everything and if anyone can see a way out of this jam, HE will."

"You are correct, my only begotten son, but there is one troublesome point I must bring up."

"And what is that, pray tell?"

"No one knows how to go to the Greatest Extreme. We will have to cast ourselves forth into the unknown void of Like Everything in search of it. It will be a long a difficult journey with little hope of success. No one has seen the Owl since he did that commercial."

"But, it is the only hope we have right?"

"Right!" God got up from his seat and adjusted his robes.

"Now that that is settled, we must address the need for Pozi to pay for the trip. Marilyn proposed that we have a gigantic Inter-Dimensional Garage Sale to cover our expenses and to pay our back mortgage payments to buy us the time we will need to complete our quest.

"Marilyn, read Jesus the list of stuff we have so far to sell."

Marilyn messed around with her computer and began to read off the list:

"Okay so far we have 22 un-ignited stars complete with solar system start-up kits, 14 various comets...those are always popular items as decoratives...lets see, there are 234 un-used sentient life kits going from thinking mold to crystal entities...also there is Jesus' crucifix and the three nails...all kinds of other junk...plenty for a decent sale."

"Yeah, I'm sure we can get some good money from the Jesus Freaks for my crucifix and the nails. They will probably break out in stigmata just hearing about it." God agreed.

"Well then" he said, "So let it be written, so let it be done."

%$#@$%

As Christ came to stand on hallowed garage sale ground, he was just in time to witness the arrival of the Jesus Freaks from the 27th Dimension. They pulled up in a giant chariot and parked right next to God's low-rider. A small slapping sound could be heard as Jesus slapped himself on the forehead in disgust.

"Jesus Freaks!" said Jesus. "I hate these guys!"

The story of the Jesus Freaks goes something like this. Shortly after the crucifixion of Christ, which was televised live on Inter-Dimensional Pay-Per-View, a boring world out in the backwoods of the 27th Dimension began a type of fan club for

Jesus. Much like the highly impressionable humans of Earth, these beings took their love of this angel to the fanatical extreme. Eventually the fan club became so big that it over-ran the government of the planet. After that, it became law that all inhabitants on their world should become genetically altered to resemble Christ. It got so bad, what with the billions of his fans sending him letters with photographs of them crucifying themselves and so on, Christ began to loath them and eventually to despise and hate them. Eventually Christ got over it and let it go but the Freaks never did. Christ thought it funny that here for the first time, the fanaticism of the Jesus Freaks was actually going to serve a purpose. Christ was hoping that the Jesus Freaks would be prepared to bankrupt the wealth of their entire planet to acquire what they must have considered the most holy of ancient relics, the crucifix and the three nails.

^%#^%$#

In the sum total of Like Everything, God's creation is but an infinitesimally small portion of it. Others in Like Everything refer to God's creation as God's Crib or God's Domain or any number of other names. The news of a Inter-Dimensional Garage Sale in God's Domain spread fast throughout Like Everything. It is written that the rate at which news may travel in Like Everything is governed by two factors. The first being the nature of the news itself and the second thing being whither or not anyone gives a crap. The ten million smackarue question NOW is what does ANYONE giving a crap got to do with it. After all, the Anyone's are just a bunch of sentient mold creatures living out near the Greatest Extreme, and who are they giving their crap to anyway? But never mind that.

Nobody got the news of the garage sale faster than the Jesus Freaks, but that was because it was Nobody's job and everybody knows Nobody can't keep his mouth shut. This is why if you want to keep a secret in Like Everything the first thing you do is say "Whatever you do, don't tell Nobody."

The word of God strikes fear in the hearts of men but only commands attention from angels. For this reason, instead of falling on his knees, Christ only straightened his posture when he heard God calling for him. In this case, he chose to use his all knowing ability to locate his Father, seeing as to how Heaven was pretty crowded just then. When he reached the Lord of Creation, he found that his Father was in a panic. God began to bark.

"Jesus Christ, is it really you? Tell me it is you, my son!" Jesus realized instantly what the Lord's problem was. There was, after all, just under two billion Jesus Freaks running around Heaven, all of whom could easily have passed for the bearded hippie. Christ chose to answer his Father's pleas with a small miracle. He turned himself into a clown with a wonkle wonkle. God smiled and said,

"I can't wait for this to be over!"

"No doubt, man" proclaimed the Messiah, "those Freaks are a complete pain in the butt, following me around all over the place." God's michealangelican chest heaved a deep sigh as he blew it off.

"Here, Son, check this out!"

Christ's feet made a flintstone patter as he came to take a peek. God was holding out his hand. There was a small tube in it. "It's Wacky Glue! explained the Father."

"Wacky Glue?" quizzed Christ.

"Right, Son, and, mark my words, it's the stickiest stuff in the Universe. Why, I used Wacky Glue to weld together the unknown forces of my infinite imagination to create the basic fabric of the space/time continuum. I used Wacky Glue to paste together the entire Universe. I used Wacky Glue to bond together my boogers to form the double helix matrixes, which serve as the fundamental basis of all life in my domain. And I used Wacky Glue to fix up my coffee cup which I accidentally broke this morning."

"WOW!" said Jesus "I did not know that."

Just then, a rude and obnoxious Jesus Freak forced his way past God and son on his way to the auction and Christ grew angry.

"Jeez! Where is a bizarre in a temple when you need one? I sure could stand to blow off a little steam." But then a sinister smile erupted across his face as he realized a method by which he could fix the Jesus Freaks forever.

Hours later the sale of the holy relics had come to an end. The Jesus Freaks had assembled themselves into a swarming mass which promptly became a violent riot as each of the millions of them vied for a chance to be crucified on the just purchased crucifix. For a Jesus Freak, being crucified on the actual cross with the actual nails used to crucify Christ would be the highest honor and pinnacle of personal achievement. God and son were pleased to see the Freaks literally killing themselves over their recent purchase.

All in all, the garage sale had been a complete success and a near sell out. The two angels were pleased because now they had enough Pozi to embark on their journey to the Greatest Extreme. There was one problem though. Judging the amount of Pozi the Jesus Freaks had just blown on the holy relics, it looked like they didn't even have enough to pay for their own trip home.

"So, this is how civilizations destroy themselves" said God having little pity for the hopeless imposters.

>%$#^%

In Like Everything, there are those you can mess with and those who can mess with you. If there is anyone who can mess with you, it's the Weirdoes, infamous gangsters and inter-dimensional criminals. A lot of folks owed money to the Weirdoes including the Jesus Freaks. It is an odd tale how the Jesus Freaks came to be so heavily indebted to the Weirdoes.

It is written that when the Freaks saw the live telecast of the crucifixion of Christ and inevitably came to base their entire civilization on the life of Christ, they soon began to demand that the crucifixion be replayed everyday exclusively on their world. Of course, to do this they would be dealing with the Weirdoes who have their tentacles wrapped around everything in Like Everything one way or another. The Weirdoes charged the Freaks a lot of Pozi for the exclusive rights to the crucifixion. But it didn't stop there. As the Jesus Freaks matured as a culture into the imposters they became, the Weirdoes found ways to squeeze more out of them. The Weirdoes offered the Jesus Freaks something they could not resist which was live replays of the crucifixion by way of time warp. The Weirdoes stated that they would position the Jesus Freak's planet in a temporal loop, flip flopping from the moment before the crucifixion up to the moment after the resurrection, then all over again for all eternity. They would do this for a price, a mere fee, a simple bill at the end of the month. Needless-to-say, the Freaks went for it despite the unfathomable cost. And so it was written and so it was done.

Nobody's phone rang. He answered and received an anonymous tip that the Jesus Freaks had just bankrupted themselves in the pursuit of acquiring Christ's holy mementos. Shortly, the Weirdoes received the news and were making calls to their accountants and bagmen, which uncovered the fact that indeed the Freaks had just gone bust. The Weirdoes were not happy about it seeing as the Freaks had been such a good source of income.

Meanwhile, Christ was stepping out of a heavenly phone booth. Soon, he found his Father who was still in the middle of wondering how he was gonna get rid of all the Jesus Freaks in Heaven now that they were too broke to leave on their own.

"Jesus Christ, what are we gonna do with these morons?" he said. Christ smiled and sat clown style next to the puzzled Lord.

"Time will tell" replied the Savior. It is written that time indeed did tell for just moments after his statement and a few moments further from his call to Nobody, the rioting crowd of Jesus Freaks were instantly as silent as they were transformed into 15-million evenly paired jars of peanut butter and jelly.

"Weirdoes always did have a strange way of getting even." remarked Christ, eyeballing the endless rows of jars. God nodded his head totally un-impressed that the millions of freaks were now millions of gallons of sandwich spread. He commented on this:

"What in the name of creation am I gonna do with 15-million jars of peanut butter and jelly?"

Jesus had it all figured out. He knew that the Weirdoes would be interested in getting back all the Pozi that the Freaks owed them. That is why he had placed a second call, after his call to Nobody, to the Weirdoes to inform them of a desperate famine, which had just occurred on the planet of White Bread and Crackers. Of course, they would be happy to purchase all the sandwich spread and no sooner had God troubled himself over the millions of jars, than did they vanish. God laughed out loud after Jesus explained what he had done.

"Ha! I never liked those Jesus Freaks myself! Good riddance."

Chapter 13
Clownboys and Indians

IN THE MORNING

Blinko woke up, as usual, before his foster parents, who were heavily crashed after the previous nights serious get together. Not surprisingly, the first thing on the kinderclowns mind was the execution of the frog. He felt a little ashamed but not for killing the frog. He felt his shame over having fallen into the trance in front of Elvis. So far, the trances were known only to his foster folks. Blinko hoped Elvis wouldn't blab to all the other kids at school about it.

Here his thoughts shifted towards his new friend. There was something in Elvis that Blinko admired. He couldn't quite place it but he felt sure it had something to do with the clown's serious nature. Blinko never really identified with others his age. Most kids his age were funny and jovial as Hell but not Blinko. His life so far had been too tragic for humor. Elvis wasn't funny either, which was why he felt closer to the tot than all the other clowns he had come by in his short six years. He delighted then in the knowing that soon he would be seeing his new friend on the clown school bus.

After dressing himself, Blinko left his room quietly and went into the kitchen. He hoped that his mother had remembered to prepare him a sack lunch to take to clown school. Searching through the refrigerator it looked like she had forgotten again. That was normal. Blinko sighed then shut the door. Quickly he opened it again in an attempt to catch the light coming on. Of course, he failed miserably in doing so as any clown would, after all, nobody but nobody can open the door that fast.

Turning to the fruit bowl Blinko noticed two Rues on the table.

"Lunch money!" thought the tot. Blinko pocketed the Rue and made his way out of the house and down to the bus stop. Elvis was already there. Blinko ran over to him. When he got there it was apparent that Elvis was angry.

"Hi, Elvis. How's it going?"

Elvis turned and replied "Like kahkah! Everything sucks right now."

Blinko was as sympathetic as he was shocked over Elvis' constant use of profanity.

"Why? What's the matter?"

Elvis answered quickly. "Well, first of all, I'm going to school and if that ain't bad enough my Dad beat my tail last night."

Blinko immediately assumed that Elvis's Dad must have found out about the frog they killed in the electric chair the night before.

"Did he find out about the chair?"

"Yeah, but that's not why he tore my patooty up. He spanked me because he broke his toe."

"But why would he spank YOU for breaking his toe?"

"Because he broke it down in the basement trying to fix the fuse we blew frying that frog. He figured out that it was us that did it right after you left last night."

"Do you think he told my Dad, too?" asked Blinko.

"Nah" said Elvis "He ain't a narc. But he smashed up my record player throwing a temper tantrum and then it got even worse when he realized that his favorite Dead Kennedy's record was on the player at the time. That's why he whooped me so bad. I ain't supposed to fool with his records and stuff."

The bus arrived.

ON THE BUS

The two kinderclowns clamored aboard the short school bus and put on their hockey helmets. The driver of the bus was an orange haired slob named Fatso. Everyone made fun of him behind his back. Fatso didn't mind being made fun of because he was a clown. Elvis and Blinko stood at the front of the bus looking for an empty seat. There was only one and it was situated right next to Apache, the indian clown who had bloodied Elvis honker yesterday. Apache could see the situation as clearly as Elvis and Blinko could. Little Elvis felt his heart begin to beat hard. He had been whipped by that Indian who was now looking right at him while patting the empty seat daring him to sit there even though he had no choice since it was the only one left. Suddenly, the two fell face first as the bus lurched forward unexpectedly. Everyone got a big kick out of that most basic form of slapstick and began to laugh and hoot. Next, the two made way to the back and sat down. Blinko sat between Elvis and Apache hoping it would keep the indian from getting on Elvis's case. It didn't work that way. Instead, the indian clown started jabbing Blinko in the side with his elbow.

"Hey!" said Blinko "Stop it, why don't ya!"

"Why don't ya try and make me, wimp" said Apache, reveling in his moment of superiority. He leaned over Blinko and slapped the top of Elvis's head. Elvis hunkered down and tried to ignore the indian who was obviously trying to start something. Apache wasn't even close to being through. He started to tease Elvis.

"Hey wimp!" he said smacking Elvis on the head again. It made Elvis's blood boil.

"Today during recess I'm gonna beat your butt, what do you think of that?"

The whole bus-load of clowns had stopped cutting up and were now focused on the little argument that was going on in back. Elvis was suddenly aware that the whole class was watching and it humiliated him. He couldn't wimp out in front of them. He tried to act as tough as he could.

"Oh, yeah? You may have got me yesterday but that was just luck. We'll see who beats whose butt at recess, Apache, just you wait."

Elvis's face was all scrunched up in anger as he tried to make himself look as intimidating as possible. It was not very effective because clown faces do not lend themselves to looks of anger very easily. Blinko knew that Elvis was secretly afraid of Apache. Apache was almost a third larger than his size and a proud warrior at that. All clownboys knew not to mess with an indian.

"You're on! Dumbo!" said Apache loud enough for all to hear. So it was all set…a fight at recess. Blinko was really feeling sorry for Elvis now. Elvis didn't say another word until the bus had arrived at clown school and let the kinderclowns off.

"What are ya gonna do, Elvis?" said Blinko, as they got off the bus.

"I'm gonna fight 'em that's what, and it don't matter if he's bigger 'cause the coach will stop the fight before anyone gets hurt. Then he will take us to the principal for a spanking and then when my Dad finds out I'll get to go out for ice cream because my dad is always proud of me for standing ground in a fight. He's a scrapper, too, ya know. But listen, you gotta back me up, okay? If that indian starts to whip me and the coach ain't around, you jump in and help, see?"

Blinko was a little worried but he'd been in plenty of fights in the orphanage. That's where he first started to fall into those weird trances. It seemed that negative thoughts or events triggered it. He had waked from trances to find himself fighting several times.

"Don't worry, Elvis, I'll back you up, dude."

Elvis cracked a smile. "Great! Then we'll both get creamed."

IN THE CLASSROOM

Then the bell rang. Quickly, the two clowns skeedaddled for their classroom. However, since they were clowns, their navigational skills were quite poor and they ended up getting lost before finally finding the right room. Mrs. Applebeans greeted the two with a sympathetic smile for lateness was as commonplace as laughter in clown school. Still, they would have to be punished, a thought Mrs. Applebeans relished because she really had it in for little evil Elvis.

"You two are tardy!" she said in as stern of voice as a clownette could muster. It was not very intimidating.

"Come to my desk" she said, as she opened a drawer and began fiddling around in it looking for two nail files, which she delivered into the hands of the kinderclowns.

"Sharpen your nails with these." she said. Quietly the tots did as they were told. Blinko had no idea what was about to happen but Elvis seemed cool. The two exchanged looks and Elvis could see tears welling up in the others eyes.

"What a wuss" he thought. Blinko was teary eyed because he found it humiliating to be singled out in front of the class like that…not because he was afraid. After they had their nails sharpened, their teacher addressed the class. "Simon says cover your ears" Mrs. Applebeans covered her ears as an example to the rest.

"Elvis! Blinko! Now, go over and drag those nails across the black board. Hurry now the class is waiting. The two did as they were instructed. Blinko's teeth nearly jumped out of their gums at the wretched sound it made and the chalky feeling on his fingertips. Elvis on the other hand seemed totally unphased. After that, they were told to take their seats.

Mrs. Applebeans had been lecturing the class for five minutes with her back to them as she wrote on the blackboard before she realized that she had forgotten to instruct the class to take their hands off their ears. She even had to tell them twice, forgetting to say "Simon says" the first time. Her lecture was extremely boring. She was instructing the class on the concepts of greater kindness and applied humor. It did not matter to her that the class was much too young to understand a word she was saying for clowns didn't learn a thing in clown school anyway. Most clowns got their education from the playground. Clown school was more like an ancient ritual to make their parents feel better for not educating their children themselves. Besides most clowns did not want to admit that they had gotten their own education at the playground and liked to pretend that they had gotten their education in clown school when they were young themselves. Clowns pretended about a lot of things.

Elvis spent most of his time that day looking over his shoulder at Apache and looking over Mrs. Applebeans' head at the clock. He knew, when the bozo's hands pointed at the number twelve, it would be time for recess and the big fight. All the children were waiting to see the big fight at recess and rumors of it had even gotten to the faculty. Violence is commonplace in clown society…violence being one of the primary ingredients of slapstick humor, dating all the way back to the Three Stooges. So even if the teachers new about the fight it was unlikely they would do anything to stop it until it was well underway. Violence was not out right encouraged but certainly not condemned.

Blinko was watching the clock as well. He could see that the hour was growing near and he wondered what things would turn out like. He was also wondering how Elvis had handled scraping his nails across the blackboard so well. Maybe Elvis was as tough as he looked after all. Then the bell rang. It was weird for Blinko walking down the hall to the gymnasium. It was the pent up anxiety of the fight along with all his other bottled up feelings…so many changes so fast.

"Don't forget to jump in if Apache starts to whip me" stated Elvis, trying to hide his own apprehensions.

"Don't worry, Elvis, I'm right behind you. Say, I wonder when he will make his move?"

"The coach always has to go to the john after we do our exercises and that's usually when clowns fight during recess, so be ready when you see him leave."

"Roger." Blinko swallowed hard. He had a bad feeling about this.

IN THE GYM

Sure enough, right after the warm-up exercises, the coach made way for the bathroom and like clockwork Apache started to shove Elvis around. At first, it looked like Elvis was going to lose right away, but Blinko could see that he wasn't getting hit despite the many punches Apache was throwing. Suddenly, Elvis landed a throw right in Apaches face, bleeding his honker. Apache seemed stunned. It was clear that he thought the fight was going to go his way with ease. He wasn't expecting Elvis to put up much of a struggle. But this didn't work in Elvis's favor because, as it turned out, Apache really hadn't been trying all that hard to begin with. Immediately after his honker got bloodied, he became a ferocious warrior and Elvis began to take quite a beating from him from that point on.

"Blinko!" called out the kinderclown. Elvis was obviously counting on Blinko's help at this point. Blinko didn't hesitate and jumped in the fray but as Apache drew back to punch out Elvis, his elbow creamed Blinko right in the eye and sent him reeling. Apache looked back and was proud that he had thwarted the second attacker, then he popped Elvis a good one. Blinko clamored up to his feet and felt his face grow hot. It was the trance coming on.

When the coach came out of the john, he noticed immediately the tight circle the other kinderclowns had made around the fighting boys. He knew it could only mean a fight had broken out and the rumor he had heard that morning had been true. He ran over to break it up as he always did, but discovered upon arrival, that the fight was over. Elvis was sitting on the floor holding his badly banged up face in his hands. Blinko was standing seemingly unharmed. He was straddled over Apache who was not moving and lying on his back between Blinko's feet. It appeared that the indian had been knocked unconscious. The coach got Blinko out of the way and tried to rouse the indian, amazed at the sight of the unconscious kinderclown. It is nearly impossible to knock out a clown. Apache didn't wake up, as the coach expected him to as he continued to shake him gently. The coach shook him harder but still the indian didn't come to. Next the coach pulled Apache into a sitting position and that was when he noticed the child's head flop backwards in an impossible manner. It could mean only one thing…Apaches neck was broken. Apache was dead!

ON THE REZ

There in the hot, dry confines of the sweat lodge, the air was sticky sweet with the sweat of Apache's elders. After the countless changes and many sufferings of these Native American Indian clowns, it was surprising how many of the ancient traditions and ceremonies were still in use. Before the reformation, these people had lost much of the greatness inherent in tradition, and the common indian looked and acted much the same as those who had conquered their nation and stripped them of their dignity in the past. But now, the old ways were back in use as strongly as ever, for clowns love to sing and dance and wear outrageous costumes. Now, the elders were singing a sad song of death over the loss of Apache, the son of Chief Falling Pants.

His people sang:

Oh, great and truthful spirits in
The circus in the sky
Take into your funhouse
Young Apache who has died
Let him walk beside you
On the shores of tutti-fruity
Keep him spirit brothers
Safe from evil in his booty
Child of our great people
Follow now your destiny
Ride on clouds of candy
Think of us all frequently
Oh, great and truthful spirits
In the circus in the sky
Keep him, spirit brothers
Young Apache who has died

As Apaches' body lay in death upon candy-cane poles in the sacred burial ground, indeed his spirit walked with his brothers in the circus in the sky. Eventually they reached the shores of tutti-fruity and Apache knelt down to drink his fill of the fizzing soda. His spirit brother knelt beside him and spoke:

"You are but a child, Apache. Here in the spirit world, there are many children your age. You will meet them soon."

Apache looked up with a puzzled expression on his clown face. "Will I ever grow up?"

His spirit brother laughed and answered. "Oh yes, you will grow up but it will take a very long time here in the spirit world."

"What will I do while I am growing up?" asked the indian angel.

"Oh, probably much the same as you would have done in the flesh."

"Does that mean I have to go to school?"

Apache's spirit brother gathered the boy up in his arms, then lifted him over his head to place him on his shoulders. He began to walk away from the shores of tutti-fruity.

"Oh, no, Apache, no school. You see, here in Heaven things are different. In your soul is most all of there is to know about everything in Like Everything you care to know about. The key to knowing most everything is simply knowing what it is you want to know. Once you know that, you will find that you knew what you wanted to know all along most of the time. In heaven, it isn't finding the answers that is hard, it is knowing the right question."

Apache thought about what his spirit brother had just said and a huge grin erupted across his face as he realized that he knew all of that already.

"So, what are we gonna do now?" asked the cherub.

"Oh...I dunno." Of course, this was only a figure of speech.

"There is a special place where all the spirit children go to live while they grow up. It's like an orphanage."

Apache flapped his pint-sized wings. "An orphanage? Aren't those places icky?"

The spirit brother laughed. "No-no...not in Heaven."

"But what if your parents are here, too? My grandfather died before I was born. Couldn't I go and live with him?"

"Why would you want to do that?" replied the spirit brother. "All that adults want to do is boss you around. You'll be much happier with angels your own age."

Apache could see that his spirit brother was right. "You know what you were saying about knowing it all?"

"Yes."

"Well, then why don't you answer my questions before I ask them if you already know what I am going to ask?"

The spirit brother laughed again. "Apache, it is true that we angels know mostly all but what fun would it be to exist in a perpetual state of knowing? It is much more interesting to ignore ones eternal knowledge and allow things to unfold unexpectedly. We save the ability for times when we need it most."

AT THE ORPHANAGE

As Apache and his spirit brother made their way over, Miss Smoochy was busy tending to the various needs of millions of cherub angels who lived in the orphanage, thanks to God's will. While in the flesh, she had often wondered what heaven would be like. Her dreams had been answered fully for now there were millions of babies for her to love and care for and she had discovered that, as an angel, her heart had become big enough to love each and all.

Presently, she was spearheading what could only have been the biggest game of musical chairs in the entire Universe. The music came to a stop as she dragged the needle of the ancient record player from the equally ancient record. It would be a small eternity before she would discover which cherub had been left without a seat, for it was impossible to see all of the players from any one vantage-point. As she waited for her assistants to find the seatless toddler, she heard a voice calling out to her. She recognized the voice as that of Jesus Christ.

Miss Smoochy stopped herself short of wondering why the Savior was calling on her by using her all knowing powers, which revealed to her that he was delivering a new cherub to the orphanage. This would have been cause for excitement for her back on Earth in Buffoonville, but here in Heaven, with the never enduing onslaught of souls, it was a matter of routine. Smoochy sat quietly waiting for Jesus to reach her as one of her assistants signaled that the "out" cherub had been found and she absentmindedly placed the needle back on the record so that the game might begin once more. Moments passed and then Jesus was with her presenting the new little angel.

"Miss Smoochy, this is Apache. He wants to live here with you and the others." Miss Smoochy introduced herself and smiled a gigantic tooth-filled grin that only an old clownette like her could manage.

"Well, Hello there, Apache. What a nice looking little clown you are. It has been a while since we had a new clown cherub. Can you imagine, Apache, that there are millions of different types of souls here and that we clowns are but one kind. I know within my heart that you are also from Buffoonville! What an amazing coincidence. I, too, am from Buffoonville. Welcome, darling."

Apache scrunched up his face. "I'm not darling! I'm a proud warrior!"

"Okay, little warrior, let's see you try your skills with the chairs. Go on."

And with that the indian cherub made his way into the teeming mass of angels his size.

"Thank you, Miss Smoochy" said Christ, "you make such a wonderful fairy godmother."

"Thank YOU!" said the old clownette.

IN THE COURTROOM

There were wrinkles as deep in the old clown's face, as deep as his disgust for clowns gone bad. Rose colored liver spots patterned his cranium but you'd never know it because of the wig. Whiter than his ancient face, it was curled in rows like cobs of corn onto his shoulders, strong muscular shoulders despite his age. These were the shoulders of one who carried the heavy burden of judgment. His black robe cascades upon his fattened blob like frame...the righteous Poobla on his judgment seat, giant clown hammer in hand, serving as the gavel of doom for all clowns condemned to face the music beneath his imposing podium. The Poobla's tongue hangs from his mouth wetting his fingers in the old tradition of wetting the corners of The Book, which contains the laws by which all clowns must be judged. How many clowns had stood looking into the towering presence of the Poobla? How many have felt meek and small before him? How meek and small Blinko and Elvis felt standing there, for in fact they WERE meek and small…just kinderclowns accused of murder. But it was an accident! That's what they had said to the coach. That's what they had said to the Keystones. That's what they had said to the Poobla. But it did not matter in the slightest. The Poobla could see right through them. These tots had gone bad early and must be sent away to Reform School.

REFORM SCHOOL

Reform School was an evil place for bad young clowns. The irony was in the name…Reform School…as though anyone who went there was reformed…refined more likely. Clowns sent off to Reform School only honed the skills that led them there in the first place. Clowns in reform school, having lost all personal freedom, could only survive by escaping into their own minds and this caused them to become thinkers among fools. Reform school was the ideal place to go bad. With the Disciples of Grand Lunacy there to force one to practice and perform the many rituals of the World Circus, clowns in reform school learned to mimic the attitudes of humorous clowns perfectly. Upon release into society they could easily pass for a complete idiot even under the most careful eyes, therefore being able to continue with their anti-social behavior unnoticed.

Blinko and Elvis came to Reform School with the advantage of having reputations as murderers. Most the kids in Reform School had merely been caught stealing or refusing to go to the circus…stuff like that. In the eyes of the others, Blinko and Elvis were some bad clowns. They were accepted into the fold instantly and respected beyond what the average newbie could expect.

Soon, the two had learned the secrets and methods of the older inmates. Had fate handed these two a different set of cards, there might have been hope but their destiny was now sealed. Blinko and Elvis, merely mischievous before, now in the environment of the Reform School, went bad for real and they liked it. After all, going bad in the world of clowns is really just an emergence from retardation and mental apathy…badness…a social blight only in the eyes of morons and fools.

It is written that Laymo and Whammo started planning to bust their kids out of Reform School just minutes after the Poobla had sentenced their sons to go there. The bailiff had hardly led the two teary eyed kinderclowns away before half of the conspiratorial plan was complete. These clowns weren't about to screw around with technicalities. The first half of their plan was simply to arrive at the Reform School and check it out. The second half was to wing it from there.

It cannot be overstated the affect of their addiction to the Obvious was having on their plans. The Obvious has a side effect of making a serious clown feel superior to the other foolish ones. Therefore Laymo and Whammo figured they could easily outsmart the guards at the Reform school, who they assumed were complete idiots for being so closely involved with the World Circus.

When Whammo and Laymo arrived on the hill overlooking the compound that was the Reform School, they set up camp which consisted of a telescope and a rig for the syrup they had brought along to help them *think*. It didn't take long for the two to begin fighting over the telescope. Both were under a lot of stress and were quite cranky. The whole ordeal with their sons getting shafted for Apache's murder had left them on edge.

Neither of them had slept a wink for several days and they had been completely serious the whole time. Soon their argument escalated into fisticuffs.

Whammo and Laymo were pretty evenly matched and soon they were rolling around wrestling on the dusty dirt road leading to the Reform School. It is written that the dust cloud created by the fight aroused the attention of a disciple in a guard tower of the Reform School and using his own telescope, he was able to see that there were two clowns on the hill scrapping it out with each other. In such a deserted area, this was suspicious even to a lame brain such as the guard was, so the dunce thought to call the Keystones out to investigate. By the time the Stoners arrived on the hilltop, Laymo and Whammo had long since finished their fight and were back spying through the telescope. Unfortunately, they had left their syrup out in the open on the hood of Whammo's Pinto and of course this got them busted. Later that day, neither of them was amused at the irony of facing the music with the same Poobla that had sent their boys off to Reform School. Laymo and Whammo got ten years on the Funny Farm each.   LAH-DEE-DA

Chapter 14
Roach Thoughts

Sicko woke early. The sun had fallen behind the hill surrounding his funhouse an hour ago which meant he was waking up three hours too soon. None of that mattered though because whenever Sicko woke up, it always felt too soon to him. Shifting restlessly on his bones, he knew that sleep was impossible. This was because the bones in his bed where old and had broken into hundreds of little pointy pains in the patooty. He yawned and this caused the roaches that lived in his bathrobe to dance an unknown roach dance. Sicko loved his roaches. Vermin and rodents reminded him of all that was good in life.

Now he was reaching for his automatic Obvious injector gun and searching the pockets of his robe for a little bottle of syrup. As he did so, one of his roaches greeted him by skittering up his forearm. Sicko spied the bug, which had come to a nervous halt next to an unusually symmetrical cluster of fleabites near his elbow. Sicko held that arm motionless and continued his search with his other hand until he had the miniature soda bottle and loaded the gun one handed, pounding a dose into his pasty neck. The candy had little effect on his consciousness, which was now in a permanently aware state. It did fend off the heebie-jeebies though.

Turning his attention now to the little roach on his arm, he paid closer attention to the strange cluster of fleabites. There was always an assortment of scabs and bites on Sicko's body, but this particular batch of bites held his attention because they together formed the letter "U." Sicko could have been mistaken, but he felt certain that the fleas were trying to tell him something. *"U as in you"* he thought. Could this be the beginning of a message starting with *you* or was it a statement in and of itself, as in an assignment of blame, with the statement of "YOUUUUUUUU" usually pronounced with a touch of contempt in a gravely tone of voice. Sicko couldn't be sure and began to wish he could ask the roaches what the fleas were up to. Of course, that a roach would answer a question put to it was about as likely as fleas leaving bitten messages on a clown. Ah, but there was the solution! The fleas had, in fact, left a message in the form of an alphabetical letter so there was just a chance that a roach might answer a question if asked. Sicko spoke to the roach still resting near the flea bitten "U:"

"Roach...what are the fleas up to?"

The roach said nothing but he did buzz his tiny burnt orange wings and began to dance a roach dance. Sicko eyeballed his little friend for roach dances were always a source of delight for him. What the clown gone bad was not expecting was that the roach bit him. Sure the ticks, fleas, and bedbugs bit him but never the roaches. Roaches don't do that or at least he had never heard of such an occurrence. Sicko was so fascinated by this event that he left the roach alone as it continued to bite at his flesh. He noticed that the roach had chosen to bite him away from the fleabites. He wondered then if the fleas and the roaches were in cahoots with each other. Was there some agreement between bugs not to disturb one another's bites or various endeavors concerning the constant infestation of his body? Could roaches and fleas be capable of that kind of thought? And what of the fleas, who are much smaller than the average roach? Was there even room in their microscopic brains for such thoughts? Sicko then began to ponder the idea that the fleas worked together using some type of collective consciousness…thousands of them acting as one mind…interconnected by mysterious forces and weird chemical combinations. What the Hell, the ants and bees were doing it so why not fleas. Then it struck him.

"So that's how them little varmints get together and start a flea circus!"

%$#%@*

By the time he came out of his lapse into reason, the roach on his arm was gone. No, not gone he realized, but submerged. The cockroach was burrowing inside Sickos arm!

"Well, I'll be!" he said. Sicko didn't care about it though. All the years of Obviousness had made him a tad too smart for his own good. Life was beginning to bore him half to death. Killing people was always fun but even that could be tiresome. Sicko scratched a bit where the roach had tunneled its way into his bicep. If the roaches were gonna kill him, so be it. Then he started to laugh. He had almost forgotten how. Now, the roach was in his neck. He wished then that he could ask the fleas what the roaches were up to. Moments later the whole mystery began to unravel when he heard a faint, buzzing whisper in his mind. He looked around to see if any of the bugs in the room were making this noise but soon realized that it must have been the roach that had tunneled all the way into Sicko's brain. This was the last thing Sicko needed because he already had plenty of voices in his head.

It was hard to ignore what the roach was saying since the roach's words entered his mind in the form of thoughts. Sicko figured that the thoughts were his because the roach was using his mind as a vehicle for its own thoughts, which of course could only appear to be Sicko's thoughts to Sicko, since it was Sicko's brain which was being utilized to think its thoughts, which were really just roach thoughts thinking to be thought of as Sicko's thoughts or at least Sicko thought he thought of the roach thoughts that way, or so he thought. The question was how long could he keep reminding himself to think of the thoughts as roach thoughts and think of Sicko thoughts as his own thoughts. He thought about it and realized that he had already lost the ability to tell the difference, which explained why he was all of the sudden feeling like an insect.

Sitting up in his bed, Sicko was compelled to hunch up his shoulders, place his arms lazily out before him, and wiggle his fingers like six antennae.

"I'ma bug" Sicko thought.

"So am I" thought the roach. *"I'm Satano!"*

Then, it all made sense to Sicko. This was all Satano's work.

"I've come to give you more commandments as a reward for all your evil deeds here in Buffoonville." Abruptly, Sicko's nose began to itch causing him to sneeze. Out came a blob of snot which landed with a splat upon Sicko's night stand. From this blob emerged the satanic roach, which hurriedly scurried off the night stand. A great and thunderous voice sounded: "KNEEL BEFORE ME FOR I AM YOUR GOD ALMIGHTY, SICKO!"

Sicko quickly jumped off his bed in an effort to kneel before his God but he stepped on a banana peel, almost splitting himself along his seam as he did impossible splits. He shrieked in pain but managed to kneel before the satanic roach. Then a great flame shot out of the roach and the air cracked in a thunder bolt as it struck Sicko's choice nose candy mirror. The flame then ricocheted off the mirror, burning away the ancient Led Zepplin logo, striking the toilet seat below where Satano's commandment was then etched. Sicko immediately ran to the toilet and, after examining the commandment upon the seat, burst into tears. Satano was pleased.

"THOU HAST SEEN MY COMMANDMENT AND SHED TEARS OF JOY. THIS IS GOOD."

Sicko turned to the roach and screamed. "Look what you did to my Led Zepplin mirror!" He was bawling. As Sicko consoled himself Satano freed the toilet seat from it's fasteners and levitated it through the air until it came to rest hanging around Sicko's neck.

"YOU SHALL WEAR MY COMMANDMENT AROUND YOUR NECK AS IT IS ON YOU NOW AS A SYMBOL OF YOUR DEVOTION TO ME. YOU SHALL PROCEED AS I DIRECT YOU AND COMMIT YOURSELF TO THE CAUSE OF MY BIDDING AND SOON AFTER, THOUSANDS OF CLOWNS SHALL JOIN YOU, EVENTUALLY, MILLIONS. YOU WILL LEAD THEM WITH ANOTHER INTO A TIME OF DOOM AND SORROW FOR ALL OF CLOWNDOM. WEAR THIS TOILET SEAT WITH HONOR, SLAVE, AND USHER ME THE DAWNING OF OBLIVION ETERNAL. GO NOW TO ROME. SEEK OUT THE CHOSEN ONE. SHOW HIM YOUR TOILET SEAT AND FULLFILL YOUR DESTINY."

And with that, the Roach erupted into flames and was gone in a puff of smoke. Sicko came to his feet and felt the power of the Devil's commandment fill every corner of his being. He read it over and over…

ALL MIMES MUST DIE

Chapter 15
Draconian Mindwarp

Satano's trip across untold millions of indescribable feats of distance seemed relatively short, in his opinion. From Earth, the road to Hell was a treacherous one to travel. But the dark-being knew all the groovy short cuts. All one had to do was hitch a ride on the back of the soul of a child molester and you'd have to pull your skin back onto your skull you'd be going to Hell so fast. Not to mention the soul of a pedophile with Satano on its back flashing that inter-dimensional diplomatic passport at every check point. The hard part was finding a child-molesting clown. Satano was still amazed that there wasn't a line of clowns at Hell's gate, what with how clowns love to have little children up in their laps all the time. For this particular ride, Satano was forced to look one up in the phone book. He found one named Molesto the Clown.

Molesto met his death that day when the Devil put the evil eye on him. Satano merely changed Molesto's shorts into bullseye brand, then dropped a twenty smackerue in his path. A jalopy, of course, dispensed with Molesto just in time for Satano to hitch a ride. They plunged into Hell like a meteor. Satano was so pleased with the punctuality of the trip that he decided to give Molesto a brief tour of Hell.

"Molesto, my friend, here in Hell we have a special place for you child molesters. I shall take you there myself!" Molesto was too stunned by the fact of his death to argue with the Devil and, after looking around for some children, fell into step behind the Lord of Maggots and Worms.

Looking out in to the vast expanse of despair that the Devil's Hell always was, Molesto could see a labyrinth of roads leading nowhere and somewhere. Confused, he looked at his new master to show him the way. Satano pointed somewhere and nowhere at the same time which didn't help Molesto in the slightest. Never-the-less, the two undead reached the location in which Molesto would spend eternity. Molesto, along the way, had seen unspeakable horrors and was beginning to wonder if all those little children he had harmed were worth it. Satano then told him that in Hell, the child molesters where held in high esteem, and not to worry, his damnation would be especially cruel and humiliating. This made Molesto feel really bad. Finally they came upon the most offensive example of architecture Molesto had ever seen. It smelled of death and rot, and happened to be Satano's mansion. The Devil led Molesto out into the rear garden and introduced him to his Hellhounds who immediately tore off a lot of Molesto's legs. Eventually the two reached the grotesque fountain centered in the garden. The Agony Column, Satano's fountain, was as impressive as it was evil.

"Well, Molesto, what do you think?" Molesto had hardly enough time to fathom a reply before two henchmen seized him, chaining him to the fountain and another shoved a feeding tube into his mouth. Fishhooks held the tube in place. Molesto knew instantly that he would never get used to the taste as the vile fluid overflowed his mouth and began to spill onto his clownsuit. He thought to himself, thankful that it couldn't get any worse, just moments before henchmen castrated him.

666

It had taken a lot of painful rehabilitation but Peg Legs had stolen enough body parts to put himself back together again. He was now serving his master with vigor. In a two fingered hand that he had stolen from a lobsterboy, who had killed his sideshow pimp, he held a message. The message was written on an old piece of toilet paper. This was not surprising since it was sent by the Weirdoes. Peg Legs gave the message to his master the moment they were close enough to exchange it. Satano examined the sheet.

"Weirdoes! What do those guys want to talk to me for? I paid them off 4000 years ago!"

"Dunno master..." hissed Peg Legs.

"When they get here, have them meet me over at Death's place. I got an appointment with him later" proclaimed the demon of a thousand horrors.

666

Meanwhile over at Death's place, Death was busy fighting with the other three horsemen of the apocalypse, War, Famine, and Pestilence. All would soon be leaving to spell doom to a planet or two. Death's wife was busy applying a fresh coat of gore onto Death's reaper. The sight of her made Death feel grim. She was an ugly woman, to be honest, and Death constantly had to lie to himself just to be able to hate her guts. He often wished in silence to kill her. But then he was Death and that was how the zombie had ended up with him in the first place.

"To think I only thought to put her out of her misery" he thought.

Despite all of the lies he told himself, he still hated her anyway and he guessed that was why he had married her in unholy matrimony so many years ago.

Death called for his son, Death, Jr. who came running to his father while screaming bloody murder. The boy was nothing more than a bare bag of bones. It looked like Jr. had studied his lessons from Famine well. Jr. constituted a miracle in Hell. The miracle had some peculiar aspects to it. The first being that Death had actually managed to get so drunk on the souls he collected from Earth after a plague that he found it in his nothingness to mate with the beast of a woman his wife would always be. The second part was that his wife's rotting eggs and his dried up manhood actually had the potency to conceive a child. The fetus itself never grew past the bones stage and was, of course, born dead on arrival, much to his fathers delight.

And tarnation, if Jr. didn't grow fast! He was a terrible ankle-biting two year old, in just three centuries, and now he was five and already making the rounds with his father. But Death didn't let his boy drink of the freshly collected souls because that was just for grown-ups.

Jr. crawled up onto his father's cartilageless knee. It creaked upon its hinges. He asked his father if he could go over to Pestilence, Jr.'s house to play. Death fathomed the time and decided this was fine for Satano would be stopping over any minute. In fact, as the youngster high tailed it out the front door, he ran straight between the visiting demons legs. Death laughed.

666

The Devil came in and took a seat next to Death. Next, Satano squint his eyes and scrunched up his nose while shaking his head.

"Death, I can never get used to the sight of your wife. Man! Leave it to you to find a horror to outdo damn near all in Hell."

Death scratched at his bony head with a skeletal finger. "She's a beauty, ain't she?" said he.

Satano took another long look. Death's wife was now putting on an additional layer of gore to the reaper. Her hands were swollen and puffy. They were covered in festering warts. Each wart had several hairs growing from them. The hairs were curly. Her head was an asymmetrical gathering of odd shaped lumps. One lump obscured her right eye while her left was missing its eyeball. Her hair was matted, clumped and infested with vermin. All together her head looked like a rotting cabbage behind a Chinese restaurant.

"A ten!" announced Satano. "But a ten on the Neanderthal scale."

Soon, talk of the monstrosity of a woman turned to talk of business. Satano took the initiative.

"Look, Death, I realize that we have much to discuss about your brother's latest scourge but I've just received message from the Weirdoes." Death shifted in his ugly seat. "OH! Then shall we put ourselves off?"

"No. I have instructed my legless servant to send them over here. I figure that they will be hard pressed to pull a fast one in the face of Death, not to mention that wife of yours." Death agreed.

"Anyway, how's that son of yours?" inquired the Lord of Ick.

"He is the spitting image of me." beamed Death. "He's got a natural eye for the sick and dying. I'd say that unless he comes back to life or something there is a great chance he will take over the family biz once he's grown. I've already taken him out in the field to learn him good."

"I see" said Satano. "I will be pleased to see him in action." Then the knock sounded.

"That must be the Weirdoes come knocking, knocking on my chamber door" said Death. "Dear, would you be a doll and answer that?"
Death's wife obediently hauled herself over. When she got close to her husband, he instinctively backed away from her. Then, she was there and gave the door a mightyheave. The ancient door gave a sorrowful creak as she opened it. The sound made Satano's teeth feel as though he was chewing on styrofoam.

A lone Weirdoe stood in the doorway. He was of medium height and a bit on the skinny. His nose was a trifle to large for his face, which was funny looking in general. His ears stuck out from the sides of his mop-like haircut. Most of his kind shared this identical image. After all, the Weirdoes were clones. Satano and Death cringed at the sight of the Weirdoe. It was by no mistake that Wierdoes were feared by all. The Weirdoes exploits ran all across Like Everything and it seemed that everyone owed them something somewhere along the line. Now, the Weirdoe was speaking in that unnerving, happy-go-lucky voice they always used.

"Mr. Satan, Mr.Death, Mam." said the Weirdoe as he took a dramatic bow. "These proceedings must be kept a complete secret. Would you mind seeing the lady out of the room?"

Death quickly shooed his wife off. Death and Satano wondered what sense it made to use code names in close quarters as his wife scampered off. Satano gave Death the evil-eye which was his secret way of telling Death to switch into full Death Angel mode. Death got into character then spoke:

"So what isss the meaning of thisssss visit?" he hissed. The Little Weirdoe did a double take and jumped two feet off the floor.

"Whoa there, Death! That is one mean tone of voice!"

"Now, now" interjected the Devil. "I think that Death here was just trying to ascertain the circumstances. It's not often that one meets Death and lives to tell about it. Take yourself for example. After this meeting, you'll be the luckiest man alive."

"ULP!" The Weirdoe swallowed hard. "I never thought of it like that."

"Don't sssssstart to." offered Death. "Now…whaaat isss the meaning of thisss visit?"

The Weirdoe took an ancient seat and sat in it. "Simple. I have just come to tell you that we Weirdoes are attempting to buy out God's Domain."

Suddenly, the door burst open and in marched a marine band of dead war veterans, who had raped and pillaged too much, playing a triumphant march. Satano grabbed Death's skeletal hands and the two began to dance a jig.

"Yeah!!" shouted the Devil over the omp-pah-pahs. The Weirdoe shouted as well.

"Yeah!" went the Devil. The Weirdoe continued:

"Oh, by the way, we Weirdoes, if successful in the buy, would like to give you your old job back."

The marine band that moment fell apart musically and then physically into a pile of torsos and limbs. Satano grew sentimental and was actually taken aback, in honest disbelief.

"My old job back?" he said, his voice…..trembling. "You're gonna give ME my old job back?"

The Weirdoe smiled. "That's right, Mr. Satan. You see, God hasn't been handling his finances very well and is virtually bankrupt. The First Inter-Dimensional Bank wants to foreclose on his mortgage. That gives us the option to buy God's Domain. We are aware that it has been your brilliant espionage and terrorism campaign that has contributed greatly to the financial problems God is having. It is obvious to us that you would be just the creature for the job of managing God's Domain."

Just then, a monster identical to Satan appeared next to the Devil. This is because the Devil was beside himself with evil. The Wierdoe spoke:

"I take it that it is a yes on the offer of employment? The two Satans nodded agreement.

"Well, then, my business here is finished. I bid you both farewell."

And with that, a rip in the time space continuum appeared, and with it a tidal wave of plasmic energy which swept away the Weirdoe.

777

Elsewhere in God's Domain, namely Heaven, the garage sale was coming to an end. While Jesus supervised the closing down of the sale, God was busy looking after the detailing of his low-rider. The low-rider was the finest example of Michealangelos work in existence. The paint job had been done in stainless steel fresco. The fresco was raw tints mixed directly with the molten steel. The result was an unbelievable series of murals totally impervious to rust or decay. On the hood was a reproduction of the "Creation of Adam" segment of the Sistine Chapel ceiling. The interior was upholstered by other master craftsmen from the era and was done in red Italian velvet and curly maple. The surround sound system consisted of a church pipe organ played by none other that Wolfgang Amadeus Mozart. The low-rider sat a mere centimeter above the ground and the seats inside lowered as well. The low-rider was powered by a Vonsydow Transwarp Drive. It had an automatic transporter system and to tidy up, the low-rider was enveloped in temporal distortion field which allowed it to exist between sheets of reality. This feature made the low-rider the lowest of lows in that it was theoretically possible for the low-rider to be lower than the ground itself.   IMAGINE THAT!

It is written that God was extremely proud of his low-rider. It had been some million years since he had last gone cruisin' and this necessary trip to the Greatest Extreme was really starting to sound like a great way to get away from it all. They were set to leave later that day and Jesus had already packed his things. His biggest problem was figuring out where he was gonna score some weed. It used to be that Earth was the best place to score big buds, but since clowns don't use pot to act silly, the cultivation of dope was no longer practiced there.

Then Jesus remembered his old friend Judas. Judas had exiled himself on an obscure planet after that crucifixion deal. The disciple was now on his 4000th generation of Draconian Mindwarp, some of the most potent pot in Like Everything. This year he would yield like three thousand kilotons of the stuff and Jesus wanted some. All he need do was convince his father into stopping by Judas's planet on the way out. Hurriedly he hauled butt to the garage where his dad was putting his own stuff in the low-riders trunk. And Jesus spoke:

"Hey, Dad, you still smoke dope, right?" he said.

God paused in his work and uttered:

"What do you think?" as he produced a massive joint from his shirt pocket. God had some pretty heavy stuff and Jesus could smell the doob from where he stood. It smelled just like a polecat that drowned in lemon juice. Jesus was now certain they would be stopping buy Judas's place. God fired up the joint and took a massive toke. When he exhaled, it came out in a billow of smoke that looked like the exhaust pipe of a jalopy. Jesus took the joint from the Lord and he himself drew a grand toke upon it. He held in the smoke like an expert before blowing perfect smoke rings. God spoke:

"It's Tibetan Prayer week."

"I know where we can get some Draconian Mindwarp on our way out" Jesus replied. God looked pleased.

"So, let it be written...so let it be done. And don't bogart that joint, my Son."

And then the Gods touched fingertips, masterfully exchanging the blunt.

Jesus reflected on the intensity of his buzz and realized that he was totally stoned out of his mind.

"I'm fried" sayeth the Savior.

"Me too" sayeth the Lord. "And we cannot go in these robes."

God snapped his fingers and instantly the two were dressed in identical outfits. Both wore kacky pants and black converse tennis shoes. They also wore brown flannel shirts buttoned only at the top…and the required black Ray Bans.

"Shall we leave then?" asked the Messiah. God spoke:

"Like, yes."

777

Now, the two were seated in the Low-rider-of-the-Gods and God was at the helm. Jesus leaned over to the internal temporal displacement field, which enveloped the master Mozart. The field allowed for a big object to be kept in an impossibly small place. Kinda like if you had two heads, one big and one small, only the big one was inside the small one. That's how Mozart fit in the console. Presently, he was playing his keyboard and this was interfaced with the amplification unit, which was attached to the surround sound speaker system. Needless-to-say, the music was as perfect as it was loud.

God began to speak to his only begotten son in mental telepathy, which could be understood clearly no matter how loud the music was.

"Which way to Judas's place?" thought God.

"That-a-way!" thought Jesus, as he pointed at a star. God revved up the transwarp engine, set coordinates and stepped on the accelerator. The Low-rider-of-the-Gods accelerated from zero to warp 9 in the blink of an eye. The Gods were stuck in their seats for several moments until the inertial dampeners snapped on. It was a short trip only a few light-years across. Soon the low-rider slipped out of warp and took up an orbit above what presumably was Judas's planet.

"We have achieved orbit, Son." Jesus was busy at the control panel before him adjusting little buttons and knobs.

"I am setting coordinates for the planets surface. This should land us a few hundred meters from Judas's compound. I want to surprise him. Energize."

And with that, the Gods were beamed the predetermined spot. As they walked in the direction of the compound, it came into view. It was a huge operation taking up many acres with totally enclosed greenhouses. The place was lit up like a fortress. Eventually they came up from the road and onto a path leading them to what looked like the front door of a medium sized hut. There was a large letter "J" on the door. Next to the "J" was a doorbell, which they rang. The door was duly answered by a Cycloptic Titan who stood twenty feet tall.

"YOU RANG?" said the Titan in a deafening roar, which was probably as quietly as the beast could speak.

"JUDAS!" shouted the Savior.

"JUDAS?" went the Titan.

"JUDAS…" agreed the Nazarene.

"JUDAS!" exclaimed God.

"Yeah right, Judas…" commented Jesus.

"No, I mean Judas!" motioned God pointing at Judas who had come to stand behind the Titan.

"Judas!" sayeth Christ.

"Who, me?" said Judas.

"Ha, ha, ha, ha Jesus! What a surprise! How good to see you!" Judas was speaking in Hebrew. Jesus made the mental switch and spoke:

"Judas, Judas, Juuuuuudas! We want to score some dope."

"Shhhhhhhhhh…not so loud…the neighbors might hear."

Jesus and God seemed puzzled. Judas' nearest neighbor was literally light years away. God offered:

"Why? Your neighbors are so far off they couldn't possibly hear what we are saying and they don't speak Hebrew, that's for darn sure."

Judas wasn't phased. "Still, they are listening and one can never be so sure. Come, come into my mighty abode and feast your senses on what's inside."

Judas turned and entered, beckoning with his hand for the Gods to follow. This they did and soon were impressed by the wonderful Arabian architecture. Judas said nothing about the surroundings allowing the others to make their own impressions. Immediately in front of them appeared a great vaulted door with an enormous cog as part of its complex lock. Judas did the combination with the cog releasing the lock and with a mighty heave threw open the vault's door. There before them appeared a vast tropical jungle complete with monkeys. Judas spoke:

"Those monkeys are the most stoned beings in Like Everything" said Judas.

"They literally exist on nothing except what grows in this room. Imagine actually living off the whacky." God took his son's sleeve.

"I never imagined it could be like this!" he said with excitement in his voice.

What he was seeing was indeed awesome. Judas' pot plants had matured generation after generation until now they were the size of trees…trees with long skinny limbs hanging to the floor, each limb festooned with buds that dripped toxic resin. It was the resin which was the primary ingredient in Draconian Mindwarp…the other ingredient being time. Draconian Mindwarp resin was placed in temporal distortion fields, which sent the pods back to the past. Found in the present, the pods would now be thousands of years old. Aged resin was what made for the Mindwarp part of the buzz…as for the Draconian part…

ANCIENT CHINESE SECRET!

"We must put on these protective chemical warfare suits" said Judas, gesturing to the dressing area to his left. Everyone began to dress.

"The resins covering the buds are toxic in its natural state. Only the aging process mellows the stuff to the point that it can be consumed safely. Even after aging, Draconian Mindwarp can only be smoked by Eternals such as we. These suits will protect us while we are out in the fields. It can be fatal merely by contact with the skin." Judas led them out to wonder among the tremendously gigantic weeds. He explained various aspects of the operation and eventually led the Gods through the giant pot trees to the other side of the compound where the robots removed their protective wear and immersed the suits in vats full of chemicals.

"Those chemicals separate the resins that were just collected on the outsides of our suits as we walked. Together we just collected enough resin to mess up 10,000 Eternals. Here is what you came for, friends. It's on me, of course, my treat."

Judas handed Jesus a baby-food jar full of Draconian Mindwarp.

"Be careful with that stuff, Jesus, its really good stuff."

"I'll do my best, Judas, thanks." said Jesus. "Sorry to score and run but Father and I are kinda in a hurry. Is there a back way to the front?" Judas nodded and the three of them set off into a maze of corridors and halls until they were once again in the front of the compound.

"Well, it was nice to see you, Jesus, you too, Lord." Judas was bidding them farewell.

Jesus shook hands with his old friend and said, "You're not still blaming yourself over my crucifixion, are you? Ya know the Romans would have found me sooner or later anyway. Besides that was 4000 years ago."

Judas shrugged. "Well, I think I will always feel guilty, Jesus…keeps me humble. You two be careful with that Mindwarp. This year's batch is really potent. We've been getting reports in from all over of accidental deaths."

Jesus flipped the jar of Draconian Mindwarp in his hands.

"Don't worry, Judas, were expert stoners." God spoke into his comlink which was automatically patched into the transporter of the Low-Rider-of-the-Gods.

"Two to beam up."

In a shimmer they were gone.

Meanwhile, Judas went back to work packing an Imperial Hyperspace Freighter to the gills full of vintage Mindwarp. The Imperial freighter had been dispatched from Boogus Maximus, the seat of the Powers That Be and capital planet of Like Everything. It would be several hours before the loading was done. Judas couldn't help but be nervous because the crew of the freighter was all human beings, not robots as usual. Considering that the payload of Draconian Mindwarp was lethal to them, it could only mean trouble. Judas then questioned the wisdom of the Powers That Be. If they were so careless as to staff a freighter with human beings, then fill it with a substance lethal to them, it was a wonder that Like Everything didn't just implode one day.

SUCH IS LIFE

Chapter 16
Down on the Funny Farm

Miss Smoochy was making fast friends with little Apache. There was always an adjustment period where she found it helped to interview the newly arrived cherubs to see how they were coping with their deaths. In the process of learning about how Apache died, she was shocked to learn that the kinderclown who had killed him was Blinko, Jr., one of her orphaned children from back in Buffoonville. She did not want to accept this revelation, yet the fact remained. She began then to think back on her days on Earth. It seemed a million years ago. She was reaching for clues as to what could have gone wrong with the sweet little clown Blinko, then laughed in spite of herself. It was obvious. Blinkos entire life was nothing more than a series of tragedies. Both his parents had been murdered. He had witnessed the massacre at the circus on his first outing and she herself, the only mother Blinko had ever known, was killed by a jalopy right in front of him. And, he came under the influence of that bad kindersclown Elvis. Was it any wonder that he had gone bad early on? Never-the-less, she was his guardian angel and she used her powers then to look in on the lad.

She was not surprised to find him serving time in Reform School. Well, at least he was safe for the moment and she thought that maybe the structure of Reform School life would do him some good. From there, she could not help herself from thinking back on all of her orphaned clowns. These thoughts caused her to think of the most unusual of all the orphans in the case of Nastina.

Nastina was brought to her orphanage by mimes. A perfectly normal clown suzie with mime parents! This didn't stop Miss Smoochy from taking the baby clownette in, but she did decide to hide the truth from Nastina about her parents. Being an orphan was hard enough without the additional burden of knowing that you were the clown born of mimes. Smoochy scolded herself for being prejudice out of necessity. Anyway, she had duly written down the facts of Nastina's origins in her best cartoon and sealed the envelope away in a file cabinet to be presented to the suzie on her 16th birthday, an age that seemed suitable for Nastina to learn the truth about her biological parents. Unfortunately, Miss Smoochy had been killed long before that date and since no other clown knew the story, it was unlikely that Nastina would ever discover the truth as to her origins.

Then Miss Smoochy used her powers to look in on the girl and found her leading a somewhat normal life with her adopted parents in a respectable neighborhood. Smoochy reminded herself that she must be especially watchful of these Blinko and Nastina as they grew up and that she should try to help them whenever she could.

AND SO IT WAS WRITTEN AND SO IT WAS DONE!

^%#^%$

Reform School was getting worse but Blinko, Jr. and Elvis were getting used to it never-the-less. Presently, the two kinderclowns were surrounded by a small gang of juvenile delinquents who were eager to pry the murder story out of them. Blinko and

Elvis had been playing up and exaggerating the story from the moment they walked into Reform School. It had so far protected them from all but the toughest clowns in the joint and they seemed content to keep their distance most of the time. Blinko and Elvis had been on the receiving end of only three not too severe shoving matches at the hands of the older clowns and those were only to show them their place. The lads were now essentially boss of their domain answering only to the old timers running the place or the clownguards, better known as Screws, because they could easily put the screws to you if you broke any rules. Today, there was a new kid and he didn't seem to be falling for the far-fetched version of events the boys were telling. However, he waited until Blinko and Elvis had exhausted themselves before offering his opinion.

"That's all a bunch of bozokahkah!" said the new kid. His name was Fudgie. The others oooed and ahhed, certain that the famous killers would easily dispense with the newbie.

"Says who?" challenged an unsure Elvis. He knew that he and Blinko were indeed full of bozokahkah.

"Says me! Fudgie! I know you two are exaggerating because I was there! Remember me? I was the quiet fat kid in back that never made for no trouble. You two are making a lot of stuff up!"

The other clown inmates abruptly made a circle leaving Elvis, Blinko, and Fudgie in its center. They were certain a big fight was about to erupt. Neither Blinko nor Elvis particularly wished to have it out with Fudgie. He was big for his age and they were not sure they could take him. After all, they were not really as tough as they were making themselves out to be. Yet what choice did they have? They would have to try and whip him or else the entire school would know what phonies they were. Fudgie decided for them in any case, using their moment of indecision to his advantage.

It was his intent to establish himself right away in the hierarchy of things. Fudgie cracked a fist directly into Blinko's honker then went after Elvis who dramatically ran circles within the circle trying to avoid a tangle with the larger kinderclown. Blinko, in the meantime, began to get that weird tunnel vision. It was the trance. He hadn't fallen into one since the fight with Apache. He realized then that getting smashed in the honker was obviously a direct way to trigger it off. Then everything went black on him. Fudgie had just caught up to Elvis and was preparing to cream him when a tremendous force spun him around. It was Blinko who apparently now had superclown strength. Fudgie instinctively brought his fists up to defend himself. They were no match for Blinko's entranced muscles. In fact, the blow that Blinko delivered to Fudgie broke both his arms sending him reeling with pain. As Fudgie howled Blinko kicked his legs from under him and pounced when he hit the floor. Blinko grabbed Fudgie's enormous ears and began to bang the clown's head on the floor in repetition. Then there could be heard a crack. It was Fudgie's skull which was letting up under the relentless blows. Then Fudgie went limp.

The Reform Schoolers stood silent, too shocked to say anything. Elvis was shocked as well for he had stood by doing nothing as Blinko killed Fudgie. Then some of the older kids, who normally did not concern themselves with the squabbles of the younger bunch, came up and they too were shocked at the sight of Fudgie in a pool of blood next too his smashed skull. Then the Screws came along and the entire group broke up except for Blinko, who was still half in a trance, eyes blinking, blood on his hands as they say.

He was shaken out of it by one of the disciples. And that was the bust. As Blinko was led away to be thrust once again into the system for further punishment, the rumors spread throughout the school. Even the big boys wouldn't be messing with Blinko from now on. The effect was so great that Elvis was granted immunity from the big boys as well. None wanted the wrath of his friend to come down on them. It is written that such was life in their first year in Reform School.

%$@#$^

Meanwhile, Laymo and Whammo were themselves doing hard time on the Funny Farm. The Funny Farm was so called because it really was an actual farm; cows, chickens, and all the rest. Aside from the tall fence, topped with razor coil, the place looked just like a typical homestead complete with a big red barn and silos where the jelly beans were stored. The funny farmers spent long hours out in "them-thar" fields tending to the candied yams and what have you. Of course, the difference between the Funny Farm and a regular farm was the Screws, sitting in the shade atop the hood of their truck-like jalopies, always with a firm grip around their cream puffs. One of those could kill the average clown and the Screws were dead ringers when it came to tossing a puff.

Invariably, the clownguard would be lazily sipping chocolate milk, which the inmates had wrenched from the udders of a chocolate cow. Whammo sometimes snuck a little chocolate milk when it was his turn at the pumping station but Laymo never did. You see, in order to sneak a drink, a clown had to take it right from the teat. It wasn't that Laymo had an aversion to that rather it was the particulars concerning the cow to which he was assigned.

Laymo had been assigned old Betsy the Cow. Betsy was nice enough but she had the annoying habit of standing on her hind legs while being milked. Not to mention that she also liked to place her front hooves on the milker's shoulders, as well. Somehow her posturing turned the innocent procedure of milking into something obscene and the idea of drinking milk from her teats while she stood there like that, to Laymo, was a trifle queer. The worst of it was the way old Betsy would softly moo while Laymo worked her over, which never failed to cause the clown in the next stall to poke fun at him. Needless-to-say, Betsy was the bane of Laymo's existence.

Whammo and Laymo had both been sentenced to ten years on the farm for those little bottles of goo. There was no question that the sentence was harsh. In a world where clowns were going bad in record numbers, the laws against hard candy were some of the most severe. You could kill a clown and serve less time than you would for the Obvious or lung candy. Even the child molesters seemed to spend less time on the farm than the candy dealers. This was because the law had decided to deem the use of hard candy as the root of all evil and this was officially sanctioned by the World Circus to boot. Besides, the Pooblas of the World Circus had a vested interest in the candy trade for it supplied them with a world wide scapegoat. The Pooblas also had a vested interest in light sentences for child molesters but that is another story.

Whammo and Laymo, when not milking the cows or tending the fields, were forced to work their patooties off with the majority of the other farmers building the new wing of the bunkhouse. There were simply so many clowns going bad that there wasn't room for them all…thus the new wing. It was here that Whammo came into possession of the splinter. The splinter was going to be his ticket off the farm, or so he thought. He had stashed the little sliver of wood inside the pant cuff of his overalls. All he needed now was a magnifying glass. The way he figured it, he could take the splinter in one hand, magnify it with the magnifying glass and then he would have a sizeable weapon. Little did he know the Screws had learned about that trick ages ago. Magnifying glasses were banned from the farm as were telescopes. Telescopes, when used backwards, enabled clowns to shrink themselves small enough to squeeze through the links of the fence.

Every day on the Funny Farm was full of activities, most of which the incarcerated clowns hated. After the work of the day was done, the farmers would be shuffled into groups of thirty to forty and then into hot, stuffy and airless rooms where the disciples would deliver the daily lessons of Grand Lunacy straight from the Holy Comic book. To a serious clown, which all clowns gone bad were, being forced to listen to such religious rhetoric amounted to torture. Yet protesting this only led a clown to face the music, and on the Funny Farm, the bagpipes were played live, something no clown wanted to experience so they had no choice but to sit there and suffer through the religious lunacy.

"For God so loved the world that he sent his only begotten son, Jesus the Clown, to show the way to the circus in the sky….and to the first Pooblas he lay down the…

Doctrines of Grand Lunacy

Hear ye, hear ye
Clowns one and all
Skinny or fat,
Short or tall
God says to laugh
Let's hear you giggle
Tickle your funny bone
Give it a wiggle

He who hath humor
Exists as divine
Loosen thou reason
Soften thou spine
Broaden thy candor
Strengthen thy grin
Goof up thy face
Like clowns among men

Dance in the streets
Thy jokers be true
Fill up thy neighbors
Shoes with glue
Slap thyself silly
Act like a fool

Relinquish thy sanity
Stand there and drool

Juggle each day
Also at night
Fashion balloons
For all kids in sight
Go to the circus
Come one come all
Skinny or fat
Short or tall

    The sermons would plod on for hours into the wee of the morning. Often the farmers would just be crawling into their bunks when the pipe organ would begin its daily revelry calling the inmates out to the barns where the cows waited to be milked. This was not to great a problem because clowns can manage with little or no sleep. The reason being that, fatigue tends to affect mostly one's reasoning skills and reaction times to various stimuli; clowns, being complete idiots and clumsy ones at that, would hardly notice the difference in that respect. However, left on one's own, the typical clown will sleep for endless hours, laziness being a clown's strongest motivation. For this reason, it was inevitable that better than half the farmers would show up late for the milking on any given day. Now, one might think that this would outrage the Screws but exactly the opposite was true. You see the Screws are, of course, clowns themselves and therefore much too incompetent to handle the full registry of farmers assigned to milk on any given day. It was all they could manage if only half the inmates arrived on time as it was. So, things worked out splendidly. Such is the beauty of untainted stupidity. Amen.

    After the milking, but before being sent into the jelly bean pastures, the farmers would have their morning allotment of fruit pies and chocolate milk. Then, they would pair off and begin the ritual daily juggling act. Usually cellmates got together having practiced with each other. Under the mindless eyes of the disciples, each performance would be judged and, if a pair did an especially good job, there were small rewards. This was what amounted to rehabilitation on the Funny Farm. Laymo and Whammo, new to the farm, still didn't really have their act together. After all, it had been years since these two clowns had bothered to pick up the pins. Partner juggling took skill and one had to be rather precise. Whammo and Laymo totally lacked precision, which was why they were often seen wrestling each other in the court yard after one or the other of them sent a errant pin into each others honker. Of course, being clowns these types of physical injuries were superficial at best but the injury to one's pride was an entirely different issue. After all, everyone was watching, and let me tell you, there is no group of beings more prepared to ridicule and laugh at failure than a bunch of clowns. Especially a group of clowns that had absolutely nothing better to do.

HAR HAR…HARDY…HAR HAR!

Chapter 17
Suzie Floosies

The lower east-side of Buffoonville was a place called home by clowns gone bad or maybe those just interested in temporarily getting serious. Most of the action centered around Slammy's Playhouse and Meemaw's Nooky Parlor. What used to be the bright and colorful center of downtown Buffoonville was now a ghetto of filth and hard candy. The taboo was the thing to do once you got past the train tracks. A clown could find young jokers on nearly every street. With a little convincing and a tickle, to see if you were serious or not, they would take you around the corner into a convenient alley and sell you a little lung candy or even the Obvious if that was your habit. Everybody was drunk on tutti-fruity or serious on something or another on the east-side.

Slammy did steady business. His dancing suzies were known to put out for rue or goo. Meemaw's girls only put out for rue *and* goo but they were also guaranteed to be disease free. A clown could catch the cooties if he wasn't careful. Meemaw's girls also always used birth control. Getting knocked up was a suzies's quick ticket out of the slums, so you were taking a risk if you trusted Slammy's suzies. Whammo got nailed that way once and Laymo too.

^$#%$@

With both their clowns in the pokey, Chesty and Dew Drop were back to their old tricks working for Meemaw. Meemaw's pimp didn't hesitate to hire the two clownettes the second they walked in. Both had reputations that preceded them, if ya know whut I mean. Presently, the two were recovering from yet another night of goo by spending hard ridden rue on some tutti-fruity at Slammy's. Dew Drop was loaded. She'd made a small fortune off the mayor who had come down to inspect Slammy's personally. Both the suzies were living high in the hog with both their husbands and children now wards of the state. The suzies did have small longings for their boys but that was nothing compared to their longings for hard candy. They were enjoying their new found freedom staying as serious as possible.

"Dammit, Dew, we gotta SCORE, Suzie-Q!"

Both were momentarily silent. Dew Drop lit a candy cigarette and inhaled deeply.

"Hey, I got an idea," she said. "Remember that weird old Sicko…the clown my husband used to be partners with?"

Chesty perked up, if that was possible. "Yeah, I know what you're getting at. If we could get to Sicko, we could by-pass these johns and small time peddlers for the sweets."

"Exactly. Maybe if we get to know a joker or two, we can get one to fess up on Sicko's location or even escort us there." Dew Drop shuffled her huge mammarian mcgillicutties.

"I know just the one! Let's book!" and they did.

Out on the street, it was like noon. The action was starting to roll in like a tide only the water was clowns. The jokers were busy fooling 'cause there were some Keystones around. The best of them hung with suzies that had the big mcgillicutties 'cause that always kept the Stoners distracted. You could deal goo right under their noses if you disguised the deal with a pair of mcgillicutties.

Blacky was good at moving candy. He was just into his twenties but had been dealing goo since before his acne cleared up. His spot was the coveted corner between Slammy's and Meemaw's. It had taken years for him to work up the reputation that had gotten him where he was and he had kicked a lot of booty to get there. Nobody messed with him anymore. Not even the Stoners. Blacky was too smart for them and it just gave the Keystones a headache to try and deal with him. Blacky would always lay some abstract bozokahkah on them disguised as a joke. For example, Blacky once walked right out of a bust when he asked the Stoner "What's the difference between an orange?"

The Stoner could only reply with "I dunno".

"A tricycle because a vest has no sleeves" answered Blacky. Then he relaxed to watch the fireworks. You could practically see the fuses in the Keystone's tinker popping trying to figure that one.

Blacky wasn't in the least bit surprised to find himself suddenly becoming the object of two floosies that had just stumbled out of Slammy's. He had seen these two hanging around the neighborhood lately and reckoned it was about time they made his acquaintance. It didn't take much convincing to get Blacky into an alley. Chesty sat on an upturned chocolate milk crate and commenced to what they went there for while Dew Drop quizzed the clown while he was under the magic spell.

"So, you suzies want Sicko" Blacky said, breathing heavy. Chesty kept encouraging and Dew Drop kept talking.

"You can get us to see Sicko?"

"Yeah babe…see I been working for Sicko ever since he took over the biz from this clown named Whammo."

Dew Drop gulped upon hearing her husband's name. "You knew Whammo?" she said.

"Yeah…why ya know 'em?"

"You could say that." Dew Drop was trying to keep a straight face which is quite hard for a clown, you know.

"Seen 'em lately? I always liked him. Least 'til he up and went foolish and married some floosie."

Dew Drop thought to smack him and was suddenly glad she was the one questioning and not encouraging. Chesty came to the rescue.

"So, what's wrong with being a floosie?"

Blacky realized instantly he had just crossed into dangerous territory. Every clown knows a floosie ain't got no legitimate excuse for being one and asking one to produce a justification by slamming their trip was a good way to get one step closer to a black eye.

"Sorry, mam, it was a poor choice of words…I just meant that he wasn't fit for moving the syrup no more after he got hitched. There's too many ways to get to a clown iffin they got a family, know what I mean…anyway ya seen 'em?"

"Sorry" said Dew, "but Whammo is keeping house for King Kong on the Funny Farm.

"Wow! What did he do?"

"Possession, dude."

"Whoa!" said Blacky, pulling out a carton of canes. He handed one each to the suzies and all three lit up off the same match.

"So, when do we get to see Sicko?" asked Chesty.

"Follow me" replied Blacky, hopping up on his unicycle. And they did.

Later, on the outskirts of town, Blacky left the two floosies standing on Sicko's doorstep. Blacky didn't want to get on his connects bad side in case the clown gone bad was not in the mood for company. Sicko was pleased, as it turned out, to find two hot and well endowed suzies unexpectedly at his door. He invited them in. And everyone got serious. It didn't take long for the suzies to establish a deal with Sicko. Now, they would be kept in goo, no problem. There was only one catch…they would have to take turns letting Sicko spank them once in a while.

WHAM, BAM, THANK YOU, MAM!

Chapter 18
Selected Readings From: The All Knowing Owl Speaks Volume 970,553,267,849,100,371: Jehovah's Domain Book 47,875: "Ruminations on Like Everything" Chapter 756,890,900 Paragraph 576,834,254,001

576,834,254,001:

It is written that Like Everything is an extremely gigantic place. In fact, with the exception of the "All Knowing Owl" it isn't even possible for one being to fully comprehend its enormous size and likewise the inconceivable amount of everything contained within it. The physical nature of Like Everything is all encompassing. Within it are that which exists and also that which does not exist. This is because even that which does not exist needs a place to be. Therefore, for everything that exists there is a place for it to go when it ceases to exist and so forth and so on. Most people who exist do not concern themselves with that which does not exist because from their point of view there is no such thing. However, there are those who do concern themselves with all the stuff that isn't, but nobody listens to them because all they talk about is nothing. Most of the time, these types have nothing to say to begin with. It would be an understatement to say that to try to control, rule, or otherwise supervise all that there is or isn't in Like Everything would be completely insane and absurd. Yet there are, in fact, those who do, by some miracle, govern Like Everything and these individuals are called The Powers That Be.

576,834,254,002:

The Powers That Be do not concern themselves with creating Universes or creatures in their own image, rather they concern themselves with creating hassles, headaches, and endless rules for the artisans and other groovy people tending to their domains. Fortunately, the Powers That Be do manage to instill some sense of order in Like Everything, if not by method, then by might. These beings, acting together as a governing body, are capable of amassing enough of whatever it might take to squash any rebellion or uprising and to settle galactic disputes and the like. At the very least, they keep nasty beings, like Satan or the Weirdoes for example, from literally ruining Like Everything. Needless-to-say, The Powers That Be are the center of Like Everything and all else moves ever outward from them.

576,834,254,003:

The physical arrangement of Like Everything can best be described as a book and one made in the form of a cube. The cubic book would be composed of an infinity of pages, each page serving as a plane of existence, dimension or domain. Beings wealthy enough in the positron/negatron currency honored by the Powers That Be may afford themselves an entire page in the book of Like Everything. Not-so-wealthy beings may simply exist or not exist within the page of their choosing. On the other hand, 99% of the beings in Like Everything are so utterly poor that they are forced to exist only on the page where their dismal lives were written to begin with. This goes for their existence even after the transition from life to the unlife after Death.

576,834,254,004:
Death is one creature whose wealth allows him to reside on the page of his choosing and even travel from page to page wherever he likes. However, the fortune to be collected in the small amount of positrons/negatrons found in souls is not enough for him to set up a domain of his own. And, what a delightful place that would be if he could, eh?

576,823,254,005:
Unlike Death, creatures such as God and Jesus Christ are quite rich and can afford nearly an entire page in Like Everything. Unfortunately for them, they must share a percentage of their domain with their archrival Satan and his Hell. Of course, the Gods are by no means the richest beings in Like Everything and must answer to those who whose funds exceed theirs…establishments like the First Inter- Dimensional Bank, for example. This brings to mind the subject of funds. The concept is much simpler than the complexities surrounding it. If one should desire something like "to be", for instance, then one must possess a means by which to do so. He, she or it would require some fundamental matter, which is a naturally occurring circumstance in Like Everything and, of course, the energy required to animate it. This matter manipulating energy, which can also be used to construct an entire Universe, constitutes the currency accepted everywhere as legal tender in Like Everything…the two acceptable forms being Positrons or Negatrons.

576,834,254,006:
The logical question here would be where do these two forms of legal energy come from? Here is the best explanation I have: The Positron/Negatron energy fields which serve Like Everything as its currency for all transactions have its origins at the root of where Like Everything began which is, of course, the beginning. As we know, Like Everything began when Like Everything was divided into just two bodies of conceptual energy, those two being the fact that at the time there was Absolutely Nothing and its counterpart Simply Nothing. It is accepted that all large sums of conceptual energy eventually came to realize their potential as they matured and because of this an argument broke out between the two. Simply Nothing realized it was a bit less of nothing than Absolutely Nothing when at the same moment Absolutely Nothing realized it was absolutely nothing, which, of course, led it to believe that it was superior to Simply Nothing. Simply Nothing as well believed itself to be superior to Absolutely Nothing because being simply nothing meant it was Something when compared to Absolutely Nothing. Albeit, a very minute something. Mathematicians see it this way:

Absolutely Nothing equals zero. Or (A.N. = 0)
Simply Nothing equals zero? Or (S.N. = 0?)

Absolutely Nothing's argument as to being the superior concept:

(A.N. - S.N. = 0)

Simply Nothing's argument as to being the superior concept:
(S.N. - A.N. = ?) ? = X (X = something)

This clearly demonstrates that Simply Nothing had Something over on Absolutely Nothing. That Something being that big ole X. Well, the X-variable wasn't really much of something compared to all the nothings put together, however, no matter how much nothing there is, it is never greater than the most miniscule amount of something. It was only moments after the argument between the Nothings had occurred than the concept of Something itself found its potential and in a blazing moment of truth that little something realized that it indeed was Like Everything. And, that is how Like Everything began.

576,834,254,007

Soon Something began to divide itself into smaller portions. Being Like Everything meant that the only room for growth was by way of compartmentalizing itself into smaller bits. Exponentially, the divisions continued until all of Like Everything's mass reached absolute division. This founded the concepts of multi-dimensional planes of existence…only there was one spectacular blob left over that wasn't big enough to be spread out into a single dimensional plane. So, this blob was itself divided and distributed evenly across the billions of dimensional pages. These teeming masses of conceptual energy, although not large enough to compose a dimensional page, were unfathomably massive never-the-less, and as with all large bodies of conceptual matter these blobs themselves came to realize their potential. In that instant, Like Everything was no longer alone as a contradiction to Nothing and for that matter its superiority was evaporated in the wake of these awesome blobs of energy called Individual Concepts.

576,834,254,008

Like Everything had godzillions, the largest conceivable figure known to modern mathematical geniuses of dimensional planes, but they were mostly like giant cosmic parking lots, as vacant as they were utterly boring. The Individual Concepts, on the other hand, were coming up with all kinds of interesting stuff. Here, in the simple beginning of Like Everything, was an endless succession of dimensional planes filled with godzillions of Individual Conceptual energy fields. The race was on! Being a vast expanse of mostly empty space was nothing to be proud of. For this reason, the Individuals began competing, trying to out compartmentalize one another. It was a slow process but now and then one of the Individuals would come up with a new and improved way to be less and momentarily be the so-called King of Like Everything until everything else copied the idea.

576,834,254,009

The first were insanely gigantic dust clouds, a simple compartmentalization of matter and energy. Then, came the endless successions of improvements on that theme which eventually resulted in the formation of galaxies. Later, as the race continued, one Individual outdid them all by massing a huge store of raw energy and then compressing it as tightly as possible into a spherical compartment called a Star. Of course the resulting superiority didn't last long as others followed suit. These first Stars were unstable and usually fell apart rather quickly until an individual perfected the idea by changing the containment process from a compression of energy to a conversion of energy. Where as before when the Stars would get bored and explode for kicks, now they had something to do.

576,834,254,010

Many others improved upon the spherical containment concept of compartmentalization and henceforth came small bodies of matter held together by the forces of gravity from their parent Star. These small units of matter would orbit the Star and were called Planets. Sometimes even smaller bodies of matter could be set into orbit around the Planets and these were known as Moons.

576,834,254,011

And so it went on and on like that until Like Everything was literally filled with Galaxies filled with Stars and their orbital pals. Eventually, the Individuals used up so much of their original conceptual energy that they became rather compartmentalized themselves. It was then that they began calling themselves Gods. At this point, the general race to compartmentalize was called off as the now much more compressed individuals (Gods) secluded themselves to concentrate on variations of the creative process. This resulted in the ultimate compartmentalization of conceptual energy when one Individual took a smidgen of energy and crammed it into a blob of matter called a Cell. Eventually, it was discovered that the Cell could divide itself endlessly further compartmentalizing the original amount of energy. The process was improved upon until finally the collection of Cells came into sentience. This was unanimously called Life. Soon it was discovered that Life was creating small amounts of conceptual energy of its own in the form of Positrons or Negatrons depending on the case. It was the eventual collection of these Positrons or Negatrons that formed the primitive economic system of Like Everything and because of this Life broke out everywhere. Furthermore Life also…

Chapter 19
Boogus Maximus

Meanwhile, in another section of Like Everything, a lost soul was trying to figure out where in the cosmos he was. Where he should have been was Hell because that is where all cannibals go because of all the people they ate. It seemed to Guh Mooga Wump the 2nd that he had been lost like this forever and he was very nearly right. The last thing he remembered was being yanked out of the flesh just after finding his cherished 13-pound bowling ball with the blue and white swirls.

"Jah moo-moo chi deeko hut yoogy dupy, lib neebu mudik log wump!" cried out Guh Mooga Wump the 2nd. *"If only I had not shed tears, I would still be king!"* And, indeed he would be, for it was his shameful act of crying that caused his own son to chop off his head. That's when Death showed up and snatched his soul. Guh Mooga Wump found himself in his current condition due to Death's son. It seems that Death, Jr. had snitched his soul out of his father's collection satchel and was planning to hide it in his room when they got back to Hell. But then, the little skeleton panicked, afraid he would get caught, and threw Guh Mooga Wumps soul out into the abyss. Fortunately for Death, Jr., his father noticed none of this. And, that is how Guh Mooga Wump ended up where he was which would have been exactly nowhere had it not been for the fact that he was positioned precisely on the trajectory of an Imperial Hyperspace freighter.

^$#%@?

After finishing up with the loading in of all the Draconian Mindwarp the freighter could carry, the ship was now warping along at an unreasonable speed. The pilot of the craft thought he saw something for a moment but he was far to stoned to do anything about it. In fact, the pilot's brain collapsed in his skull seconds after the sighting. Had he lived a little longer he might have seen Guh Mooga Wump the 2nd out their floating in space. But, he didn't because he was dead. This left the pilot's duties to the co-pilot. The co-pilot had also foolishly done a bong hit of Draconian Mindwarp and was currently experiencing the complete failure of his nervous system. There were five others on board who might have been capable of flying the craft, but, alas, they were all stoned to death as well. Stupid humanoids!

Anyway, as fate would have it, the co-pilot fell dead, face forward onto the console and just by luck his nose engaged the automatic pilot. Now, the craft would hurl itself blindly and directly to it destination, Boogus Maximus, where it was certain to crash.

In another bizarre twist of fate, the freighter passed so close to the marooned Guh Mooga Wump that he was caught up in its warp field bubble. Now, he too would travel at an unreasonable speed to Boogus Maximus. Of course, he had no way of knowing that. However, he was relieved to be going somewhere even if he had no idea where that somewhere was.

^$#%@

Boogus Maximus got its name due to the unusual formation of its star system and cosmic dust clouds which together looked exactly like a colossal nose. The planet, Boogus Maximus is but one of many booger like satellites found in what would be the nostril of the formation. It is, however, the largest therein and therefore its name.

On Boogus Maximus, the Powers That Be were in session in the labyrinth like building serving as the capitol of Like Everything. In the far end of the unbelievably massive room, where the representatives of a godzillion civilizations assembled themselves to make all the big universal decisions, stood the Prime Minister of All, Lord Emperor of Much, Regal Personage of This, Maharaja of That, Sultan of Somewhere, Overlord of Underdogs, Crowned Head of Lots, Prince of Polecats, Monarch of Most, Tyrant of Totality, Shah of Something or Other, The Absolute King of the Hill, Rikki-Tikki-Timboo-No-Saw-Rimboo-Chari-Bari-Richy-Pip-Pari-Pimboo the Third.

Despite this enormous title, most people did away with the formalities and simply called him Hey-Dudes. This was because he unwaveringly greeted everyone that way. Hey, Dudes began to pound his gavel to bring the session to order.

"Hey, Dudes!"

Bang! Bang! Bang!

"Hey, Dudes!"

It seemed hopeless for poor Hey-Dudes. Try to imagine the noise created by a godzillion beings all in one place. Hey-Dudes stood there banging away but one could hardly hear his pathetic little hammer strike over the deafening roar. Finally, things began to settle down when one of the representatives said something so loudly that everyone was forced to listen. This was because his race was composed of sentient unnecessarily large public address systems. It also had to do with what he said.

"I call for the immediate impeachment of Hey-Dudes!"

Hey-Dudes instantly began to look nervous as silence draped over the teeming masses. He fielded a question. It sounded like a mouse fart.

"What for?" he squeaked. The P.A. systems response to this was loud as Hell.

"Because, Sir, your name is way too long and I think I speak for all of us when I say that if I have to hear you say "Hey, Dudes" one more time I am going to blow a cone!"

Hey-Dudes looked upset.

"Hey, Dude, you can't talk to me that way why I am the…"

"There he goes again! See he can't help it." The P.A. looked pleased with itself. Hey-Dudes tried to argue his way out of the spot he was in. It might seem at first that being the leader of the Powers That Be would be a coveted position. Nothing could be further from the truth. It was truly a thankless job. This was Hey-Dudes point.

"If you impeach me, then who the Hell is going to be my replacement, huh? Tell me that big mouth!"

Hey-Dude was pleased with himself. A stir made its rounds in the room as untold millions of beings whispered the words "Not me!" in a million languages. Nobody wanted Hey-Dudes thankless job. The un-necessarily large P.A. muttered as quietly as he could which meant nearly everyone could hear him trying to think of a suitable retort. Hey-Dudes was right. Then he had it.

"Hey! Nobody may want your job but that doesn't mean there isn't a replacement out there somewhere."

@$%&%$

It is written that at that moment, a little hunchbacked bug-eyed old humanoid woman was awakened from a deep sleep in her deep seat in the big room. Evidently, her latest invention had begun to act up. It was in her pocket and it was squirming around. She took it out and began to examine the odd little device. The invention could best be described as a cybernetic slice of throbbing gristle capable of forecasting obscure yet galacticaly important coincidences before they happened. Hmmm…

#$#@^%?

Hey-Dudes was now jumping up and down behind his podium mocking the P.A., screaming "For all we know, my replacement could come crashing through the ceiling but so what!!"

And, that is when the runaway Imperial Hyperspace freighter full of Draconian Mindwarp crashed through the dome of the big room and impacted directly on the spot where Hey-Dudes stood. He was killed instantly and with irony. Fortunately for the others, the shields went up and they emerged unscathed. Then, began the talk of how incredible the coincidence was, for standing in the rubble, right where the podium used to be, was a tired looking cannibal.

Needless-to-say, the crash created plenty of confusion. It took some time for the robots to clear away the wreckage and rubble. The big room was filled with a dense fog, which came from the burning tons of Draconian Mindwarp. This resulted in the deaths of several interns and pages all of whom had not graduated from the flesh. All of the representatives there were flesh graduates, for that was required. No one could expect to understand the complexities of holding a seat in Boogus Maximus without literally a lifetime of experience. The smoke had gotten them all incredibly stoned. Nobody was more stoned than Guh Mooga Wump the 2nd, who began to freak out when he was suddenly surrounded by hundreds of weird beings all of who were wanting to know if the stranger from the stars would take the thankless job as ruler of Like Everything. They felt certain that he would because coincidences of that magnitude were nothing short of prophecy. Hey-Dudes himself had suggested that his replacement would come falling through the ceiling.

As Guh Mooga Wump the 2nd gathered his wits, he became frightened at the sight of an enormous collection of boxes and humming shapes with little fires all over them which was his visual interpretation of the un-necessarily large P.A. system. When the system began to wave at Guh Mooga Wump, the savage tried to think of something polite to say through his fear, confusion, and unbearable buzz. The only thing that came into his mind was atypical cliché used when meeting strangers in the jungle.

"Zoot Locka!" said the savage.

If the P.A. System could have understood Guh Mooga Wump's language, he would have blown a fuse for the savage had just said *"Hey, Dude!"*

Fortunately, he didn't understand and he then began calling for a translatorbot who quickly came forward to interpret.

The P.A. said "Ask him if he wants to be King of Like Everything."

The robot nodded then approached Guh Mooga Wump the 2nd. Abruptly the robot slapped the savage cannibal across the face. The P.A. was shocked by this and demanded an explanation.

"What'd ya do that for?"

The robot answered calmly. "In order for me to translate, I must first hear the being's native tongue. By slapping it, I hope to illicit a response."

It worked. Guh Mooga Wump began screaming..

"Unga-Umlup!! Lib-Hugi-Teega-Noon-To- Ung-Obgut-A- Zoogie!!" He was harmlessly kicking the robots shins. The P.A spoke up.

"What's he saying? What's he saying?"

The robot's brain could be heard to think in little clicking and whirring noises. "He said, and I quote, "*I will teach you to mess with a warrior!*"

The crowd cheered for this was one fit to be King. The P.A. shouted over the cheers of the crowd easily.

"Ask him! Ask him!"

The robot turned to the cannibal. "Gump-noon. Hooky-noon-choud-to-log-wump? Wump-pee-ooga-whoa?

"Hey, there. You want to, be King? King of Like Everything?"

Guh Mooga Wump the 2nd could not believe his ears, he was so excited. His answer was swift. "Chi-hugi-log-wump…Wump-pee-ooga-Whoa!

What'd he say? What'd he say?" said the P.A. Again the robot translated.

"I will be King! King of Like Everything!"

AND SO IT WAS WRITTEN AND SO IT WAS DONE!

Chapter 20
Death on the Double

It was a busy day for the Buffoonville Keystones. Every available squad jalopy had been dispatched to investigate the situation empty, as well, was the fire station, for all of Buffoonvilles fire clowns had been called to the scene down to the very last Dalmatian. Presently, all were gathered around the invisible ruins of Mime Manor, which was in the process of burning to the ground. The soil around it was muddied and water logged from the pressure hoses the fire clowns had used to douse the inviso-flames.

The Fire Chief was a fat one among fat ones…like a plumped link of sausage ready to explode. With a helmet on his head, the funny kind that fire clowns wear, he kinda looked like a giant wiener. This was why the others in his unit called him Hotdog behind his back.

"Is it out yet? What a disaster! How are we supposed to know if it's out if we can't even see the flames?" asked Hotdog, waddling around the area making sure everyone noticed him as he made his observations. He came to the spot where the victims lay. There was about twenty of them lying about squirming in what must have been their idea of agony. Despite the pretenses of their reality, the flames had been all too real and had roasted most of them beyond recognition. Still, they wore that idiot's grin, something that deeply disturbed Hotdog. They looked like demented skulls staring out in agony from lid-less eye sockets.

Besides these poor wretches, the only evidence of a fire was the great black pillar of smoke billowing from where ever the jets of water made contact with the inviso-flame. It was a strange sight for all practical purposes because it looked as though the smoke was merely a side effect of the huge jets of water, which arched high before falling into the ruined silent home. But it was the silence that was the oddest part of all. With the exception of the officials, the fire hoses and the sounds their jets of water made, it was nearly completely quiet up on the hill. No roaring inferno. No crackling of burning timber. No hissing where water met flame. No screams of agony. For the most part, it sounded like a gathering next to a waterfall.

"Is it out yet? Somebody tell me it's out!" The sausage was talking.

"God, I hate mimes. This is not funny. Not even remotely humorous. All this inviso- nonsense. For cripes sake, you can't even see the flames!"

The sausage was really frothing this time. His crew was used to it but he was getting on the wrong side of Keystone Sergeant McDoodle who had heard enough of the Fire Chief's racist bozokahkah. McDoodle made his way over to the sausage and got right up in his face.

"That's it, Chief! I've heard enough of your clown supremacist malarkey! These people got as much right as the next clown to the services of the Fire Department. You guys sure took your time getting over here. I don't want to find out you was dragging your tail because it was Mime Manor that was torched!"

McDoodle punctuated himself by giving the Chief a solid shove. Of course, the sausage was top heavy to begin with so he fell right over, landing six inches deep into the muddy soil. The chief's face turned bright red with anger and he hurled his insults at the Sergeant.

"It's bleedin' hearts like you, McDoodle, that's gonna come crawling on their knees to us when the mimes take over. Then we'll see all about your mimes got rights theories." McDoodle came over to tower above the sausage.

"Just who exactly is US, Chief? You're not implying you're one of THEM are you? The Notsees are our prime suspect in this fire, ya know. Why, I oughta run you in for questioning…you ever face the music, Chief? Why, we got us a live piper these days that will blow your sox off!"

Hotdog went to get himself up out of the mud but his weight only caused him to sink even deeper. "You ain't got nothing on me or my boys, ya hear!" Suddenly, there was the sound of a tremendous fart as the air pocket beneath the sausage burst. The Chief sank in the mud up to his neck in one mighty heave. He began to plead with McDoodle.

"Don't just stand there, Sarge. Help me! Can't you see I'm sinking over here?"

McDoodle laughed. "Help you? Why should I help you? I don't even like you and by your logic that's all the reason I need to stand here and watch you drown in the slop. Where are your cronies now, Chief? Better hope they don't mind getting their hands dirty!"

And with one final burp the sausage was gone.

@#$%^&

Next door to Mime Manor, of course, was Sicko's house. Sicko leaned back out of his upstairs windowsill, from which he had been watching the commotion next door, and turned to face the small group of Notsees who were in his house in the process of hiding out. Sicko picked a booger and then began an exercise in futility trying to dislodge it from his dirty digit. It ended up being smeared onto the front of his bathrobe, already a veritable booger graveyard.

"Alright, who's volunteering to go dig that fat slug of a clown out of the mud puddle?" Nobody spoke up. Sicko stamped his foot, causing a handful of cockroaches to flee across the floor.

"C'mon, you guys, we need the Chief. He's the only one that can cover up the many arsons we will be committing. Like today's for instance."

Still nobody seemed interested. Some of the group kind of smirked because the really didn't like the Chief anyway. Sicko lost his patience which was really too bad because he had just found it watching Mime Manor burn next door. In his rage, he absentmindedly threw the first thing he laid hands on out the window. It was his cat. The cat landed on it's feet, went down another life, then scampered off for good.

"Dammit! You idiots should be ashamed of yourselves. Did you think you could just waltz in here, hang a toilet seat around you neck, and take an oath to do what ever it takes to kill all the mimes without committing yourselves to the well being of your comrades? You fools, this is WAR! Now who's gonna dig the sausage out of the mud?

It should be pointed out that clowns are extremely susceptible to "jumping on the bandwagon". Speeches like the one Sicko had just made were just the sort to cause clowns to climb over each other to join the cause.

"I will!" said the Mayor of Buffoonville.

"Me too!" said his honor the Judge.

"And me!" said the Commandant of the Keystones.

"I'll get him!" said the Reform School Poobla.

"No, I will!" said the Funny Farm Warden.

"Let me go!" said Meemaw.

"No. I want to!" said Slammy.

"I'll dig him out!" said the Ditch Digger. Suddenly, the volunteers stopped in their tracks. Now, they had a thousand excuses to back out and leave the chore to the Ditch Digger who was best suited for the job anyway. The Ditch Digger made his way to the stairwell leading to the ground floor. Sicko spoke up.

"Hey, you stupid clown! Aren't you forgetting something?" said Sicko.

The Digger quickly began to ponder what it might have been he'd forgotten. Then it dawned on him. He had forgotten to give the Notsee salute. Abruptly. he thrust his right arm out at a 45-degree angle. Then, he brought his right hand thumb to his nose, wiggled his fingers, stuck out his tongue and gave the group a solid raspberry.

"Thank-you brother" said Sicko, "but don't you think you'll look a little bit too serious if you go out there with that toilet seat around your neck?"

The Ditch Digger smiled and politely removed his sacred toilet seat hanging it on the empty nail beneath his name.

Now, with all that rigmarole put of the way the group got back to business. The Mayor opened the discussion.

"Well, Sicko, I must say your plan went off brilliantly. Burning down Mime Manor has sent the mimes back into the woods or wherever it is they go to. How do you come up with these plans? I can never pay attention long enough, it's a chore for me just to remember how to tie my shoes and I think I speak for everyone when I say that."

The group all nodded agreement. This was a fine collection of morons if there ever was one. Sicko was searching through his bathrobe and then eventually produced a little bottle of syrup.

"I do it with this!" he said, showing off the little bottle to the group.

The Commandant exclaimed. "Hey, that's Obvious! Why, that's illegal!"

Sicko was ready for that tired old argument. "So's murder and arson but that didn't stop any of you today now did it?"

The stoner was beaten by logic…something he and the others were desperately short of. Surprisingly, the Poobla of the Reform School came to Sicko's defense.

"Look, clowns, this is war. The mimes are the only thing we need to worry about. We've all sworn an oath to destroy the mimes no matter what it takes, whither it's murder or arson or getting serious. If Sicko thinks we should get serious, then I'm with him!" The band wagon thing went around the room like a rumor.

"Darn Tootin!" said the Mayor.

"Here, here!" said his Honor the Judge.

"Hell, yes!" said the Commandant of the Keystones.

"Me, too!" said the Poobla.

"Always wondered what was all the fuss!" said the Warden.

"Finally!" said Meemaw.

"It's about time!" said Slammy.

Of course, the last two had been serious the whole time. Sicko handed out little syrup bottles and the guns to shoot up with till everyone had one, then he showed them how to load up the shooters and bang the goo home. The group did as they were instructed and all fell silent as the rush of intelligence hit them. Sicko waited till everyone was good and serious before starting his rhetorical speech.

"We all know that the mimes have evil powers which they use to disrupt our daily lives. They leave their invisible objects all over the place. I doubt there is any one of you that hasn't bashed his honker on some inviso-house or wrecked his jalopy trying to park in a space occupied by a mime wagon. I have found in my obviously enhanced state of mind that studying the mimes has been very useful. I discovered that all I had to do to fight them was turn their evil powers against them. You saw how well that worked with this little operation to rid Mime Manor from being in the vicinity of our headquarters."

"Yeah, there was nothing to it!" said an excited Slammy, as he deftly took another syrup bottle from its place on the cocoa-table. "I pretended to run out of go-go juice and this filthy mime comes along in his inviso-wagon and I called to him for help. It wasn't nothing to talk him into giving me his inviso-can of juice. Then, all I had to do was paint it so we could all see the can."

The Mayor cut in. "That's right. Then, the fire chief copped a book of inviso-matches from a mime disco by pretending he was there to inspect the place. He couldn't see a thing but the mimes went along with it."

Meemaw took her turn. "I had to bandage up the fat clowns fingers. He burned himself pretty good trying to get the fire going 'cause he couldn't see the flames."

Sicko was bored listening to the others recounting the day's events.

"You will all find that your ability to use mime power against them will grow the more serious you become."

Sicko was tossing little bottles around. Just then the ditch digger came in with the muddied sausage in tow. Sicko instructed him to take a shower (even though he himself hadn't bathed in years) and told Slammy to get them both set up with the Obvious. It was time for Sicko to make his daily report to Satano.

Sicko made way into the basement where his secret chambers were located. The Devil had created a two-way com-link out of Sicko's toilet. Sick flushed three times to call upon the demon. Peg Legs received the call and instructed Sicko to hold on while he fetched the master.

Peg Legs hobbled into the chamber where the Prince of Darkness was entertaining three Weirdoes, numbered 13, 23 and 20,332. The Devil himself had taken the form of a Weirdoe just to annoy the three Weirdoes. His shirt bore the numeral zero.

"What I want to know is why you are so interested in Jehovah's domain for anyhow?" The Weirdoes shifted uneasily in their seats. This was mostly due to the fact that the cushions were filled with pins, needles, and broken glass.

"Sorry, Satan, Ancient Chinese Secret." Satano quickly began wondering what the deal was with Ancient Chinese Secrets. Then, he remembered this was the same tactic used by God whenever he didn't feel like revealing sensitive information. It was also a tactic designed to disrupt ones train of thought. Satano had already forgotten what he wanted to know because of it. It was then that Peg Legs came stumbling into the room.

"Master, Master, there is someone on the toilet that refuses to get off the pot until he speaks with you. Satano leaped out of his throne which was situated behind an obnoxiously huge, cherry-wood desk and grabbed Peg Legs by the nostrils.

"Who is it?" he demanded.

"It's some clown named Sicko!" pleaded the amputee. Satano cast his slave into the abyss. Then, he turned to the three Weirdoes.

"I'll be right back. I just need to use the bathroom." And the Devil vanished in a minor explosion of blue and green flames. The Weirdoes waited for the smoke to clear, then Satano went into his bathroom and lifted the seat of the filthy toilet there. He could see Sicko's head surrounded by the toilet seat he had been ordered to wear.

"Sicko, this better be important! I was in a meeting."

"Sorry, Master, but I do have important news."

"Yes? Then, what be it?"

"I have successfully attracted the local government to the Clown Supremacy Movement. They are getting serious as we speak!" Satano was pleased.

"What about the Poobla? Did he also fall into the trap?"

"Yes, Master! And there is more to it. This Poobla is also the principal of the Bufoonville Reform School. He is single handedly responsible for the rehabilitation of delinquent youth!"

"Ahhh, this is indeed good news. If he is turned far enough, he may take it upon himself to instruct the inmates of the Reform School in the rhetoric of the Clown Supremacy Movement. We could end up with a sizable youth army. Good, good. Your reward is that I will not have you castrated like the others when you arrive in Hell. Anyway, work on that Poobla and see to it that he becomes your right hand man. You will need someone in authority in Buffoonville when I call you to Rome. Now be gone!"

The Devil flushed his toilet causing Sicko's to backfire then overflow. The clown gone bad made haste to leave so as not to leave a clean spot on his slippers. There was a fine layer of scum on them that he was extremely proud of. Standing on the first step, he watched helplessly as the toilet overflowed sending about an inch of water on the basement floor. He felt bad about the filth that was being washed away. But at least it WAS toilet water and who knows maybe it would mildew or something.

When Sicko arrived back into the room where the others were seated, he noticed immediately that the slaphappy attitude of the clowns had been replaced with the stern awareness and requisite quiet of serious clowns. Everyone was silently reading Sicko's treasured and ancient encyclopedias.

"So, what do you clowns think?" said Sicko, adjusting his toilet seat.

"You're absolutely right, Sicko" said the Judge. "I do find myself thinking quite a bit."

"That's obvious. But, what about?"

The Judge's peepers glazed over as he replied. "I was just thinking that's all. Never did that too much before. I guess you could say I was thinking about thinking. What about you guys?"

Everyone sort of looked the Judge's direction and sent a look that said *"Don't bother me, can't you see I'm thinking?"*

Sicko smiled at the sight of them. Nothing finer than to see a bunch of clowns going bad and getting serious. *"Who's laughing now?"* he thought.

666

"The reason we are here, Mr. Satan" said the Weirdoe, "is because something important has taken place on Boogus Maximus that has sent every Weirdoe into a state of panic." Satano leaned back in his throne and propped his grotesque feet up on the obnoxiously huge, cherry-wood desk. The Devil was barefooted and the Weirdoes could see the stench rising from them. They tried to ignore the smell; seeing it was bad enough.

"You don't look like your panicking" said the demon.

"Don't judge a book by its cover. Why he just pooped his pants only moments ago and I am currently peeing in mine."

The Devil was visibly pleased by this. He smiled then spoke.

"Glad to hear it. So what exactly has happened on Boogus Maximus. I so rarely pay attention to the Powers That Be, you know."

The Weirdoes spoke in turn. "Just after our most recent meeting with you a mere ten years ago, the Prime Minister of All, Lord Emperor of Much, Regal Personage of This, Maharaja of That, Sultan of Somewhere, Overlord of Underdogs, Crowned Head of Lots, Prince of Polecats, Monarch of Most, Tyrant of Totality, Shah of Something or Other, The Absolute King of the Hill, Rikki-Tikki-Timboo-No-Saw-Rimboo-Chari-Bari-Richy-Pip-Pari-Pimboo the Third was on the verge of impeachment."

Satano held out his hands and placed them behind his head. "Oh, my, what for?"

"Because his name was too long and he kept saying "Hey, Dudes" all the time."

"Sounds logical" said Satano squeezing a back zit that really hurt. "So, what happened?"

"An Imperial Hyperspace freighter crashed through the ceiling and landed on Hey-Dudes killing him instantly."

OH! Is that all? said the Lord of Spiders.

"Not quite" replied Weirdo 23. " A survivor was found in the wreckage."

"And…" the Devil was working on another pimple.

"And, it seems that the survivor was part of a monumental coincidence, one seen as prophecy by the Powers That Be. It was because of this that the survivor was crowned King of Like Everything."

Satano sighed as the pimple he was squeezing popped satisfactorily. "Well, I'll be. That's one Hell of a good story. What I want to know is what does that have to do with me. I could give a crap who the King of Like Everything is unless he's messing with me somehow."

The Weirdoe squirmed and continued. "That's exactly how we feel, Mr. Satan. The new King IS messing with us. We had invested a lot in the former ruler, if you know what we mean, and now all of our connections have been broken as new alliances form under the new king. Can you see how that might mess with us?"

The Devil nodded, he didn't like to be patronized. "Yes, yes, but what has this to do with me?"

The Weirdoe removed a small note pad, referred to it and spoke: "You might be interested to know that the new King of Like Everything, Guh Mooga Wump the 2nd was scheduled to arrive in your Hell the summer of Earth 2073 A.D."

The Devil kicked his feet back and sat up. He was suddenly taking an interest in the Powers That Be.

"No way! One of mine, huh? Well, we lose a few now and again…hey wait a minute, the Weirdoes aren't blaming me for this…"

The Weirdoe hissed. "The Weirdoes are indeed blaming you, after all, it's your fault this flesh graduate escaped to end up where he has….now quite untouchable."

The Devil leaned forward and touched his intercom. His secretary answered. Nearly under his breath he said:

"I want Death on the double!"

It didn't take Death long to arrive once he got the message. It took the message quite a while to reach him though where he was collecting souls near a battlefield on the planet Remulak. When he got the message, he hauled his bones back to Hell as quickly as he could. It wasn't often that Satano insisted he come "on the double" as they say. His biggest problem was who was gonna watch the kid. His ugly wife was out for the day, getting even uglier he imagined, which meant he would probably just have to bring the little skeleton along. After a few more minutes trying to see if any of his sisters would sit with the child and discovering that none where home, he moseyed on over to Satan's office, child in tow.

The three Weirdoes were careful to move their seats as far away from Death as they could. Death, Jr. was tugging at his father's tattered cloak pointing at them. Death patted his head saying:

"It'ssss not nice to point, SSSSon….remember you're Death. Pointing at ssssomeone is liable to killllll them."

It was true. One of the Weirdoes was practically having a heart attack. Death noticed that there was a Weirdoe sitting in the Devil's seat. He could not have known it was just Satano in a Weirdoe suit. Death confused his son by pointing a bony finger at the Weirdoe in the Devil's chair.

"You sssshouldn't be sssssitting in other people seatsssss!" he hissed.

The Devil was not amused. "You shouldn't be telling people what they should or shouldn't do."

Death realized immediately that the Weirdoe was really the Devil.

"Ssssorry Sssssatan…I did not recognize you."

"You got a lot to be sorry for today, Death, and you can start with yourself!" The Devil punctuated his words by slamming a frail Weirdoe's fist on the top of his obnoxiously huge, cherry-wood desk.

"Whatssss all thissss?" demanded Death who had no patience with other peoples bozokahkah. The Weirdoe was eager to dispense with the situation and quickly began explaining the particulars of the crisis to Death all the while careful not to look the specter in the face. Death had taken a seat half way into the dissertation when Satano took over and outright accused Death of losing the soul that had wound up as the new King of Like Everything. Everybody in the room was trying to pin the whole mess on Death.

"Man…. I just don't ssseee how thisss could have happened…." pleaded Death, as his son quietly began to sneak towards the chamber door. The Devil took notice of the suddenly nervous child and gave him the crusties, something no normal being could stand. Jr. was however the son of Death and the crusties had no effect on him.

"Now letssss see…I picked up his ssssoul…and the three of us were coming back…"

"What do you mean THREE?" inquired Satano.

"Me and Jr. had gone out together that day…" Death's sentence was cut short as a door slammed. It was Jr. making his getaway. Satano lifted a brow and exchanged looks with Death. Both knew what had happened.

"Allow me" said Satan, blankly as he snapped his fingers. Instantly, a tiny skeleton appeared, hanging in the air, still running above the obnoxiously huge cherry-wood desk.

"Jr!" barked Death, in a shriek that caused all three Weirdoes to cringe and shiver. Jr. was visibly upset and could be seen crying. Little puffs of dust were emanating form his empty sockets.

"I didn't mean to! Honest, I didn't" screamed the little banshee. He followed his cries with a full confession.

"….and then I got scared and threw it away."

A Weirdoe protested.

"Honestly, bringing a child along to collect the spoils of Death…really it's unprofessional!" The Weirdoes nodded in agreement. Their petty triumph did not last long as they soon found Death looking them in the face.

"How am I ssssupposed to train the boy if I don't take him into the field? Hmmmm?" The Weirdoes were cowering.

"Gentlemen PLEASE!" commanded the Devil. "None of this is accomplishing anything. At least now we know what happened. It was a simple mistake, and accident! Death grabbed his son out of mid air and began to scold him. Death was going to give the tot a good skinning. The Weirdoes couldn't understand how such a thing were possible seeing as to how the boy was nothing more that bones as it was. Death explained he was going to put some skin ON the tike. Evidently, this was something Jr. hated. Satano dismissed them to go about their business feeling confident that Death would be sure that his son paid for what he had done. He then turned to the Weirdoes.

"Well, now that the mystery is solved, what are we going to do about it?" Satano was visibly relaxed at this point in the melee. The Weirdoes on the other hand were unable to relax due to the broken glass in their chairs and the horrible smell of the Devil's feet which were presently propped up on the obnoxiously huge, cherry-wood desk. A Weirdoe spoke:

"What we Weirdoes plan to do about this fiasco is not at issue here. What is at issue is what YOU are going to do about it."

Satano was outraged at the insolent tone of voice the Weirdoe had just addressed him with. Had he not been a Weirdoe, he would have cast him into the abyss. Being bent over a barrel was not one of the Devil's best positions and it showed. Still he managed to be as polite as anyone with pure evil running through his veins could be. He forced out the words.

"What ….do…you want?" the Weirdoe replied.

"It isn't clear at this point what course of action we must take to undo the damage but time will tell. Just consider yourself in our debt for the time being until we can determine the extent of that debt."

With that, the Weirdoes bid the Devil farewell and caught the inter-dimensional tidal wave which passed before Satano's lair with a rip in the space time continuum. Then, they were gone.

Satano felt a surge of relief wash over him. That was the longest he had had to mind his manners in a million years. He would have liked to torture those Weirdoes slowly and personally but he needed something that only they could offer, which, of course, was his old job back. He needed their inter-dimensional clout if he wanted to ruin Jehovah's domain forever. Now this new King of Like Everything business had to come along and put a bad taste in his mouth. Well, maybe he couldn't torture a Weirdoe but he could torture the image of one. Satano stepped out of the body of the Weirdoe he had worn for the meeting to annoy them and took the form of a giant henchman with rippling muscles. He then placed the soul of a rapist in the body of the Weirdoe, which he promptly grabbed by the hair and dragged into the dungeons of Hell…there, to take out all his pent up feelings on the effigy of his benefactors. As for the soul of the rapist, well he had it coming, didn't he? After all, this is Hell we're talking about.   DUH!

Chapter 21
Suicide Birthday Cake

There was a suzie who was about to have her sixteenth birthday. Her parents had a big party planned for her. Her mother, Billy Jean, had baked a cake so sweet it would make your sweet-tooth scream. The cake was three feet tall and filled with jelly and strawberries and candy corn and chocolate morsels. Her father, Billy Billy, had taken the cake into the living room and set it upon the serving table right in front of the giant banner of the Notsee Party. The top of the cake landed dead center of the swastika. He stood there admiring it as he rubbed the stubble of his shaven head, rocking back and forth in his giant jack boots, thumbing at his red braces which held up his oversized khaki's. The scene brought tears to his eyes and he took out his hanky to wipe his honker above his Hitler mustache. His wife came to stand next to him sharing in the emotion filled moment.

Nastina, the birthday suzie, entered the room quietly through the kitchen. She stopped in the doorway and looked at her misty-eyed parents. Her innocent heart began to swell at the sight of them framed by the giant red, white, and black Notsee banner. She sobbed along with them because she hated them. She hated them and she hated the Notsee party. She decided that after the supposed festivities of her sixteenth birthday party was over, she would go into her bedroom and hang herself to death.

She was serious, too. Yesterday, she'd gone out and gotten a nice length of jump rope and, with trembling hands, she'd fashioned a noose on one end. Nastina entered the dining room and approached her parents.

"Mommy, Daddy…I want to open my presents."

Billy Jean and Billy Billy snapped out of their sentimental trance and came over to their darling little suzie.

"Happy sweet sixteen, Nastina, open mine first!" her mother said.

"No! NO!" said her father, "Mine first like we planned it B.J. Billy Jean quickly remembered the long talk they had had the previous night about their daughter's refusal to join the Notsee Party.

"Oh…that's right, Bill, baby…Nastina go on and open your father's gift." Nastina faked excitement for she already knew what the gift would be. Undoubtedly, it would be what every party member gave their children on their sixteenth birthdays. She tore off the wrapping paper and, upon seeing it, held back tears of disgust. It was a copy of Mime Kampf by Sicko the Clown, leader of the Clown Supremacy Movement, the Notsee Party. Of course, this was just her parent's way of hinting for the millionth time that she should join the party.

"Thanks, Dad" she said weakly, hardly disguising her true feelings.

"That's my girl!" said Billy Billy, knowing she was lying. He wished he could turn her in…the little traitor. His heart was filled with anger, sadness, and frustration.

"Now, Nastina, open mine next!" Nastina gave her mother a kiss and wondered if she was in the party because she wanted to be or because her father made her join. Nastina opened B.J.'s gift carefully because she knew her mother wished to save the wrapping. Her father's gift had been wrapped in swastika print wrapping so she had done her best to thoroughly ruin it. The present turned out to be a Mime Concentration Camp

Dollhouse with built in Easy Bake Oven. Nastina said nothing and just looked at it. Her mother broke the tension.

"Oh, I know you're too old to play with a dollhouse, Nastina, but I thought that you could give this to your own daughter after you join the party and marry a nice skinhead clown." Nastina forced a reply.

"Uh…thanks Mom...that's just what I'll do…I…guess."

The tears she was holding back made her eyeballs hurt from the pressure. Somehow she survived the ordeal and went to her room with a piece of cake on a plate also festooned with swastikas. When she got to her room, she threw the plate out the window and placed the slice on her nightstand. The plate sailed to land on a growing pile of Notsee junk down there.

Nastina prepared herself for the hanging. She felt fortunate that there was a nice beam across the funhouse ceiling for her to toss the jump-rope over. This she did and then she stood on a chair beneath the noose, which she placed around her neck. Then, she remembered she hadn't written a suicide note.

Nastina got down from the chair and got out some stationary and a pen. She made a big letter X over the party logo, which was printed on the right hand corner and began to write:

> There's no place in this world
> For a suzie like me
> I try to hate mimes
> But I can't, you see
> They seem so gentle and
> Nice from my view
> I don't understand
> How to hate what they do
> So, goodbye cruel world
> I think I'll feel better
> 'Cause I will be dead
> If you're reading this letter
>
> Nastina

Nastina left her note in the most obvious place she could find, then, once again, climbed on top of the chair. She began to have slight second thoughts but she paid no attention to them. Then, with the noose tight around her neck, she prepared to kick out the chair. One… a drop of sweat ran down her forehead…two…

It was over.

Nastina could see the golden tunnel of light. It filled her completely. There was a chiming sound in the room like tinkerbells. The sound was vaguely familiar. Then she saw what could only have been an angel. It WAS an angel as a matter-of-fact…her guardian angel, Miss Smoochy. It took a moment for Nastina to recognize the angel but as soon as she did, the light faded and she found herself still standing on the chair, noose still around her neck.

"Guess I never made it to three, huh?" said Nastina. Miss Smoochy said nothing but removed the noose.

"I remember you. You were my mother at the orphanage. You got killed by a jalopy. Then these clowns adopted me." Miss Smoochy was busy smoothing Nastina's hair, fawning over her.

"I couldn't let you kill yourself, Nastina. Not on the most important day of your life."

Nastina became sarcastic. "Oh, give me a break! It's just my lousy sixteenth birthday and my life sucks right now."

Miss Smoochy was unfazed by Nastina's remark and she spoke her turn.

"Oh, now-now! Everything is going to be better from now on. Listen to me carefully, Nastina, I want you to go down to the old orphanage. There is a sealed package with your name on it in one of the file cabinets in the basement. You must go there tonight and get that package. It's your destiny, do you understand?"

Miss Smoochy was smiling. Nastina seemed puzzled but understood what the angel wished her to do.

"I'll go" she said. The angel began to fade.

"Good" said Miss Smoochy and then she was gone.

Nastina felt weird right after Miss Smoochy disappeared. She wondered if it had even been real but couldn't think of any reason why she would concoct such an unlikely chain of events in her mind. She hadn't thought of Miss Smoochy in years. There was only one thing to do.

^%#$^%

MEANWHILE IN REFORM SCHOOL:

Ten years is a heck of a long time. A lot can happen in ten years. Let us now visit Blinko and Elvis. Remember them? They have been locked away in Reform School all this time. And let's not forget that they have been under the supervision of a clown supremacist, the Warden. Two kinderclowns, sentenced as murderers, now grown into teenage clowns the likes of which the world has never seen. Take Blinko, for instance. Blinko is all of sixteen years. He is huge for a clown. Nearly six-foot tall and a solid 250 pounds, all muscle. His impish looks have been traded in for a chiseled clown's face. He wears a scowl. No smile on this one. He is a stern and disciplined individual. His tinker is full of the rhetoric of the Notsee Party. He is the leader of a small army…an army created by the Warden out of the social misfits and lost youth sent to his Reform School.

And, what about Elvis? Turns out he is no wuss, but not quite as big as Blinko, and with twice the brains. Elvis is the mastermind behind everything Blinko does…Elvis, hater of mimes…Elvis so full of hate that he needs to fill Blinko's head with it just to have room for his own.

We are talking about two serious clowns here…powerful clowns. Two clowns that every clown in Reform School looks up to…role models…Sicko's boys.

Yes, Blinko and Elvis have heard all about Sicko. He is their hero. He is the clown that's going to be there for them when they get out of Reform School…Sicko the

Clown, who wrote the book on clown supremacy…"Mime Kampf"…Blinko and Elvis's Bible. Yes, a lot can happen in ten years.

"It's midnight," said Elvis. "Time to go man, they'll be waiting for us."

Blinko was wiping the last bit of shaving cream off his head while Elvis was busy combing up his greasy black pompadour.

"Hand me my toilet seat, would ya?" asked Blinko.

Elvis handed it to him. Carefully and honorably Blinko slipped the toilet seat over his head to hang around his neck. His and Elvis's were special party seats of shiny black wood with golden swastikas on their centers. The two teenage, skinhead clowns were in full ceremonial dress. It was a grand day for both for tonight they would be served their walking papers.

Now ready, willing, and able, the two walked down the cell block towards the auditorium. Elvis followed Blinko. Elvis now stood five foot nine and weighed in at 175 pounds. His feet were impressively huge for a sixteen year old. He was lean and strong and one of the most dangerous clowns in the school with the exception of Blinko, who was THE most dangerous clown. Elvis was a good looking bozo and the floosies who visited him, one of the perks of high rank in the party, really liked the way his upper lip curled whenever he said "Baby" in his deep alto voice. His blue eyes and ink black hair made most of them old floosies just melt and that was only half his charms.

Blinko, on the other hand, didn't like the floosies much. He didn't like anybody much except for Elvis who he probably liked a little too much. But that's to be expected in juvenile prison. Blinko had been working out for ten years and was a tough clown. He had more gusto than a keg of malted tutti-fruity and was so macho that he felt that cavorting around like a pansy with the floosies was beneath him. When the floosies came to his cell, he usually made them lie on the floor like a rug so he could prop his feet up on them like furniture. In fact, that's what he had been calling the floosies for years…furniture.

Blinko had the whole Reform School under his right boot and was saving his left for the outside. Today was the first day of the rest of his life. He and Elvis were walking out of the joint. Now, the two stood at the outside of the double doors leading into the auditorium. Blinko straightened himself from the top of his shaved head to the bottom of his knee high jack boots. Elvis spoke:

"I'll push the button" which he did. It rang an alarm in the auditorium so that the troops would snap to attention. Elvis turned to Blinko.

"Chest out, shoulders back, chin up…lets move!" And they burst through the doors to the sound of applause.

The auditorium was elaborately decorated with Notsee Party logos and paraphernalia. Huge swastikas emblazoned on giant red banners hung from the rafters. There were over 800 inmates present in the auditorium. They were arranged in neat rows in order of the youngest to the oldest, every clown wearing a Notsee Party toilet seat around their necks. Even the littlest kids had potty training seats for a perfect fit. Every boot spit shined, every pom-pom puffed, every brace taught, every head shaved. It was quite a spectacle. The room was full of electricity. There was a certain power in all this ceremony and stilted imagery.

The room fell silent as Blinko and Elvis, the highest ranking clowns there, inspected the legions for the last time. Blinko barked an order to about face. Had this order been given to a similar group of everyday clowns, the troop would have fallen all over themselves in a pile of idiocy. The fact that this did not happen stood as a testament to how well the years of training and mind conditioning had worked. Sicko and the Warden watched the proceedings from a secret window in wait of their own grand entrance. Sicko turned to the Warden saying:

"You will, of course, be handing the boys directly to me."

The Warden grunted an acknowledgement as he shot a much-needed sobering blast of Obvious into his jugular. Sicko smiled at the sight of it all. His master's plan was proceeding well.

It was now time for Blinko's speech. This made him nervous. Despite how tough he was, Blinko had trouble speaking to large crowds even if he had it all written down so he handed his speech to Elvis who had no such phobia. This was how it usually went so Elvis said nothing and simply took the paper from Blinko.

Elvis stepped up to the podium and began clearing his throat. Elvis spoke out in a clear and deep voice of a timber:

"Two, four, six, eight, just who is it that you hate?" said he.

"One, three, five, seven, kill a mime and go to heaven!" said they.

"Blood, guts, kah-kah too, see a mime, what do we do?" said he.

"Broken teeth and bloodshot eye, pretend to kill 'em, watch 'em die!" said they.

Then, in unison and in time with clapping and stomping of boots, the entire 802 strong clown supremacist army began to sing:

Sicko won't you lead the way
Guide us each and every day
How we love you through and through
We will even kill for you!

WE WILL EVEN KILL FOR YOU
(Stomp, Clap)
WE WILL EVEN KILL FOR YOU
(Stomp, Clap)

The doors crashed upon the walls as though pushed open by a titanic ill wind. All turned quickly to face the opening. An intense white light burst forth from the hallway spilling into the auditorium. There was a silhouette in the light. Silence dropped. Even Blinko and Elvis were stupefied by what they couldn't explain that was happening. *"Who could it be?"* they thought. Then came the familiar tune of the Notsee Party Anthem sung just loud enough for all to hear. The stranger's song gave away the stranger's identity to Blinko and Elvis immediately. They answered by repeating the anthem at the top of their lungs. Soon the rest joined in. It was only when the entire room was singing the mesmerizing tune that the stranger stepped out of the light and into the auditorium. He could be seen clearly now. It was their hero there in his utterly soiled bathrobe and matted fuzzy slippers. Around his neck was the original toilet seat with the law burnt upon it in bold lettering…ALL MIMES MUST DIE!

La-la-la-la
Lolly-la-lolly-la
Loyal we will be
To the Notsee Party
Sieg-hiel and Raspberry.

Sicko raised his right hand, arm out at 45 degrees, and then brought his right hand thumb to his nose and gave the raspberry. It was the salute of the Notsee Party. Eight hundred and two young clown supremacists returned his salute with their own raspberries. They continued to sing the tune over and over. Sicko began to lead them. His powers of persuasion were irresistible. He commanded a fraction of the crowd to be silent while the others sang the anthem. Then with a bold gesture he would call the other fractions in until he had them singing a round. This was nothing short of a miracle for never before in the history of clowns had such a large group successfully managed to sing a round, clowns were simply too retarded to pull it off. Everyone realized it was happening and this only added to the general euphoria and awe of their leader, Sicko. To them the clown gone bad really WAS a hero. This moronic little song of Sicko's had shown everyone the power of the individual within the group. You can't sing a round by yourself but you also can't sing a round unless you have individuals doing their own thing. This anthem was a perfect slice of propaganda.

Many skinheads began to break ranks compelled to slam dance as the others continued to sing. Soon there was a ferocious pit. One could hear it as heads smacking against heads, honkers bled with pleasure, bones broke under foot. But this type of violence was not that dangerous for clowns are quite indestructible. Blinko and Elvis watched as the pit grew larger and larger while heading their direction, towards the stage. Now in stage diving range, Elvis could resist no longer so he vaulted himself of the back of a fallen comrade. He landed perfectly on top of the teeming mass and floated there for a time before sinking into the tangle of arms and legs. Next, it was Blinko's turn. Blinko readied himself for what he intended to be his greatest dive ever. Eagerly, he shoved the podium out of the way and pushed the button that caused the diving board to slide out of its compartment. Then he was off. Sicko watched his protégée with an obvious induced slow-mo.

Blinko bounded towards the board and leaped four feet off the ground, sailing to that precise spot on the board for maximum recoil. Sicko could see that the board bent impossibly far down as all of Blinko's 250 pounds impacted on it. Then the clown assumed the ideal launch position as the board inevitably recoiled from its spine crushing position near the floor. Blinko reached the point of no return and flew from the board faster than a thrown cream pie. He twisted his body as gravity began to take hold at the apex of his jump. He looked down. They looked like ants down there. He began to calculate his landing. He judged the motion of the pit…estimated where the thickest of clowns would be seconds from now…then he went into his dive… jack knifed into a triple back double twist head first gainer then a backwards mobius followed by a neat tuck into a clown cannonball (the only safe way to land from such an altitude).

Blinko's impact with the slam-dancing clown supremacists was nothing short of spectacular…in perfect form and in complete devastation of those beneath him. All told, Blinko was totally unconscious with a triple concussion, three broken ribs, fractured jaw, two lost teeth, broken honker and big toe, broken right arm, bruised pelvis, and a dislocated shoulder and hip. When the quacktitioners arrived at the crater, it would take them twenty minutes just to untangle his pretzel-like condition. Those in his immediate vicinity were in a similar condition and those beneath him...well, they weren't in working order to say the least.

"Good show, Blinko!" said Sicko. "Good show indeed.

Blinko woke up a few hours later in the Reform School Infirmary where the nurse had just brought him some cereal and an envelope bearing the wardens seal. Elvis groaned as he sat up in the next bed over from Blinko's.

"It's our release papers, bro! We're free clowns!" Blinko tried to move. Even his hardened resistance to pain was no match for what the concrete floor had done to him, even if there had been a layer of clowns under him to break his fall. He tried to speak but his jaw was wired too tightly. Elvis could still talk though his collapsed lungs and brain damage made it difficult. He looked at his badly injured friend and spoke:

"Who was it that said that the price of freedom is high? I'll agree to that, ya with me?"

Blinko could only wiggle a toe.

Chapter 22
Ding-A-Ling Supreme

It was some of the most oppressive weather the Supreme Ding-A-Ling could remember. The humidity made his awkwardly fitted joints ache and he had been wearing a sad face since he had gotten himself out of bed. Now, he sat within the walls of the most humorous place on earth, deep inside the Vatican's Golden Big Top. He was looking up at the most wonderful mural painted on the ceiling, 15 meters above. His eyes followed the length of its brightly colored depiction of the Lord and his heavenly deeds throughout the centuries beginning with the Clown Reformation. He gazed in awe of the size of the Lord's gigantic clown boots. His tiny brain burst at the sight of God's plaid pantaloons. He savored every tiny painted fiber of the Lord's pom-poms. But he used his imagination to fill in the misty spot where the Lord's face should have been.

It was said that the artist left out the Lord's face, for he had never seen it. He must have thought it blasphemous to make one up. The truth was that he had fallen to his death from the high scaffolding before completing the work, but that was not the stuff of legend. Anyway, the Supreme Ding-A-Ling did his best to fill in the misty spot and being that he was the stupidest clown on the planet, a requirement to achieve his rank in the World Circus, his idea of the face of God was utterly unoriginal and cliché. Therefore, his version of the Lord was a silver-headed, bearded old clown with a crinkled and fading red honker. The Supreme Ding-A-Ling also imagined the Lord's eyeballs, which were not surprisingly large, and unknowing and blank, suggesting his infinite retardation.

"As it should be" thought the Ding-A-ling, a thought that used up the last bit of brains he had after imagining all that.

The Supreme Ding-A-Ling's thoughts on the mural were then erased when he realized that he had looked upwards, head tilted as far back as his neck bone allowed, for so long that he had gotten it stuck that way. This was not unusual because clowns could get everything stuck that way if they were not careful. There wasn't a clown alive that as a kinderclown hadn't gotten his eyes stuck while crossed. Of course, this happened to his neck every time the Supreme Ding-A-Ling looked at the mural so there was already a Disciple of Grand Lunacy there waiting to fix the Poobla.

The disciple mounted the clown's face forward and grasped his head in both hands. Then, he placed his left boot on the Pooblas chest for leverage. As usual, there was the obligatory count from one to three. A loud popping noise resounded in the great hall and immediately the disciple slipped out through a back door. Fixing the Supreme Ding-a-Lings neck hurt the Poobla like anything and he didn't like for any clown to see him cry. There in the vast expanse of his sitting room, his sobs and sniffles echoed and reverberated until the room sounded like a handful of cry-babies had joined him.

Presently and without warning there came a deep and bellowing voice from out of nowhere.

"Aw…quit your crying, my faithful fool!"

The Poobla was visibly shocked and began wiping the tears from his freshly bloodshot eyes.

"Who said that? Who's there?"

"It was I, you dummy! Do you not recognize the voice of thou Lord?"

"Oh my God!" shouted the Ding-A-Ling, as he fell out of the chair and onto his knees. He clasped his hands together and began to plead. "Forgive me, oh, Lord! I had lost my sense of humor and was crying in thou temple. Please have mercy!"

The voice answered promptly. "Fear not, my servant, there is a plain and simple reason I have manifested myself here today and it has little to do with your crying in the temple."

There was a deafening thunderclap and the Lord appeared before the Poobla. The Supreme Ding-a-Ling gazed upon the Lord who towered as high as the ceiling before him in gigantic boots, plaid pantaloons and pom-poms. To his amazement, the face of the Lord looked exactly as he had imagined. Suddenly, the Poobla was overwhelmed with shame and he prostrated himself before the Lord so deeply that he mashed his honker on the floor, breaking it.

"*I like this clown...*" thought Satano, realizing with this kind of cooperation and blind faith, his task that day was going to be easier than he thought. His charade came easier now that he knew the subject was completely convinced he was in the presence of God rather than the Devil himself.

"Have not thou noticed a predominantly blue feeling within ye ridiculous being?" harkened the Devil.

"Uh-huh" said the groveling clown. Satano didn't bother to tell him it was merely a symptom of the Poobla's badly swollen neck vertebrae that was causing him to feel depressed, due to the constant nagging pain. The Supreme Ding-A-ling had gotten his neck all out of whack looking up at the mural over the years.

"And, what about the general population of faithful followers of the Doctrines of Grand Lunacy world wide who await your guidance in these troubled times? If you're feeling sad, imagine how they must feel!"

"I know…I know!" the Poobla moaned.

It was taking enormous concentration for the Devil not to laugh at this pathetic clown prostrated before him. "It's the end of the world!"

"Huh?" said the Poobla, "What? Now?"

"Well, almost anyway."

The Poobla was as deeply confused, as he was frightened out of what little wits his poorly designed brain could manage. Now, he was totally open to suggestion.

"You can save the world, my child. Fear not. It is not too late."

The Poobla began to boil over with thankfulness. He crawled to the Devil's position and began licking his gigantic boots. It made the Devil feel particularly evil.

"Oh, thank you, Lord…thank you…thank you…thank you! Tell me. What must I do to save the world?"

The Devil smiled at the clown. "Nah, I'm not telling you, you'll just screw it up."

The Poobla became hysterical, clawing at the Devils pantaloons. "Please, Lord, please! Give me a chance…"

"Nope can't do it. I need a real clown not a big cry baby like you."

The Poobla came to his feet. "I'm not a big cry baby, really I'm not…"

The Devil was just getting started as he toyed with the easily manipulated Poobla.

"Not a big cry baby, huh? Well, then, let's see you punch yourself in that broken honker of yours without crying."

The Supreme Ding-A-ling knew all about the tests of faith that god had asked many times of his faithful children.

KA-POW!!

The Poobla's fist landed hard on his honker. First, a small explosion of sugary blood. Then the recoil as the honker collapsed under fist. Synaptic messenger impulses shot out across nervous pathways, erupting into the pain center of his under developed mind. The response was swift...red alert...battlestations...all tweety birds on deck...birds which promptly flew out of his ears to orbit his skull as his honker popped back out from its inverted state. Then came the unbearable urge to spill tears as the relief valve for the super heated sting burst open. Yet somehow, and to the Devil's amazement, the clown didn't cry. He couldn't for he thought the whole world was depending on him.

"That idiot ain't crying!" thought the Devil. A snap of the fingers and suddenly the clown's arms became possessed and with another snap the clown's arms began to violently punch him in the face like a stampede. Each blow skidded the clown back an inch until eventually he was backed up against the wall, his body held up by the force of the never-ending blows. Finally, the Devil released his control over the poor Poobla's body and the clown's arms fell limply to his sides exhausted from the thirteen rounds worth of punches thrown. This revealed his face which looked like a plump roasted hotdog married to ground beef with two wrinkled raisins for eyes. Still, the clown shed no tears for his tear ducts had been thoroughly destroyed by the punishing blows.

"Ow!" said the Poobla.

The Devil took a good look at the clown's face. This would never do. The Poobla would be permanently disfigured. Even clowns would never follow a freak like this one. He would have to fix him up.

"This might hurt a bit" said Satano as he grabbed the clown's head in both hands and shoved it completely inside his torso, submerging his arms up to the elbow. They made a squishy sound as he removed them. The now headless clown tore off running around the room crashing madly into the walls and various articles of furniture. Again, the Devil found it hard not to laugh, which he did this time. Eventually, the clown's head popped back out of his body. It was covered in a thick mucus membrane, which he clawed at. When it came away, the Poobla had a brand new head and one ten years younger at that. He eagerly ran to the golden bathroom with its golden toilet and golden wash basin to look in the golden mirror.

"Yuck!" exclaimed the Poobla. It was not an unusual remark coming from a clown unaccustomed to seeing a fresh head where the old one used to be. Fresh heads always appear a little too moist and plump as it takes several hours for one to cure properly. He felt his forehead. It moved with ease under the pressure of his fingertips like a sponge. Then he noticed how much younger he looked and forgot all about the pain and horror of it all. He ran out of the bathroom to fall before his Lord, kissing the god's gigantic boots saying:

"Thank you, thank you!" The Devil was only slightly amused by this.

"Shut-up and quit groveling. Don't you want to know how to save the Earth? Don't you want to know what is wrong with it?

"Yes, Lord, I will shut up and listen now."

"Have a seat" said the Devil. The Supreme Ding-a-ling plopped heavily into his throne. After all, with the pain from his ordeal and getting a fresh head, he thought about forgetting to ever get up again. He gazed at the Lord and was thrilled beyond words. He had met his maker and lived to tell about it. He would now be placed in a position to save the world. He would be a hero and they would erect statues of him so that pigeons could sit on his nose. The Devil could see that the Poobla was day dreaming. He began to snap his fingers.

"Hey!…hey!..pay attention here, idiot!" The Poobla sat up straight in his throne. Then the Devil's body disappeared and he became as a floating head growing bigger until it had filled the room. The enormous face grew solemn and serious, the sight of which cast fear in the heart of the Ding-A-Ling. The Devil could see that his words would sink in.

"There is a great force of evil at work on this world…so evil that those who practice it are literally left speechless. These witches and warlocks weld great powers… powers so great and beyond the realm of all that is good that it cannot be seen by clowns. They hide from society as they plan their evil deeds. Do not let their peaceful mannerisms fool you. These are the children of Hell…the spawn of Satan himself. Their potential for destruction is without measure. The time has come for all of my clowning children to know the truth. You are the keeper of the faith. You are the latest Supreme Ding-a-Ling to sit on the throne overseeing that the Doctrines of Grand Lunacy are spread to every corner of the globe and that the World Circus shall forever ride the holy choo-choo tracks spreading my word and my will as law to all sinners. But alas, nothing in the circus can save the souls of Satan's wicked servants. Now, you must lead the faithful to destroy them."

The Poobla, who had been listening with his eyes wide open in awe, blinked at the conclusion of the Devil's monologue. It hurt. His brain was at the point where it would usually be completely filled yet somehow it wasn't this time.

"Must be bigger than the last one" he thought. Unfortunately for him, his new brain was still no bigger than the pointy end of nothing sharpened so he still had not figured out who the evil THEM was despite all the clues.

"But, who are they, Lord?" pleaded the Poobla.

The Devil smacked his hand against his forehead in disbelief at the utter stupidity of the clown.

"They are the mimes, you frothing numbskull, who else?" Satan tried not to catch fire, which was the usual manifestation of this type of frustration. The Poobla was stricken then by the fact that he had not the slightest idea how to go about doing what the Lord bid him to. The Devil was way ahead of him.

"Do not worry. I don't expect you to lead the battle. Your job does not concern such things. You are expected only to lead the complete reformation of the World Circus.

"Reformation?" cowered the Poobla.

"Correct. The World Circus is dead. It only attracts clowns who are already so foolish from learning what the Doctrines of Grand Lunacy taught to them, that it only reinforces belief systems they already have."

"Huh?" said the clown, totally mindblown at this juncture. His brain was falling behind in the race for comprehension. The Devil continued:

"A new system of delivery is needed if we are to defeat the clever evil of the mimes. We need a place that will attract all clowns. A place that will satisfy the clowns need of reckless abandon and cerebral stimulation…a place that does away with the pretensions of the circus with all its tired rituals and get directly to the point. I am talking about the real thing…satisfaction guaranteed or your rue back… I am talking about the Carnival… the Carnival of Despair!"

The Poobla was of course puzzled.

"The Carnival of Despair? Why despair?"

"These are desperate times my friend."

"Oh."

Satan knew, of course, that everything he had just said had been absorbed into the dilapidated synaptic pathways of the Pooblas brain only to be lost in a jumble of confusion. Never-the-less…

"Got all that?" he asked, already knowing the answer was a resounding no. The clown lied.

"I think so…" Satan shushed him up as he took clown form in order to hand something to the Supreme Ding-A-ling. It was a little syrup bottle… the Obvious.

"For me?" said the Poobla.

"For you" replied the Devil.

"What is it?"

"It is the Obvious, that's what it is."

"What's it for?" quizzed the Poobla.

"It is for all my children here on Earth. It will clear your mind of impure thoughts and help you see the light. It will purify your soul and help you find the way to despair. Through this desperation, you will find the strength to defeat the evil miming forces of Satano. With the help of the Obvious, you will create the new rituals of the Carnival of Despair.

"How do I use the Obvious?" asked the clown.

Satano had perfected the confection. The new Obvious was one hundred times more potent, could be absorbed readily through the skin, and its effects where practically permanent.

"Simple. All you need do is bathe in it. A baptism you see. Accordingly, one of the main attractions at the Carnival shall be the dunking booth where all faithful clowns shall be baptized in the Obvious. This will be the primary step towards eternal salvation."

"You mean they will be saved by the Obvious?"

"Exactly. One way ticket to Heaven non-stop ."

"Give it here!" shrieked the Poobla swiping the tiny soda bottle.

He eagerly splashed the contents upon his face. Instantly, he was blasted into utter awareness so strongly that he nearly passed out as everything the Devil had said suddenly made perfect sense. The former fool thrust out his chest, shoulders back, while putting on a serious face. The Devil, still in disguise as a clown, was pleased as he produced a black book emblazoned with a shiny red swastika. It was a special edition of Mime Kampf by Sicko the Clown.

"You will find a complete overview of my plan here in this book. The book will of course act as the replacement for the Holy Comic book. Have it printed and distributed to all the Pooblas of the World Circus who shall take it upon themselves to distribute it freely to clowns at large. In the courtyard outside you will find that I have manifested a magic fountain that will supply you with a never-ending source of the Obvious. Baptize your disciples immediately and begin to spread my word."

With that, the Devil began to fade from view as the Poobla again fell to his knees repeating the holy law of God…"*all mimes must die…all mimes must die…*"

Then only the Devil's voice remained.

"One more thing…" said the voice.

"Anything, oh Lord!" said the Poobla.

"Shave your head."

The seeds of evil were now planted within the most sacred sight on Earth and into the planet's most respected and listened to clown…an Obvious clown now capable of spreading the Devil's evil plan world wide, all the time tricked into thinking he was serving God. How easily fooled a fool can be. It was the perfect plan.

AND SO IT WAS WRITTEN AND SO IT WAS DONE!

Chapter 23
Patooty and Petunias

When Nastina reached her destination, she was surprised to see that the orphanage, where she had spent her earliest years, was boarded up and abandoned. She had never heard of an orphanage going out of business. There most certainly couldn't have been a lack of orphans in Buffoonville. It's common knowledge that clowns make whoopi as often as possible and the fact that clowns are extremely accident-prone has always made for a steady supply of orphaned kinderclowns. Still, the condition of the place spoke for itself.

Nastina's adopted parents had told her that she had been found on the doorstep of the orphanage and that was all anyone knew about her natural parents. She had often wondered whom her biological parents were and what they might be like, if they were still alive. Privately, she wished that she could find them one day and go and live with them instead of her adopted parents, who she disliked for being so hateful.

Somehow, things were beginning to look on the up and up. The quest to find the mysterious package Miss Smoochy had told her about was taking her mind off the mess her life had become. Now, she could tell that from here on her life was about to be very different…just as the old angel had said.

Nastina had a natural high as she inspected the old abandoned building for an entrance. When she got around back, she discovered that the ground floor window by the door had recently been relieved of its boards. This was convenient for her. She wondered if Miss Smoochy had arranged it that way somehow.

Nastina tore her tutu a little on a half-bent rusty nail as she climbed in. The floor inside creaked as she hopped down onto it. The place smelled of dust and mildew. It was completely dark inside. She wished she had thought to bring along a flashlight but then she had not been expecting to go rummaging through a vacant dark building all alone.

It occurred to her to pray for some heavenly guidance from her guardian angel. Nastina was not really expecting an answer so she was pleasantly surprised when there came into her consciousness a kind of voice. It was in her mind like a fleeting thought. She found that she had to ignore it to hear it…kind of like peripheral vision. The voice was not giving clear directions but somehow she just knew where to go in the dark. It was like following one's nose.

She found a stair-well that went down into what she thought was most likely the basement. She used the handrail as a guide in the dark. When she arrived at the bottom, her feet made splashing sounds. There must have been a thin layer of water covering the floor, presumably from some leaking pipes. It was entirely dark down there and it was as though she was blind. Nastina felt around in the dark not knowing what exactly she was searching for. Again she was trying to rely on the weird sense she had recently come to possess. She found what felt like a file cabinet. She opened it and it made a terrible sound like the ones old, creaky, metal file cabinets make. She hesitated to put her hand inside not knowing what manor of creepiness could be inside. She swallowed her fear and plunged her hand in. She screamed as what must have been a bug ran up her arm. She shook it off, as any clown would, fearing that the bug might crawl inside her ear, something that all clown's fear.

It was a bit harder to reach in the second time after that scare, but she did. She found a package inside and took it, hoping that it was the one she was meant to find. After that, she made her way out of the building as best she could in the pitch dark where she intended to inspect the package by the light of the moon. It was old and covered in dust…a long forgotten file in an even more forgotten file cabinet. Carefully, Nastina went about untying the string which bound the top flap to bottom half of the envelope style folder. The string broke off instantly, being rotted. She lifted the flap which also broke of instantly. Then she pulled out the contents and began to examine them. At first glance she could see that it was mostly official papers relating to orphanage business. Then, Nastina found something that caused her eyeballs to pop out of her head.

Abandoned kinderclown, female, name: Nastina

As she put her eyeballs back in their sockets, Nastina couldn't believe what she was seeing. It was the official record of her arrival at the orphanage. Eagerly, she skimmed over the documents looking for the answers to all those old questions about where she had come from. The papers described how she had been found on the doorstep of the orphanage one rainy night. She liked that "rainy night" part because it sounded all mysterious. But that much she already knew. She was blown away by what she read next.

"…the child was dropped off by a couple of mimes. Apparently, a mime couple had given birth to a clown and were unable to care for it…"

After that there was little else of interest, mostly legal mumbo jumbo. Nastina set down the folder and placed her pretty head in her nimble hands. This revelation was some really heavy stuff. Her biological parents were mimes! No wonder she could never relate to her adopted parents and all their Notsee rhetoric. She WAS a mime or at least one on a genetic level. This simple fact went a long way explaining all the turmoil in her life.

Nastina remained there for a while, submerged in thought. She applied this important fact to all the equations and soon experienced a fundamental epiphany…a moment of truth. It was clear that she could never go back to her old life. She decided to be a runaway from that very moment on. To Hell with her fascist folks and all their bozokahkah. She knew then what she must do. As crazy as it seemed, she wished to seek out the mimes and try to find her biological parents.

The first order of business was clear. She was going to need a place to stay. Nastina probed her mind for a solution to that problem and decided her chances would be best down on the lower east-side. But, that was miles from where she was. She would need a ride and the bus wouldn't be running until morning. What she needed was a place to crash until then. Where to do so was pretty obvious. The cemetery was right across the street. Nastina gathered up the folder and made her way over to the cemetery. She ventured past the front gates on into the jumbled tombstones until she found a secluded spot. Then she lay down using the folder as a pillow.

It occurred to her how ironic it all was. Two hours ago, she was trying to put herself into the grave, now she would be sleeping on one. But, whose? She sat up and read the tombstone by moonlight. GRANNY SICKO "Granny Sicko," she said. Then she lay back down. She closed her eyes and let her mind wander. Eventually she slept…like a corpse.

%$#@$%

She dreamed: *There were mimes marching off to die in prison camps. Her adopted parents were at the gates prodding mimes into line with hot pokers. Then she was in the line crying…she was to die also…in the ovens…the silent screams of mimes burned alive….*

Then she awoke. Her thoughts were focused on the dream and the events of the previous day. She thought about what Miss Smoochy had said about destiny. Maybe that was it. Maybe her destiny was to find a way to lead the mimes out of their persecution and to start a mime rebellion against the Notsee's movement…to liberate the mimes from the camps that had recently been built. But, it was all beginning to be too much to deal with. The needed to focus on one thing at a time and that meant getting herself situated down on the lower east-side. This would mean getting hooked up with the other runaways and outcasts like her. In the distance, she could hear the busy morning traffic.

"I'm a good looking suzie, so getting a ride should be no problem!" she thought as she dusted the leaves out of her long, frizzy, blue hair. When she got out to the street, it seemed that she had been absolutely correct about that. No sooner had she stuck out her thumb and a decent portion of her patooty, than a three-jalopy pile up occur as the driver in front unexpectedly slammed on the brakes causing the others to crash into him. The clown sat in his jalopowagon as Nastina got in and he didn't even notice how badly damaged his jalopy was, for he was entirely concentrating on this blue haired suzie. He was in love.

Nastina played it cool, which was hard because the young clown had a tremendous stutter.

" Juh…juh…juh…jew…sh…sh…sure are..puh…puh…pretty good lookin!"

"Thank you," replied Nastina, as the stuttering clown stomped the gas peddle, the jalopy leapt forward, pulling into traffic.

"Wuh…wuh…wuh…wanna..guh…guh…get…mare…married?"

"No, thank you." Nastina smiled.

"Puh..puh..puh…please?"

"I'm under age." Nastina turned the rear view mirror her way and examined her face for pimples to prove her statement. It turned out that there was one on her chin so she pointed to it. The stuttering clown saw it and stuttered:

"That's..guh…guh…guh….gross" he said. Nastina smirked and raised an eyebrow.

"Still want to marry me?" she asked.

"Suh…suh…sure!"

"No, thanks." Nastina sighed.

The stuttering clown shrugged.

"So wuh..wuh…wuh…wuh,…"

Nastina could tell he was never going to stammer his way out of this one and answered the question she suspected that he was trying to ask: "My names Nastina."

"Nuh…Nuh…Nastina! That's a …nuh…nuh…nice name."

"Thank you, wanna know where I'm going?" The stuttering clown nodded yes.

"The lower east-side…you going that far?" Again, the stuttering clown nodded yes. Nastina risked another wasted minute by asking "What's your name?"

"FFFrank!…Frank FFFFurter…buh..buh..but you can cuh…cuh…call me Frank."

"Pleased to meet you, Frank. Thanks for the ride. You gotta job?"

Frank nodded yes out of practice avoiding speech wherever possible.

"Good!" exclaimed Nastina, "would you give me some money?"

Abruptly, Frank pulled over to the curb and slammed on the brakes nearly causing another pile up. He leaned over Nastina's lap and opened her door.

"GGGG…ggget out!" Nastina was shocked at Frank's sudden turn of opinion about giving her a ride but she got out quickly. The stuttering clown puh…puh…putted away.

"Oh, well, I can see the lower east-side from here" she thought and began walking that direction. Unexpectedly, an ice cream truck came screaming to a halt beside her. The driver leaned out and stammered…

"Nuh…nuh…nuh…need a ride?"

Nastina sorta freaked out about another stuttering joker, but nodded yes, and went around to climb into the passenger seat.

"I'm going to the lower east-side okay?"

"Kuh…kuh…kay."

Nastina stared at the clown then asked "Hey, you got a brother?"

The clown shook his head no, then said:

"Would you…muh…muh…muh..."

"NO! I don't want to marry you?"

"Nuh…nuh…no! Would you muh…muh…mind going in back and…guhh...guh…getting us some ice cream sammichs?"

Nastina laughed and climbed into the back of the truck to hunt down the sammichs.

"It suh….suh…sure…is hot, ya know!"

Nastina returned shortly with the treats. By the time they were finished eating the sammichs, the ice cream truck was right in the middle of the lower east-side of Buffoonville. Nastina thanked the stuttering clown still quietly amused at the coincidence of riding with two stutterers that morning. She was standing in front of what could only be a titty-dancing joint. This was clear because of the painfully obvious façade. She read the sign: SLAMMY'S PLAYHOUSE.

There was a massive, two sided, metal, and half naked suzie with royal blue hair hanging above the side walk. There was a big red light bulb serving the suzie as a nose and two more red bulbs right where any respectable floosie joint owner would think to put them. The words koochie koochie koo blinked on and off in neon inside a giant bubble attached to the suzies mouth, which was wide open revealing its massive red tongue. She was missing several teeth, a feature which appealed to most clowns.

Nastina examined the posters inside the marquis. Each featured a topless clownette. Nastina could see her reflection in the glass. She looked a lot like the giant metal suzy right down to the royal blue hair. That's when Slammy himself came strolling out of his dive into the morning sun. He was after his morning paper, which he always bought from the paperboy that had taken over the business from the paperboy that Sicko had killed a decade ago. Then, Slammy laid eyes on the nubile young Nastina.

"Holy moly!" he said. Nastina knew he was talking about her. She was no stranger to the remarks of perverted clowns concerning her hot little body.

"You like?" she said, sliding her hand along her torso showing off the merchandise as it were.

"Like it? You're hired, lady!" said Slammy taking a few steps in her direction.

"Who says I'm lookin for a job?"

Slammy wasn't fooled by Nastina's tease in the slightest degree. He continued to sleaze his way over to her leaving a sleazy trial on the sleazy sidewalk.

"Well, excuse me, suzie, but there ain't exactly a large inventory of nice girls in this part of town and all the bad ones work for me. Tell me…are you bad?"

Nastina smiled. "As bad as I need to be."

Slammy shifted the toothpick in his mouth to the other side and slipped a sleazy arm around Nastina's waist.

"You match my sign sweetheart so I'll let you work for me and I won't even ask for the required proof of age, I like it that way."

Nastina smiled then swallowed hard. She needed the job if she was going to make it on her own and, even though she was technically a virgin, she knew she would probably have to sleep with this scumbag. But, he wasn't bad looking at least. What she didn't know was that Slammy wouldn't have touched her with a ten foot pole. He might hire an underage clownette but he wasn't stupid enough to make whoopee with one. They went inside the joint.

"So what's your name, chick?" said Slammy.

"Nastina, Sir."

"Well, Nastina, I'll introduce you to our girls. We got some really bad clownettes working here so you'll fit right in. You get serious? Plenty of candy 'round here."

Nastina tried to see in the dark because her eyes had yet to adjust to it. Slammy had no such problem because he had the layout totally committed to memory. Not to mention that his pupils were permanently dilated thanks to the Obvious. They made their way back to the dressing room which smelled of incense, perfume, lung candy. Slammy brought her to the last door and barged in without knocking. Slammy let out a whispered "oh boy".

"Got a present for you, girls. Nastina, this is Chesty, and the other is Dew Drop. Chesty, Dew…this is Nastina." Slammy gave Nastina a gentle shove in the direction of the dressing room, then left in search of a few bottles he could smash.

Chesty looked at the clock and said…

"It's nine o'clock, chicks…lets dance."

^%$#@^

SEVERAL MONTHS LATER

Nastina found her new job at Slammy's fulfilling, and it was the filling part that she liked best. Well, much could be said about that. Her relationship with Chesty and Dew Drop gave her sense of belonging, which was much needed in her upside down world. She discovered her own power over the clowns that patronized Slammy's and she thought she might like to lose her virginity to one of them when she got the chance. The problem there was that most of them were rather disgusting beings that smelled dirty with breath like cheap soda.

Regardless of the complexities of her job, the gig afforded her with plenty of rue which she spent some of on training herself in the martial arts of nincompoopery. In just a few months she had graduated up to plaid belt which meant that she was more than able to take care of herself. She felt it necessary to learn how to defend herself in light of what she was planning to do. Nastina's master at the nincompoop school was amazed at how fast she caught on to the art. Neither of them realized that she was genetically superior being the child of mimes, who although scapegoated to death, were superior in everyway in comparison to the average clown. That, of course, is why the clowns hated them so much. Then it was time for her to begin her secret mission.

The Notsees were all over the place these days and any mime foolish enough to get caught by one ended up in the camps if it lived at all. The only thing worse than being a mime left at the mercy of the party was being a clown caught hanging around with one. The enemy was one thing but being a traitor was another.

Nastina packed the few belongings that she had acquired while working at Slammy's and took off without saying goodbye. She had no idea how long she would be gone, and thought it best to leave things open-ended in case she had to come right back or something. Besides, being flaky was the most basic feature of the average floosie.

Nastina had learned that mimes had been forced underground ever since the first wave of fascism had swept the lands. Buffoonville's mimes were no exception. So, that is exactly where she went…underground into Buffoonville's sewer system. Nastina had squeezed herself down a storm drain on the street corner right in front of Slammy's. She peered down the length of the pipe, which was big enough for her to stand erect in. She could see the sunbeams, which came in from the subsequent storm drains down the street. She could see okay and began to traverse the pipes length. Deeper and deeper she worked her way into the complex maze.

The foul smells within a sewer are familiar to all. Multitudes of sinister germs, who take great pleasure in creating the offensive odors, live and multiply within the bile, their stench matched only by the excrements they call home. Clown poop just happens to be some of the stinkiest poop there is. Their diet being entirely sugar-based makes for some truly rotten kahkah. When Nastina took a turn down a particular pipe, the wicked smell hit her honker like a spring-loaded boxing glove. Her honker actually tried to climb inside her skull but to no avail. The smell was inescapable and the signal made it to her brain anyway. The message was then relayed to her stomach, which then politely heaved its contents, which only added to the mess already living in the pipe. Nastina barely had time to lean over and avoid vomiting on herself and her perfectly color coordinated clownsuit. She was soon thankful that she had voided the contents of her stomach early for the stench only got worse the deeper into the pipe she went.

Nastina was now depending completely on her flashlight and even it seemed to be attempting to recoil from the stink. Then, she thought she would die from asphyxiation when her lungs began to refuse to breathe the soiled air. But then, just as she thought she would keel over, she found that her honker could detect the faint smell of petunias. Petunias? She decided that she must be going mad. Never-the-less, the smell of petunias intensified as she trotted on.

Nervously she fidgeted with her flashlight and accidentally shut it off for a sec. To her astonishment, she noticed a dim illumination coming from way on down the pipe. Leaving the flashlight off to follow the dim sparkle, she made her way in that direction until she bashed her head on something really hard. Turning on her flashlight, she discovered she had banged her head on a pipe. There was a little sign on the pipe that said…WATCH YOUR HEAD.

Boy, it really hurt too. Nastina found a dry spot and sat down to rub the knot, which was getting bigger by the second. Her tinker throbbed and the sharp contrast of the flashlight against the darkness in the pipes was also giving her a headache. Rubbing her head, she listened to the sounds inside the sewer pipe. Countless different plinks and plops and drips and drops and that ever present flushing sound off in the distance somewhere. And then, she held her breath when she thought she heard footfalls splashing in the little river that ran the length of the pipe. Calming herself, she thought to turn on her flashlight but remembered some of her nincompoop training and thought better to leave it off. Chances were that they would see her light before she could see them so doing so would only have served to give her position away…whoever they were.

The footsteps were coming clearer now and suddenly two flashlight beams erupted into the darkness 20 meters from where she huddled. Often the beams of light jiggled and crossed paths, which told Nastina that they were being carried by more than one person. The beams continued to fatten as the strangers got closer to the junction where she was waiting. Nastina lay down on her stomach, stretching out flat, to minimize her surface area against the imminent illumination of her present location. Then, it occurred to her that her spot would be the most likely place the stranger's beams would land once they turned down her junction. She reckoned that one would turn his beam to the left the other to the right to inspect the tunnel in both its directions. The only safe place to be would be dead center of the junction itself. This would in effect be the blind spot and might afford her with a slight advantage should she have to tackle the two who were nearly upon her. Quickly as she could, she crawled to the optimum position.

Her plan worked, and no sooner had the strangers snapped their beams down the two sides of an empty tunnel, than did she leap up snapping her own flashlight beam in the faces of two mimes, momentarily blinding them. The two made no sound whatsoever but then being mimes, they could do nothing else but stand their with these dramatically horrified faces…miming their surprise, no doubt. Nastina, on the other hand, was so shocked she had screamed at the top of her lungs, making a sound which echoed a hundred times in the myriad of pipes. Two seconds later, she came to her senses and realized SHE HAD FOUND THEM!

The first thing she noticed about the two before her was how long they stood there looking shocked. They were really playing it up good. She could not identify their sexes but assumed the one she was looking at was female, for some reason. The next thing she noticed was her flashlight. The suzie mime was standing their holding out her arm in proper flashlight holding fashion, only her hand was empty, but her fingers appeared to be curled around something round…like a flashlight. Never-the-less, three inches from the end of the hand was a bolt of light just as if she was holding a flashlight, even though it was completely clear to Nastina the suzie was indeed holding on to nothing at all. *"Evidently, the mimes imaginary world manifested itself to some degree in clown reality,"* she thought. But then, that was the whole problem to begin with, wasn't it?

The male mime was now attempting communication. He draped his arm dramatically over his brow and patted his chest directly over his heart. Then the suzie pointed at herself and aped the male's mime, adding her own where she wiped imaginary sweat from her brow and began fanning herself. Then, the two of them began to clap their hands in Nastina's direction as they started to dance in a tight circle. Nastina seemed to understand what they had just said to her, IN MIME, and she then mimicked them with her own pantomime as if to say…"*you guys scared the Hell out of me, too, but I am glad we have found each other.*" By then all three of them were dancing. Clowns dig that.

Now, the mime suzie was giving Nastina the universal *come with us* hand signal so she did precisely that, as she followed them into the tunnel from which they came. Here, she learned the origin of the glow, which turned out to be imaginary lightbulbs hanging from the ceiling of the pipe in imaginary light fixtures. She also noticed that the smell of petunias had become much stronger. When they reached another junction, the mime suzie did the pantomime for *"I'm getting tired"* by throwing her arm over her brow and fanning herself and then walking in place stooped over, tired like. The male nodded in agreement and then reached into his pocket to produce a bit of nothing. Nastina tried to imagine what it could be. Then the mime placed the end of the bit of nothing into his mouth and began to huff and puff on it, obviously blowing the bit of nothing up into a much-inflated version. As he did this, he began to lean over as though the thing he was inflating was getting heavy. Finally, he mimed the sealing of the imaginary spout and then stepped back to admire his handiwork. Then he walked back over to the spot where he had left it and stepped over, mounting whatever it was. Dramatically, he lifted his right foot and then stomped down hard. It was then that Nastina had figured out what he was doing…the little mime was trying to start his imaginary motorcycle. He gave it another kick and then his whole body began to vibrate as he revved the imaginary and completely silent motor. Somehow, Nastina could swear she heard the motor running. She wondered if her genetic link to the mimes was allowing her to perceive their imaginary stuff. Then she had another epiphany. All she need do was imagine and she was one step closer to understanding how it all worked for them. She had mime power.

The mime suzie hopped on back of the imaginary cycle and, for a moment, Nastina wondered if they were going to make her walk. But then, she noticed the gestures of the mimes and she realized that there would be room for three on the cycle if there was a side car. She went to the spot where the sidecar should have been and thought hard to picture it in her mind. Shortly, she could see a ghost like image of the sidecar and it was into this ghostly image that she climbed into to find herself sitting six inches above the ground and for all practical purposes, suspended in thin air. The mime flipped an invisible scarf over his shoulder and they were off at great speed.

Nastina could feel the wind on her face. She could feel the intense vibrations of the motor. She could feel the bumps wherever the pipes joined. Then, she noticed the flowers. They were growing out of the cracks and nooks and crannies and wherever they could manage to cling to the surface of the tunnel walls.

> They grew upon the heaps of poop with toilet paper soil
> They grew in dried up urine, too, and thrown up castor oil
> They grew in places that no flower really oughta should
> It really made things cheerful and, for that reason, was good.

The flowers seemed to bow to her as they passed by. And, the further they went, the thicker the petunias grew until it was nearly impossible to tell they were deep in the bowels of Buffoonville's sewer system. Eventually, they came to what looked like a dead end.

Nastina stepped out of the sidecar as they came to a halt and likewise the two Mimes dismounted the cycle. The mime kneeled down and undid the valve stem of the inflatable imaginary motorcycle and his hair flew back as the air rushed out. It ended by making a farting sound. Then, he stuck the little bit of nothing back in his pants pocket and looked at Nastina then shrugged.

"End of the line, huh?" she said. The mime, of course, said nothing in reply and only nodded to her a negatory. Nastina was puzzled but didn't let it bother her for she figured these mimes knew what they were doing. Then, she looked down the pipe and noticed that all the imaginary lightbulbs and flowers were disappearing one by one and in their direction. She used her noggin and decided that there must be some actual limitation of the mimes imaginary power field. Then, she decided to ignore that and train her attention on the mimes. She turned around just in time to see the mime suzie step through what appeared to be a solid brick wall. Then, the male mime did the same but stopped short of finishing the job so that half of him stuck out of the wall. He was making the universal signal for "*follow me*" again then disappeared altogether.

Nastina stepped up to the brick wall and tried it with her gloved hand. It was solid as one might expect from a brick wall. So, this was to be her big test, huh? It was clear to her that all she needed was to exercise her mime powers to walk through the solid wall, just as the mimes had done. This she did, imagining that there was, in fact, nothing there to stop her and boldly she took a step right into the wall. She banged her honker up pretty hard and was no further along than before. Still, she kept trying imagining different things and eventually after imagining herself to be something like a liquid she managed to pass through.

The patient mimes where standing their waiting for her…thousands of them. Thousands of mimes, all dressed identically in black pants with stripped shirts, ballet shoes and berets, red suspenders and white gloves. There appeared to be a village there and the green hillsides were completely filled with flowering petunias. She ran down the hill and into the swarming mass of them. All wore smiles from ear to ear as they welcomed her into their clan. She felt light on her feet and, after looking down at them, found that somehow her gigantic and heavy clown boots had transformed into gigantic ballet slippers. She also found that she was now dressed in a mime's outfit rather than her garish clown's suit.

"I've made it!" she thought as she visually inspected those around her. It was then that she learned about how the mimes called the sewer system their Reality Well and used it for their own safety knowing clowns would never venture in. Nastina felt at home and perfectly at peace. It was then that she remembered an old nursery rhyme Miss. Smoochy had told her as a little girl:

Dreams will come true
As all dreams do
If you believe
You want them to…

Chapter 24
Where's My Dentist

Blinko and Elvis, now fully recovered from the injuries they had suffered during their release party, had gone through several bizarre episodes in the short amount of time they had been out of Reform School.

Reform School! Everything these two skinheads knew about life they had learned in Reform School. Both clowns had been so young when they were sent to Reform School that neither of them would ever realize they had been carefully brainwashed by the warden over the years.

The warden, being a Poobla of the World Circus, as well as one of the founding members of the Notsee Party with Sicko the Clown, had known what his mission was from the beginning concerning those two. That's why he had held loads of private discussions with them over the years disguised as therapeutic rap sessions. It was during these rap sessions that he had turned the boy's initial guilt over the death of Apache, the indian clown, into a base of power and self esteem for the two. As he said once:

"Indeed, it was wrong for you to have killed that little indian clown but had it been someone else, the murder may have been justified. You see, it is sometimes okay to kill someone if that killing serves the greater good of clown's civilization on the whole and serves God. That's right, sometimes killing serves the Lord."

It was this type of bozokahkah that created, in the two kinderclowns, the type of belief system one might find in a soldier and that was precisely the warden's mission: to create a war-like army of young clown supremacists to serve the party and its Fuhrer, Sicko the Clown.

The warden could tell that these two young and impressionable clowns, rather sophisticated for their age, would never fall for the teachings of the ridiculous World Circus, even as they pretended to accept circus teachings trying to fool him. Therefore, the warden, himself, used this knowledge of their true motivations to fool them. His mission called for a radical approach. So with these two, he left behind the comic styling of circus doctrines and experimented with a new form of rhetoric. The warden had begun the process with the concept of God.

"Tell me, Blinko...Elvis...who is God?"

"Some old clown up in Heaven" answered Elvis. It was as creative a response as he could muster. Being little clowns, neither had a real idea who God might be and could have cared less if not for having been forced to play the warden's game.

"Ah, but you see, children, that is a common misconception. Foolish clowns often place the Lord into a position of greater power when, in fact, this has no basis in reality."

At that moment, neither of the two had had any idea what the warden was talking about. The warden was simply using too many big words. Because of this, he gave them candy cigarettes to smoke. For the kinderclowns to be able to grasp these concepts, they needed to quit clowning around and get serious. The warden had giggled to himself watching the two cough and choke as they tried to smoke lung candy for the first time. At any rate, despite their amateur attempts, both did become quite serious in the end. The candy changed their perception of everything, of course, and from then on played a key role in their spiritual awakening.

"God does not reside only in Heaven, not always, it is the part of God that resides within you that's what's important. When you look in the mirror, it is not his judgment that should concern you, it is your own self-judgment that matters most. That is, in effect, how God judges us...by giving us the power to govern ourselves according to our beliefs."

And thus did the warden fool the two clowns into listening to him instead of them just pretending to. He knew they would like the idea that in a small way they were actually God. The fact, they were now completely serious sealed the deal.

The years passed and the rhetoric became the truth to them. They, as elders in the reform school, spread these new ideas and truths to the others. As they got older, the warden introduced them to the Obvious which produced a dramatic change in their ability to make use of what they had learned and he gave them certain powers over the others, ultimately setting up a system inside like that of a true military. They were the Notsee Youth.

^%$@$#

The Obvious made Blinko and Elvis as serious as two clowns could be and its use encouraged the boys to develop their personal power trip...build upon it...until they were as powerful within the reform school as they believed themselves to be. At the base of the power trip was an infallible belief in God. Not to believe in God was to not believe in one's self. Accordingly, to do God's will was to do for one's self. And doing God's will was a simple matter. There was really only one idea that the warden had instilled within the two, as Sicko had told him to do, as Satano had told Sicko...the primary commandment of God: ALL MIMES MUST DIE

Mimes were the minions of the Devil. Mimes were the true source of all the evil in the world...mimes, who left their invisible landmines all over the place. Blinko and Elvis were taught to believe this practically all their lives.

> To hate a mime was to obey God.
> To obey God was to be true to one's self.
> To be true to one's self was to be honest.
> To be honest with one's self was to be without sin.
> To be without sin was to live in innocence.
> To live in innocence was to create habits by its grace.
> And, by those habitual graces to create a lifestyle.
> And, by that lifestyle to create a destiny.

These two were well on their way to that self-created destination. All they need do, to be rewarded within the system, was hate mimes. To hate is a simple thing really. Not to the average clown, of course, for they are too foolish for that, but to those who have gotten serious....that's different isn't it? And, these two had been serious since they were kinderclowns, so it was easy for them. Hate was serious business and business was good, thanks to Sicko.

Anyway, after leaving the Reform School hospital, right after bidding their underlings a final farewell, Blinko and Elvis caught a cab down to the lower east-side of Buffoonville where they were to meet with Sicko. Blinko and Elvis were extremely excited about it. From now on, they could be at Sicko's side whenever they liked.

The original clown gone bad had given them directions to his favorite east-side floozie joint. Being Sicko's soldiers was one reason why Slammy didn't charge them a cover for the afternoon show. Blinko, upon entering the club, being a total party member down to the core, totally ignored the half-naked floozies and made a beeline straight for the first bald clown he saw, thinking that any skinhead clown would be eager to talk propaganda with him. Elvis, on the other hand, went directly to the bar to get a stiff soda.

As it turned out, the bald clown was just a drunken old fart too sloshed to interrupt Blinko as he barked out lunatic party slogans and hate drivel. The drunk just said "Yeah…yeah…" now and then, as Blinko ranted and raved.

Meanwhile, Elvis had his eyes peeled on the dancing floosie who was lying on her back gyrating against a chrome pole between her legs. Elvis folded some of the rue the warden had given him for release money, down the length-wise, and made way to a front row seat. The regular drunks were used to getting thrown around by young jokers and being clowns only laughed it up when Elvis tossed a few aside to steal their seats. Elvis took his attention off the dancing floosie for a second and looked for Blinko. He found him looking kinda out of place with a toilet seat around his neck standing erect sieg-hieling some old clown who was just starting on a fresh soda.

"Now, that's one loyal party member!" he thought, amazed that his friend could ignore the gyrating floosie. He took the folded rue and stuck it under the floosie's garter.

Slammy watched his business carefully with Sicko at his side. Both were on the secret side of the two-way mirror. This gave them an ideal and concealed vantage point within the club. Had a regular clown done what Elvis did next, they would have watched a gigantic bouncer beat the clown to his senses but instead they just watched Elvis, one of Sicko's boys, snatch the floosie off the stage, throwing her over his shoulder. The floosie didn't seem to mind and told the handsome Elvis clown to make for the back door where her dressing room was. After all, Sicko had given her a miniature case of miniature soda bottles for her troubles.

Sicko knew what his boys would be after. Sure the warden had always brought floosies to the Reform School to reward certain inmates with from time to time, but that was never enough to satisfy the appetites of the youth, which was why he had staged this first meeting with his best soldiers at Slammy's.

Sicko had gone over the boy's files from Reform School in depth. He had played an outside but strong role in their upbringing and wasn't about to stop with their education now that they were free. These two were going to be commanders in his youth brigade. Being the genius that he was, his trickery and strategy were excellent and he had had it arranged so that everything these two would experience, immediately upon their release, would only serve to reinforce their loyalties to the party and Sicko personally. He knew that Elvis' thing centered around clownette flesh but that Blinko got off on power alone. That was why Blinko was ideal for leadership…nothing could distract him from party politics, Hell, that's all he cared about, that's all he was inside. Notsee to the bone.

Sicko had seen to it that there was no one in Slammy's that could be recruited. Nothing but pickle-brains and sore-noses, this would leave Blinko ripe for some real action. Sicko gave a nod to a waitress who quietly left as he watched her jiggle her way over to Blinko who was now completely bored to tears.

She tapped his shoulder.

He turned.

She spoke:

"Follow me. Sicko will see you now."

Blinko grew noticeably excited and stomped his boots behind her as she led him past the two-way glass and into the office. He entered and was not repulsed in the slightest at the sight of the wretched clown gone bad. Any normal clown would have run to the phone to call the meat wagon for the stiff. But Sicko's corpse like appearance was not unusual for a clown as addicted to the Obvious as he was…not to mention the wear on his soul from being in league with Satano and all.

"Get serious, Son" said Sicko, pointing at a syrup shooter sitting on Slammy's desk. Blinko did as he was told. After, with his tinker throbbing in complete sobriety, Sicko led him outside to a waiting Jalop-o-zeen.

"But what about Elvis?" inquired Blinko. The two had not been separated for more than a few minutes in the past decade. The thought of leaving without Elvis was unacceptable.

"Lets not worry about him for now, Blinko…he is in good hands, I assure you…come now."

The two were forced to squeeze in the jalop-o-zeen for there was already a third in the back seat. The jalop-o-zeen was four times as large as the average clown's jalopy but it was still three times smaller than the smallest pre-reformation economy class vehicles. When he got in, Blinko at first thought the third clown was the warden, for the clown wore the robes of a Poobla. But as it turned out, it was someone else.

"Blinko" said Sicko, "this is the Supreme Ding-a-ling." Blinko was completely blown away by this announcement and also at the sheer size of the jalop-o-zeen. He took the Supreme Ding-a-ling's hand and kissed the Supreme Ding-a-ling's plastic Supreme Ding-a-ling's ring, which was in the shape of a toilet seat. It matched the full sized golden one he was wearing around his neck.

"Your worship…it is truly an honor" he said. Sicko looked at the two of them and was thankful that his funny bone had disintegrated. The situation was calling for hysterics. Here was a young clown and an old clown who both thought that they were serving God, thanks to careful manipulation on his part and on the part of Satano, himself. The situation was truly laughable but Sicko had forgotten how to do that. It was times like these, when the perfection of his master's plan was so evident, that really made him love being a minion of the Devil. Sicko spoke:

"Blinko, I am sure you are wondering what brings the Supreme Ding-a-ling, himself, to Buffoonville."

The jalop-o-zeen started on its way as Sicko continued:

"See, the Supreme Ding-a-ling here saw God a couple months ago, and God told him it was the end of the world!"

Blinko choked on his own spit as it went down the wrong pipe. The Supreme Ding-a-ling began to pound on his back. Red-eyed and hoarse, he croaked:

"End of…the world? What? Now?"

"Well, sort of," replied Sicko, "But, God told the Supreme Ding-a-ling…Hell, old man, you tell him yourself." The Supreme Ding-a-ling sat up straight as he could manage in the cramped compartment of the jalop-o-zeen and composed himself, in a saintly fashion reserved for pompous fools in funny hats, then said:

"God, himself, came to me in the Vatican and told me that I must reform the World Circus. There is a great force of evil at work here on Earth, the mimes. God told me that I should make a pilgrimage to Buffoonville to begin his work."

Blinko had his voice back and posed a question: "Here? Why here?"

The Supreme Ding-a-ling was quick to respond: "Because…all mimes must die, my son. They are the wicked spawn of Satano and Sicko the Clown, here, just happens to be the best chance this world has of ridding itself of Satano's evil scourge as is God's will. For he is the leader of the Notsee Party, author of Mime Kampf, the definitive authority on this matter and you, my son, are to be his second in command!"

"Congratulations!" said Sicko, handing Blinko a box, which had somehow gone unnoticed by him in the confines of the jalop-o-zeens miniscule coach. Blinko tried to open it but was unable to move enough to do so. The feat was accomplished only after the Supreme Ding-a-ling to his left and Sicko to his right opened their windows and leaned out.

Inside the box was an exact replica of Sicko's holy toilet seat. Blinko was moved almost to tears.

"It's…it's just what I've always wanted…and I solemnly swear to serve the party as is my duty towards God and…" Sicko cut him off, not being one to go for the pathetic speeches of brainwashed teenagers, saying:

"Okay, we get the idea."

Sure he made up all the rhetoric of the party but that didn't mean he wanted to have to sit there a listen to his own bozokahkah. The Supreme Ding-a-ling broke out a gilded cigarette case and then all three partook of what could only have been the finest smokable candy Blinko had ever tasted. After all, he was used to that Reform School low grade lung candy. He could tell already how much he was gonna enjoy life on the outside.

"Your Holiness, that's some tasty candy!"

The Supreme Ding-a-ling took a toke then replied: "Freakin' A! My office does have its rewards." He passed the confection over to Sicko. Soon after, they arrived at their destination.

It took some work for them to untangle themselves from their pretzel like positions in the back of the jalop-o-zeen but in the end they managed to do so in record time. Then the three solemnly walked from there over to Sicko's funhouse before them. The place was entirely surrounded by scaffolding swarming with skinheads who were obviously doing some type of construction work.

"You'll have to excuse this mess, fellows, but I am converting my funhouse into a type of bed and breakfast" said Sicko.

The Supreme Ding-a-ling responded: "I imagine it will make entertaining your many guests more convenient."

"Precisely, your Eminence. With the place being the headquarters for the party and the conversion of the World Circus, it is going to get pretty busy around here and I do need my privacy. Guests will have access to all areas with the exception of the basement which will serve me, as it has for years, as my private domain. The penalty for invading my space will be death."

By then the three of them had entered the funhouse. Sicko removed his toilet seat and hung it on a meat-hook protruding from the wall. The Supreme Ding-a-ling and Blinko did likewise. The Supreme Ding-a-ling also took off his stupid hat, placing it on the merry-go-round. Sicko messed around in the kitchen then came into the playroom with a bottle of bubbly.

"A toast to the beginning of our salvation!" he said passing dirty glasses to them. They held the filthy things up.

"All mimes must die!" said Sicko.

"ALL MIMES MUST DIE!" repeated the others. They drank deeply.

Sicko pulled a drape, which was separating the room from the adjoining one, which had up to then been hidden from view. Standing in the center of the room was a mime! Blinko instantly pushed his way in front of Sicko and the Supreme Ding-a-ling and assumed the defensive posture of a nincompoop, which explained why he was standing on one leg with his thumb in his mouth.

"Don't worry, Blinko…" said Sicko, "he can't get to us. You see he is trapped inside an invisible box."

"Clever!" said the Supreme Ding-a-ling. "Using his own wicked sorcery against him, are you?"

"He's using it against himself" said Blinko, flatly as he relaxed a bit and removed his thumb adding: "We can't use their powers but we CAN trick them into using them to our advantage. I learned that in Reform School."

It was Sicko's turn. "Ever seen a live one, your Holiness? I know that Blinko, here, hasn't."

Blinko spoke: "Only in my copy of Mime Kampf…you know the one…the picture of the mimes running off with a clown baby for their sacrifices."

The Supreme Ding-a-ling shuddered noticeably. "I have seen the little Devils but never this close!"

Sicko swept his hand in the mimes direction. "Why don't you both take a real good look?"

Blinko and the Supreme Ding-a-ling made their way to the mime trapped in his invisible box. The mime stood there testing all sides of the box desperately seeking an escape. There wasn't one he could imagine.

"Don't get to close or you might get stuck in there with him" said Sicko, as he shot some syrup into his jugular. Upon approaching the mime, Blinko began to feel strange. It was the void. The empty place he was helpless against in emotional moments like these.

His eyelids began to spasm.
Veins bulged from his forehead.
Smoke poured from his ears.
Two jets of flame erupted from his nostrils.

The Supreme Ding-a-ling had no idea what was happening to the young skinhead. He jumped back shouting: "Look out, he's possessed!"

Sicko shook his head no then said: "Hell, no, he's not possessed, he's just foot-stomping mad is all!"

Blinko stood directly in front of the mime that was cowering in an invisible corner of his box. It's child-like face was a contorted mask of horror and fear. It knew that the end was near. Blinko's arm began to rise until he was pointing an accusing finger in the direction of the mime.

"YOUUUUUUUU!!" he said, in a sinister voice, "MUST DIEEEEEE!!!" Blinko's hand formed an imaginary gun.

666

Somewhere in the ghettos of Hell, Death got a call from his Inter-Dimensional Answering Service. He pulled out his file-a-fax but there were no appointments.

"Crrrrap!" he hissed. It was beginning to become difficult to keep up with all of the souls he was to collect lately. He was wishing that Death, Jr. were old enough to help out. He couldn't wait for that. He grabbed his reaper.

"Gotta go!" he said spitting in his ugly wife's face.

"*HE SPIT ON ME!*" she thought as little hate bubbles gurgled their way out of her moldy head.

Death got to Sicko's funhouse by way of materialization in a flash but was unseen by all clowns except the mime whose soul he had come for.

"*AW!*" thought death. He knew that the mimes soul was destined for Heaven and lately Heaven didn't pay, just another example of God's financial troubles. When the mime saw Death it pretended to poop its pants.

^%$#@$

Blinko's hand trembled.

"BANG! You're dead!" said he.

"Die! Die! Die! Die!" Blinko's thumb snapped repeatedly on his index finger.

He was filling the little mime full of imaginary lead. The mime of course imagined everything perfectly and reacted as though he had, in fact, been shot to death quite dramatically being the little actor he was. Finally, the mime took one last breath then exhaled his soul into the waiting hands of Death.

Death promptly gathered the mime's soul and then hauled patooty over to Heaven to drop it off at the Pearly Gates. St. Peter was there. Peter didn't like Death any better than he had the first time they met, which was on the day of his own departure from the flesh. Still, he didn't enjoy having to send Death away with yet another voucher for a soul received in lieu of hard Positrons/Negatrons.

Meanwhile, Blinko was getting back into his head. In the old days, he might have asked the others what had happened but he was sixteen now and had his pride to think about. Besides, after all those years, he had learned to exercise a certain amount of control over the trance and he was now able to remember most of what happened during one. Still, the trance turned him into a killing machine. Evidently, this time he had killed the little mime pretty good.

"All mimes must die" he said in a whisper.

"Shouldn't be no problems 'round here with you around!" said Sicko to Blinko, who was then rejoining them in the front room. The Supreme Ding-a-ling was terrified never having seen an act so terrible. Being a stupid clown, he had completely overlooked the reality of the "DIE" part of God's commandment. Obviously, it wasn't going to be a joy ride. He thought hard about it for the few seconds he was able to concentrate and decided that for the sake of a clownkind, he could probably kill one himself. No doubt in the end, he would probably have to. Whatever had to be done to obey his god would be done. Still, the violence repulsed him.

It wasn't the first mime to die at the hands of the party but it was Blinko's first kill and he really liked it…liked it a lot in fact. It went down good like cold fruitys on a clowndog afternoon. Old clown tendencies tried to force their way into his consciousness. A tiny drop of guilt fell into his heart. He felt it pang. But the warden had taught him well. Silently, he thought the right thought. *"It's okay to kill if the killing serves the greater good of clown civilization and the will of the Lord."*

^%#@^%

Later, Elvis left his floosie when Blinko showed up all hot under the collar. Elvis was still pretty hot under his own collar and eager to brag. He mistook Blinko's enthusiasm for something other than what it was.

"You get you some too?" he said.

"No…No…Elvis… I killed a mime!"

"What? Where? Tell me!"

"At Sicko's…dude! The Supreme Ding-a-ling was there! I killed that little mime right in front of the Supreme Ding-a-ling!"

"The Supreme Ding-a-ling? You're kidding me."

"Nope, right in front of the Grand Poobla of them all!"

"So, you killed a mime right in front of the Supreme Ding-a-ling, huh?"

"Yup. Liked it too. You'll see. Wait till you get your chance to kill one. I did 'em just the way they taught us. I made a pretend gun out of my hand and blew him away simple as pie!"

"Clown…so what's up anyway?"

"Sicko sent me back here to get ya, and, dig this…Sicko's got a zeen, dude."

"A zeen? Propaganda, huh? You seen it?"

"No, bro, I mean a jalop-o-ZEEN, wait till you see how big it is. We could almost fit all three of us in the back!"

"Wow, then Sicko is really gonna have us stylin' it, huh? This is so rad clown. I'm freakin'g out."

"Me too, bro, and dig this…the Supreme Ding-a-ling and Sicko made me second in command of the entire Notsee Party here in Buffoonville! Can you believe it?"

Elvis felt a little bit jealous and kicked a bottle that was lying on the floor.

"Cool" he said feebly. Blinko could see that Elvis had his feelings hurt.

"You're gonna be my first officer!" Elvis perked up quick like.

"Right on! So, where's the ride?"

"Right out front." And they left.

On the ride back to Sicko's bed and breakfast, Blinko tried to inform Elvis with what little he knew about the reformation of the World Circus headed up by the Supreme Ding-a-ling. He didn't have many details to give but the two high fived it over the fact that they, by a bizarre twist of fate, had ended up in cahoots with the two most powerful clowns on Earth. This was history in the making. Why, they would be war heroes!

This revelation suddenly wore into them and Elvis prepared a whizz-bang to add to their mental awareness before getting over to Sicko's. There is a type of honor and self-evidence that can only come from being part of a lofty and noble cause. That is to say nothing of the enemy, which, of course, get crushed in support of such achievements. To this end, both clowns were busy imagining the future…a future where they were the rulers of a giant-clowns boot-stomping on the face of the mimes forever. It was then that they placed their youthful thoughts aside and took on the full responsibility that came with their destiny…bred from the age of five for this very moment in time, and now here they sat, at sixteen, welcoming their fate like a lost friend. Sadly, this friend would one day betray them for they knew not what they were really doing and for whom. Unbeknownst to them, time would eventually screw them over just like everyone else. STUPID CLOWNS!

%$#$%@

Anyway, the two went on, spending the next few weeks alternating between Sicko's bed and breakfast and Slammy's, where Elvis had gotten a little thing going with an older floosie.

&^$#^%

Ya know, there was another set of clowns in this story that had just served ten years on the Funny Farm. Whammo and Laymo, fathers of Elvis and Blinko.

The Farm was a whole different story than Reform School. Reform school was overseen by World Circus Pooblas, while the Farm was run by law enforcement officials...the REAL criminals.

Buffoonville County Funny Farm was run by Sargent Bilko. Bilko had taken the job two years after Whammo and Laymo's incarceration, under pressure from the Chief. The job of warden was dead-end and boring, consisting of filling out endless streams of paperwork and sometimes getting to yell at the convicts if the kitchen ran out of pudding and stuff like that. Bilko had lots of time to think, always stuck in his tiny office, not much bigger than the convict's cells. Bilko knew the reason he was serving his own brand of time on the Farm was due to the fact that he had foolishly taken his conspiracy theories to the D.A. in Buffoonville. He was hoping that the D.A. would take him seriously but the D.A. only called in the Chief who joined the D.A. as they both laughed in his face. After all, Bilko's report named almost every elected official and officer of the Keystones as co-conspirators. The trouble was that he was dead on right. He knew it and they knew it. That was why the Chief put pressure on him to resign his post on the force and to waste away running the Farm, a job nobody but nobody wanted.

But Bilko didn't let that stop him. For the past eight years, he had carefully documented all the corruption in Buffoonville. Now, with the arrival of the Supreme Ding-a-ling, and the knowledge of the Supreme Ding-a-ling's association with ringleader and head of the Notsee Party, Sicko the Clown, he had come to the conclusion that everyone in the world, but him, was in cahoots. This was why, after signing Whammo and Laymo's release papers and walking them out to freedom, he set his ballpoint on top of his 9000 page report and slapped a pie in his own sad face. AN HONORABLE DEATH FOR A TOTAL LOSER!

Whammo and Laymo, on the other hand, felt that this particular day was the happiest day of their worthless lives. And, just think how happy they would have been if they had known that total jerk of a warden had just committed suicide. Presently, the two were literally skipping down the deserted road back to town. The years on the Funny Farm had hardened them a bit but they didn't care about all the misery they had been through, preferring to embrace their new found freedom. As free clowns, they could re-enter society and do as they pleased within reason. But these were not reasonable clowns so they mostly had two things on their minds. First, was getting serious and the second was finding and killing their cheating wives who never once came to visit them on the Farm in ten years!

But all of this had been planned long ago, so neither of them were talking about it.

"Wonder what our boys are up to?" said Whammo.

"Wow, I almost forgot about them. They was why we ended up on the Farm in the first place," replied Laymo.

"Yeah. But they never answered our letters…wasn't that why we quit writing them?"

"Something like that…but maybe we'll run into them…they ought to be freed by now, just like us. Probably won't even recognize them little jokers who'll be full grown by now." Whammo socked Laymo in the arm.

"Screw you, Laymo! I'll damn sure know my own son when I see 'em. But we can do that later. First, I want to get serious and find my no good wife. Cheating, no good floosie!"

"Likewise…" said Laymo "Clown! I have a serious itch for the Obvious. It sure ran thin down on the Farm. I ain't been serious for so long, I damn near took up juggling." Whammo was about to respond to that when a jalopy truck full of pie-toting skinheads sped by them. The skins all had toilet seats around their necks. Laymo spat a lougi.

"What was that?" he said "Must be some kinda gang or something. You see all them toilet seats they was wearing?"

Whammo socked him in the arm again.

"Them's Notsees…shoot, clown, you oughta heard of them by now…they're supposed to be everywhere trying to wipe out the mimes or something."

Laymo punched Whammo back.

"Give me a break, dude, you know I spent most my time in solitary for killing that moo cow that kept standing up when I milked her. You know, I couldn't hardly remember my own name by the time I got out."

"Aw, clown, I'm sorry. I didn't mean to remind you of your isolation ordeal…you ain't gonna have one of your panic attacks on me now are you?"

"Don't break my heart, knucklehead. 'Sides, if these Notsees is such a big deal, then how come you never said nothing to me about 'em anyway?"

Whammo fidgeted a little then replied, "Well… they all take their orders from this one clown named Sicko. Me and Sicko used to be partners dealing candy. Remember? Now, he's this big shot and I'm a total loser. Hurts my pride to think 'bout him. Those Notsees just serve as a reminder of what a screw up I am."

"Wow! I didn't know that. We been friends all this time and I still don't hardly know you, I reckon." Laymo was wiping sweat off his brow. "So, anyway what do you know about them Notsees?"

"Not much really, only that they are on this clown supremacy trip all racist against mimes or something."

"Oh. Well, to Hell with them and all that bozokahkah! Listen we gotta catch us a ride into town. What time is it anyway?"

Whammo looked at his classically designed clowns watch with the little mouse whose arms pointed out the time. "It's about 4:30."

Laymo put his hand over his brow to shade his peepers and squinted. "I can see the choo-choo tracks. I'm pretty sure the circus is due through here any time now. We oughta get smart and walk along those tracks and see if we can't catch a ride on the choo-choo when it rolls by."

Whammo nodded in agreement and they made their way across the green pasture to follow along the tracks. No sooner had they got there than did, as if on cue, the circus train came barreling down the tracks. The race was on as the two ex-cons ran as fast as they could, with their giant feet, to hop aboard. Whammo got on first and turned to offer Laymo a hand. Soon, they were both stowed away on the train for what would only amount to a quick 15 minute ride the ten miles into Buffoonville. Lucky for them, the choo-choo would be passing through the lower east-side on its way, which was just where they intended to go. After all, that was the only place where two clowns could get serious in relative safety. Before they knew it, they were standing in the shadow of the gigantic metal floosie outside Slammy's Playhouse.

It's funny how a clown locked up, stripped of his freedom, begins to cherish even the smallest memories from his life on the outside. This includes even the most mundane things like old jobs and stuff like that. This is why it is often hard for the ex-con to adjust right away to the new found freedom once released. Often, the individuals involved in the memories don't share in the convict's nostalgia, which can be a disappointment to the poor slob just out of the joint. Needless-to-say, Whammo was disappointed that his old boss Slammy didn't recognize him right away. In fact, it was all Whammo could do to get Slammy to listen to him long enough to refresh his memory.

"For cripe's sakes, Slammy, you was best man at me and Dew Drop's wedding!"

"Dew Drop?" said Slammy.

"Yeah! She's my wife!"

"Oh yeah…I think I remember now…uh….look it's been good talking to ya, Whammo, but I gotta split…I got important business…"

Whammo grabbed poor, skinny, old broken-down, waste case Slammy by the shoulders and got into his face.

"I know you…always the first to try and leave when something's up…so what's up, Slammy?"

"Uh…like hey…Whammo…like we go way back, clown. No need to get violent."

"Yeah…well, two minutes ago you couldn't even remember my name…now spill it 'for I break your scrawny neck."

Slammy was scared and started trembling. He was wondering where his bouncer was. Seemed like, it was always his luck that the bouncer was never around when he really needed him.

Whammo was looking him hard in the eye. Slammy had guilt written all over his face.

"She's here working for ya, ain't she! That's what's got you all uptight, isn't it? She been whoring for you all these years? Huh! I oughta…"

Slammy spurted out the truth. "She's in back clown! Same old room as the one she kept back when you two first met…go on, she's back there… I'm clean, clown!"

Whammo eased up and loosed his grip on the clown, then shoved him aside as he made way for the rear of the club. Laymo was right behind him. Whammo turned. "Hey, bro, this is a private matter, you dig?" Laymo nodded and stopped where he was, besides there was a relatively hot floosie on stage at the moment and he hadn't seen a suzie in a decade.

Whammo made his way down the hall to the second to the last door on the right. He barged in without knocking. There he found his wife making whoopee with some strange clown. Whammo wanted to kill them both but soon thought better of it.

"To Hell with this, clowns, I am outta here!" Nobody tried to stop him.

Whammo felt like he was gonna freak out as he barged his way back down the hall and into the stinking club. He found Laymo making small talk with a fat floosie that looked like a giant pair of mammerian mcgillicutties attached to a circus tent.

"C'mon we're leaving!" Whammo said, literally pulling Laymo off his barstool. Laymo could sense the rage and fury boiling off of his friend and considering all the diabolical plans they had made in the joint about what they was gonna do to their wives once they found them, there was no way to tell what kind of scene he was so anxious to leave. Laymo figured he would hear all about it later but couldn't help but wonder what was going on, when Whammo passed by Slammy only to stop, turn around, and lay the poor clown out it in one mighty blow. Laymo could actually hear Slammy's front teeth hitting the back of his throat. Leaving the dental disaster behind, the two made a quick getaway on foot and they didn't stop until they reached the old forlorn tree house, still there after all those years. They relaxed there, after beating up and throwing out the jokers who were presently using the old tree fort as their hideout. Whammo felt kinda sorry for what he had done to Slammy but figured that Slammy had it coming one way or the other.

BESIDES, HE JUST HAD TO HIT SOMEBODY!

Chapter 25
Pizza, Pizza

The Low-rider of the Gods traveled through the Lonely Abyss. It careened the Waves of Emptiness and paused to partake in the dismal view of the Vortex of Misery. It lurched within the Quagmire of Sadness and skimmed the surface of the Eternal Cesspool. It ventured the fathoms of the Bottomless Nebula and probed the floating wastes in the Valley of Broken Wills. It is written that during this portion of their trip, Jehovah and Jesus Christ were both very depressed.

The low-rider cruised into the beyond, and beyond that, it explored beyond the beyond until it had ventured beyond even thinking of a place which it could go beyond, and beyond that, it came crawling to a stop because Jesus really needed to use the bathroom and there happened to be an All Being Rest Stop there. The rest area was situated in the shadow of the rock that had a sign on it that read: "This rock is here for no good reason, even if its peak extends beyond the furthest reaches of that which was never really reachable in the first place"

It was written in every language spoken in Like Everything. Obviously, the rock was quite proud of itself to have gone to so much trouble.

In the rest area, was a ridiculously enormous bathroom, which contained every conceivable kind of toilet designed to fit every conceivable kind of portion of a creature's anatomy where waste materials are voided. Jesus went inside in search of an apparatus designed to fit his particular humanoid butt. As he searched through the endless rows of toilet like apparatuses he finally found a standard style toilet and immediately parked his hiney upon it to relieve himself. Being a god, his bowels were in perfect working order so it did not take him long to finish the job. When Jesus got back to the Low-rider of the Gods, he noticed that his father had fallen asleep. Well, he had been gone for some time, and God had a right to be tired, but that was not what was remarkable about his sleeping Father. What was remarkable was the fact that in a million years, Jesus could not recall ever having seen his father sleep. Evidently, God was a twenty four-hour a day type dude. The fact that he was actually asleep served as a testament of how grueling their trip had become. Afterall, they had been searching for the Greatest Extreme for almost ten years now.

Jesus slammed the door of the low-rider and said…

"Wake up!" God was startled by the sound of the slamming door and snapped awake instantly.

"Huh? What is it?"

"You were asleep that's what."

"Asleep? So, that's what it was." God yawned. The action surprised him. "What was that I just did?" he pondered out loud.

His son explained, "That was what's called a yawn. People do that when they get tired."

"Oh" replied God, as he placed another Draconian Mindwarp capsule in the resin coated pipe while trying to wake up. But God wasn't fully awake yet and the Draconian Midwarp wasn't helping since it tends to mellow one out so God completely forgot to warm up the Positronic Navigational Computer Brain and fired the low-rider into warp with out setting coordinates. This was not a very good idea. For one thing, it was incredibly rude to the navigational brain and it might not want to speak to you for weeks. The other was that without coordinates there was no telling where you might end up after dropping out of warp. You could end up materializing inside a star or solid rock somewhere. God and son didn't realized this mistake for several hours after committing it because to the fact that the Draconian Mindwarp they smoked had given them both temporary amnesia. By the time they had come to their senses, there was nothing to do but drop out of warp and hope that nothing messed up.

After dropping out of warp, the first thing the God's noticed was that they had splashed down in some kind of yellow goo. Jesus rolled the window down and stuck his finger into the stuff. He brought a small glob of it to his nose and sniffed…

"Hmmm…smells like…cheese." He tasted it.

"Tastes like cheese…mozzarella actually." God rolled down his own window and sampled the surf.

"You're right about that, Son. Imagine that! We are sailing on a sea of cheese." The situation was so truly weird that both sat silent as the low-rider softly bobbed up and down over the smallish curdled waves. Then God spotted what looked like and island up ahead. Jesus could see it too. The current was taking them directly to it. Soon they found themselves beached. Both got out eager to stretch their legs and explore the island.

Upon exiting the pot-laced atmosphere of the low-rider, the smell of the island was unmistakable. Jesus was quick to comment.

"Pepperoni!" said he.

"Pepperoni!" said God.

God had a hunch but was not yet certain enough to say anything. He spied a medium sized mountain that was apparently a massive peppercorn.

"Let's climb up that mountain for a better look, Son."

"Agreed" said Christ, and they made their way to its base.

The surface of the peppercorn was all craggy and made for a splendid climb, free of risk or hard labor. Upon reaching the summit, one could see quite clearly all the other pepperoni islands spread across the vast sea of cheese and way off in the distance what could only have been the perimeter crust. The Gods looked skyward. It resembled grease stained cardboard.

"I know where we are, Son!" said God.

"Where?" replied the only begotten one.

"Pizza, Pizza!"

"Pizza, Pizza?"

"Pizza, Pizza."

The story God told after announcing his discovery went like this: Long ago, God had been physically much larger than his current diminutive size. This had to do with the massive amount of Positrons he possessed back then. Apparently, there was this one time when God had decided to flood a planet called Earth in the Sol System of his creation, and for reasons he didn't want to get into right then, he had ordered a couple of pizzas to eat during what would probably be a pretty good show. They never got delivered and he could only assume that the twin pies were out there somewhere in Like Everything.

Now, God was pretty sure that he had found the two pizzas, after all these years, only since he was so Positronically poor, as his smaller size depicted, the pies were gigantic monuments to his financial failure. He was now literally reduced to the point that a peppercorn on one slice of pepperoni on just one of the pizzas was a mountain to him…quite an explanation which Jesus could hardly begin to believe. But, believe he did because he believed in God.

It was a moment of reckoning for both. God sat down on an outcropping and invited Jesus to join him. Both sat quietly for a moment gazing at the spectacle of it all. God leaned back placing his left arm behind him for support. His hand landed in something cold and wet.

"Eouuuu, what the…?" God was inspecting the mess on his hand. Suddenly he leapt to his feet.

"Son, your never gonna believe this, but look what I just stuck my hand in." Jesus looked at the blueish-white stuff on God's hand.

"What is it?"

"Well, if I am not mistaken I am pretty sure its owl poop!"

"OWL POOP! You mean…"

"That's right lad, Pizza, Pizza must be the Greatest Extreme! Somewhere around here, we will no doubt find the All Knowing Owl! I suggest we start looking for him immediately."

Both began to walk around looking over the various crags and boulders. Soon they in fact did find the owl. The little bird was sitting on it's nest reading what looked like a owl sized newspaper. They caught him by surprise.

"Holy smokes!" shrieked the owl upon discovering the two angels so rudely interrupting his reading.

"Can't a bird read in peace? Where in Like Everything do I have to go to get away from you people, always coming around to ask your stupid questions. One would think that the Greatest Extreme would be sufficient. But nooooo…someone's always got to come around and spoil everything!" The angels did not know what to say. Jesus offered an apology.

"Please, excuse us, Mr. Owl. But we have traveled far to seek your advice…" The bird cut him short…

"That's just what they all say. Okay, now that I have been interrupted, let's just get this over with and please try not to waste my time with explaining to me all the boring little details about your problem. Don't forget that I am the All Knowing Owl and I probably know more about your problem than you do. So you are?"

"I am God and this is my only begotten son, Jesus of Nazareth."

"God …hmm yes, yes you are one of the originals aren't you…well just look at you…haven't been doing so well lately, have you…judging from your size, I'd say you're here to ask for financial advice."

God and Jesus were impressed with the Owl's reasoning skills. He was absolutely right of course. God spoke:

"In a nut shell, our problem is this…I took out a huge mortgage on a portion of my creation called Heaven. Heaven is a place where all my beings go after they graduate from the flesh. The overhead to run it is tremendous. Anyway, a former employee of mine has been out to destroy my creation for several million years and thanks to him and my own bad decisions, we have gone bankrupt. The First Inter-Dimensional Bank is going to foreclose on my creation and sell it to the Weirdoes from the Fifth Dimension, who plan to turn over my creation to my main competition, the former employee who will, no doubt, destroy its natural beauty just to spite me. We come seeking a solution to this problem. You're our last hope."

God sighed, shrugged his shoulders and began to weep. He had up to this moment been in a state of denial but after telling his woes to the little bird he couldn't see how the Owl could help. That is if the Owl even took the time to help them at all.

The Owl was silent and it was clear that he was thinking over what God had said. Finally, he broke the silence.

"I am familiar with your creation, God, and I am positive that I have a solution to your crisis."

God came to kneel before the Owl, anxious to hear his words. Jesus also came to kneel beside him. Both had big dreamy eyes in awe of the speed at which the Owl had found the solution, which had so far eluded them for over a decade.

"The answer to you problems is simple. The Platypus."

"The Platypus?" said God.

"The Platypus?" said Jesus

"The Platypus" said the Owl, rolling his big round eyes. It was clear to the Owl that these two Gods could not reason how the Platypus could save their creation. Evidently, he would be forced to explain it to them.

"Now, listen carefully. No doubt, neither of you are familiar with the Laws of Redundancy so let me tell you what they are. In Like Everything, because of its sheer scope and size there is a redundancy somewhere for everything that exists or does not exist. Never in all its history has there been a non-redundant thing…until you created the Platypus. The Platypus is such an absurd and unlikely little creature that, believe it or not, it does not have a redundant partner anywhere in Like Everything as far as I know and believe me I know everything. So, here is how you can use this interesting anomaly to save your creation. First, you must travel to Boogus Maximus, seat of the Powers That Be, and register the Platypus with the Department of Redundancy Department. Once you have done so, you may then appeal to the Environmental Protection Agency to have your domain deemed a wild-life refuge. This should effectively void the First Inter-Dimensional Bank's claim. The Powers That Be will be obliged to compensate the bank for its losses and, although you will no longer own your domain, you can still reside over it as park rangers. Git that?"

Of course! It made perfect sense. Somehow that little bird had nailed the whole thing down in reasonable do-able terms. God and Jesus were overjoyed.

"Thank you, Mr. Owl…thank you! How can we ever repay you for solving our problems?" said they.

"Simple, just get the heck out of here and never reveal the location of the Greatest Extreme…for you see Pizza, Pizza is MY wild-life refuge.

777

When the angels reached the beached and cheese-incrusted low-rider, God had a momentary nervous breakdown. He just couldn't bear to see her like that. Anyway, there was nothing to do but get in and make for the crust. Despite the cheese, the low-rider's hyperdrive came on line without incident and, before long, the Gods were well on their way. Finding Boogus Maximus would not be a problem due to the fact that there were millions of broadcasts emanating from the planet. It was a simple matter to let the navigational computer home in on the signals and set coordinates. There was nothing to do now but ride out the countless hours it would take to get there.

The approach into the spaceways of Boogus Maximus was treacherous to say the least. The three-dimensional trajectory systems surrounding the planet where like a bowl of spaghetti piled on top of a mess of baby snakes on top of a jumble of yarn. It was as though the systems had been designed by a truly sadistic and maniacal being outwitted only by the maniac that had painted the signs, which seemed to give headaches instead of clear directions. Not to mention, the various hazards encountered along the way like inter-dimensional gravitational potholes and stuff like that. There was also the fact that the whole thing was under reconstruction so there were millions of dead ends and switchbacks and floating orange barrels…quite impossible to navigate. Yet, it had to be done. God and Jesus at this point had no other choice but to carry out the Owl's plan.

By then, however, neither of the angels was in the mood to care. The journey to the seat of power in Like Everything had been so long that by the time they got there they were like two zombies, brainlessly traversing the insane and impossible pathways, in their search for the surface of the planet, where the administrations they were seeking would, no doubt, be located. Consequently, they roamed the wasteland of interchanges, on/off ramps and merges with out batting an eye. Had they not become zombies, they might have noticed the countless rotting corpses littering the roads and heaped along its sides among the barrels and over-passes…not road kill but suicides.

Finally it got to the point where it seemed they where the only ones left on the pathways. This was, in fact, the case for less than zero percent of beings trying to reach the surface actually make it. They, however, had somehow beaten the odds, which explained why they were all alone. Still the space-ways were as confusing as ever and the insane sign painter seemed to have reached a zenith with his work. But then, just as they were ready to lose all hope, they came upon a pristine service station.

The robot that ran the place was extremely polite to them. He even remarked that they were the first beings he had encountered in ages that had gotten this close to the planet's surface. He went on to explain that there was actually a direct route in but that it was reserved for official government vehicles only.

Jehovah and Christ found it odd to meet a robot that was capable of expressing an emotion like surprise. Evidently, the technology being used on Boogus Maximus was state-of-the-art. When asked, the robot seemed to be an authority on directions and he stood there patiently reciting a 10,000 word oratory on how to get there. God and Jesus where as lost when he finished as they were when the robot began. Still, in their zombie like state they could hardly care and they thought of what the robot said as words of encouragement. The robot certainly seemed confident that if they followed his directions they might actually stand a chance of getting there. It was all the support they needed.

Eventually, they came to the fringes of a sprawling and unbelievably complicated metropolis. Here, the signs became even more sadistic in their approach than the ones out on the spaceways. Still, the zombies endeavored to find the government buildings they needed so the search continued. After a few years of searching, they finally made it to what looked like a capitol building. It was surrounded by millions of life-forms all of whom, the zombies suspected, must have been pretty serious about their own reasons for being there, considering the kind of Hell it was to get there at all. It was amazing to them that so many had actually made it. Then, they were thankful almost that the brutality of the journey was so particularly evil otherwise there would be billions waiting to be seen and heard rather than millions.

After parking the low-rider in a parking garage the size of the planet Neptune, they set out on foot, walking for months, to get in what would be the first of many thousands of lines, hoping to get directions to the Department of Redundancy Department. After a few more months of waiting, the zombies came before a robot who was not very nice and obviously irritated by the literally millions of questions it answered every day. Somehow they talked the robot into giving them the address of the D.O.R.D. and immediately set out once again on another long journey by foot to get there.

The Department of Redundancy Department was located directly above a place called the Paradox Superstore. There were two things they noticed about the Paradox Superstore. One was a sign that said that there were no longer any paradoxes being sold at this location and the other being the fact the store was closed for business even though there was a sign stating it was open 24-hours a day.

God and Jesus entered the building and made a beeline for the elevator. Once inside God pressed the number two button for the second floor. Nothing happened. Pressing the button again got them on their way. A redundancy. When they arrived on their short trip up one floor, the elevator stopped and before they could get out, went back to the first floor, forcing them to repeat the entire procedure. The second time through they managed to get out. There they found the double doors of the Department of Redundancy Department. They knew they were in the right place because there were two signs telling them so with the D.O.R.D. logo printed twice on each. In fact there seemed to be a redundancy of everything. Two door knobs on each door even.

God opened one of the doors and Jesus followed him in. There they discovered that they were in an identical hallway facing two double-door knobbed, double-signed doors. Again they entered. This time they came upon two desks behind which were two, two headed humanoids.

"May we help you?" said the twins on the right simultaneously. Immediately, God and son took seats before the twins.

"Yes" said the Lord. "We are here to register one of my creations with the Department of Redundancy Department."

The two-headed twin on the right said, "Really?" followed by the one on the left who said, "Really?"

"Really" said Christ, "only our creature is without redundancy anywhere in Like Everything."

"Impossible!" said both twins in unison.

"No, it's not impossible…" said the Lord. "The creature is called the Platypus and if you check your records carefully you will certainly find that the Platypus is without a redundant partner. You people must have over-looked it. This fact is known to us on the highest authority in Like Everything, the All Knowing Owl."

"Which one?" said the twins.

Neither God nor Jesus were gonna let the two headed twins trap them in by making them explain which one of everything they were dealing with.

"OURS" said they.

Then the twins reached inside their desks and pulled out a mighty stack of legal forms which were no doubt to be filled out by the Gods.

"You must fill these out" said the twins.

God and Jesus looked at each other, pain evident on their faces. Both disliked doing paperwork of any kind. However, this was pretty important so they took matching pens from matching penholders and began to fill out the forms in duplicate. After a couple of hours they were finally finished and handed the paperwork back to the twins.

"Now, what do we do?" asked Jesus.

"Go over to the desk on the left and ask them" the twins said.

God and Jesus looked at each other with worried faces as they made their way over to the second set of twins.

"May we help you?" said the twins on the left simultaneously. Immediately God and son took seats before the twins.

"Yes" said the Lord, in an irritated voice. "We are here to register one of my creations with the Department of Redundancy Department."

The two-headed twin on the right said, "Really?" followed by the one on the left who said, "Really?"

"Really." said Christ, "Only our creature is without redundancy anywhere in Like Everything."

"Impossible!" said both twins in unison.

"No, it's not impossible…" said the Lord. "The creature is called the Platypus and if you check your records carefully you will certainly find that the Platypus is without a redundant partner. You people must have overlooked it. This fact is known to us on the highest authority in Like Everything, the All Knowing Owl."

"Which one?" said the twins.

Neither God nor Jesus were gonna let the two headed twins trap them in by making them explain which one of everything they were dealing with.

"OURS" said they.

Then the twins reached inside their desks and pulled out a mighty stack of legal forms which were no doubt to be filled out by the Gods.

"You must fill these out" said the twins.

God and Jesus looked at each other, pain evident on their faces. Knowing they had done this before, they sighed and took matching pens from matching penholders and began to fill out the forms in duplicate. After a couple of hours they were finally finished and handed the paperwork back to the twins.

"Now what do we do?" asked Jesus.

"WAIT" said the twins.

God slammed his fist down on their desk.

"WAIT? For what?"

The twins seemed unconcerned with the angel's sudden display of anger. Of course, they were used to people getting fed up with all their redundant nonsense.

"Well, if you expect us to check ALL our records you are just going to have to wait. Do you have any idea how long it is going to take us to verify what you say?"

God and Jesus were afraid to ask. They waited and waited and waited and waited until finally, after what must have been another couple of eons, both sets of twins came back into the room to seat themselves behind the redundant desks only to get up and reseat themselves. The twins on the right informed the angels that in fact they had verified the Platypus as being non-redundant and that they would have to fill out another duplicate set of forms to register it with the Department of Redundancy Department. This, the angels were obliged to do. When they were finished they, of course, had to repeat the entire procedure again at the other desk.

Once finished, all of the twins got up to make duplicate copies of the duplicates then came back to give God and Jesus duplicate duplications of the duplicated duplicates. The twins then bid the Gods farewell with a duel, "Have a nice day."

Once inside the elevator, God spoke:

"I'll think twice before I ever go back to that place."

"You can say that again" replied Christ.

777

God was busy cramming paperwork into his pockets.

"Well, I guess we better head back to that capitol like building and see about getting directions to the Environmental Protection Agency from that unfriendly robot. Thankfully, so far the Owl's advice has been right on. Think they will actually deem my creation a wild-life refuge?"

Jesus was rocking back and forth on the ball of his feet. The elevator stopped on the first floor. For some unknown reason, it did not force them to repeat the trip on their way out.

"I don't know Dad, the Owl's been right so far, like you said, so I can't think of any reason why he won't prove to be right about everything."

"I hope you're right" said God, as he opened the outer door for his son."

God and Jesus thought that the worst of their problems were behind them now that they had escaped from the Department of Redundancy Department with the proper paperwork. Of course, there was no way for them to know what lay in store for them as they attempted to navigate through the bureaucracy of the Powers That Be.

After spending another couple of months waiting in line, they were finally able to talk with the same robot they had spoken to the first time. He informed them that indeed the Environmental Protection Agency was located inside the tremendous Capitol building but that they would not even be allowed to get in the proper line to wait to enter the building unless they brought along their own red tape and paper clips. The robot explained to them that there was so much red tape involved in going through the system that the Powers That Be could not be expected to supply it to everyone. The paper clips were needed to bind the endless streams of paperwork and they had to bring paper clips themselves for the same reasons as the red tape. Fortunately, for them there was a red tape/paper clip vendor near by ready to supply them with the articles. Unfortunately for them, there was no way they could afford the price she was asking and so after much bickering and eventually begging, she traded them the minimum of tape and clips for their clothing. This explained the laundry truck behind her labeled "The Shirt Off Your Back Cleaners" and why two-thirds of those in line were nude.

Things could have been worse, though. At least it was summer and warm there on Boogus Maximus and for that reason God and son felt a little optimistic. However, this was not to last. Evidently, the change of seasons on Boogus Maximus happened almost instantly. This was because the planet had long since been developed to the point that artificial structures covered every square meter of the globe. Therefore, the natural changes of seasons had been eradicated. Now, the changes were created artificially by the central computer and when it was time for winter it was simply time for winter. There they stood, naked, and freezing to death in a blizzard. Not to worry, for as it was with the red tape/paper clip vendor, so it was that there were vendors now providing warm coats, pants or snowsuits....again for a price. God and Jesus looked at the coats for sale and saw that they were flawed, most having only one arm or one leg. Some in line simply froze while others paid the price and hobbled back in line trying to balance on one leg or hang on to someone with one arm. Jesus and God decided they might out smart the vendor by promising him a new job as a park ranger back in Heaven in exchange for a warm robe. The Arm and a Leg vendor agreed to loan them robes and think over the offer until they returned from EPA with proof of the deal. God and Jesus got back in line. On and on it went, until after the passing of many seasons, they finally found themselves walking through the front doors of the Capitol building.

Once inside, they came upon another robot behind a desk. It was obvious what they were expected to do. They handed their meager supply of red tape and paperclips to the metal individual. The robot took the tape and cut of a few centimeters then pasted it to a form. Next, the robot scribbled a signature on the bottom of the form then placed a paperclip over the tape. Then, he handed the form back to the waiting Gods. Eagerly they took it and read the printed words upon it. This is what it said:

Welcome to Boogus Maximus!

Now let's get something straight. We do not care who you are or why you are here. It is your job to make us care, not ours. You better have a good reason for coming here. If we find out that you do not have a good reason to be here, you will be arrested, imprisoned, then executed.

Have a nice day!

"Well, that don't sound too good" remarked a hopeless Christ.
"Don't give up, Son, we got the only non-redundant creature in Like Everything...if that ain't a good enough reason then what is?"
"Okay!" agreed the Nazarene. "Let's ask the robot where the E.P.A. is located." God stepped forward.
"Excuse me..." he said, "but could you please direct us to the Environmental Protection Agency?" The robot was clearly irritated. It replied in its monotone voice.
"All directions are printed clearly on the map on that wall." The robot was pointing to what looked like a really bad abstract painting. Upon closer inspection, the Gods discovered that the abstraction was actually layer upon layer of little dotted lines and arrows pointing the way to the untold millions of official offices inside the colossal building. They both sighed deeply as all hope again slipped away. Finally they decided their chances were probably better if they simply just wandered through the building in search of the correct door, instead of trying to spend the rest of their lives decoding the map.

Like madmen on acid, they marched through the endless corridors and halls. Along the way they encountered many lost souls, emaciated and dressed in rags. The lost would often fall to their knees before them begging for directions they could not give. Periodically, official looking robots would demand red tape from them or paper clips. This caused the deities to fear they might run out.

The hours turned to days, the days to weeks, the weeks to months, the months to years. By then, they, too, were emaciated and dressed in rags. Eventually, they gave up looking all together and just wondered the halls aimlessly with the rest. It was in this all too familiar zombified state one day that Jesus happened to look upon one of the millions of doors they had come past through his bloodshot and yellowing eyes. There he saw the initials "E.P.A." printed boldly on the glass! Against all odds, they had found it at last!

After convincing themselves that they had actually found the E.P.A., the ragged Gods wept tears of joy. Gathering their wits, they wished that there was something they could do about their appearance but all was lost. They would have to present themselves in their rags as best they could. God was busy trying to smooth out the paperwork he had carried all those years from the Department of Redundancy Department. The forms were in pretty rough shape but were still legible.

Now, it was time to enter.

They knocked.
No one answered.
They knocked again…still no answer.
They barged in.
The man inside said "Who art thou?
"I am God" said God.
"I am his only begotten son" said Christ.
"What is it you want then?" said he.
"We want to register our creation as a wild-life refuge!" said God.
"Ha! Get outta here!" said he.
"We ain't going nowhere!" said they, backing the man into a corner.
The man looked into Christ's eyes.
There was no saintly innocence left in them. He had the eyes of a deranged lunatic.
The man decided it was in his best interests at the moment to participate.
"Come into my office" said he.
They followed.
The office was huge.
Its floor was carpeted.
Wall-to-wall.
This only served to burn the blisters on the angel's feet.
The man sat down behind an obnoxiously huge, cherry-wood desk. The Gods sat down in two plush velvet upholstered chairs shaped like upturned human hands. The animosity seemed to be over.
"How may I help you, gentlemen? And, let me introduce myself. My name is Fred…Fred Zeppelin."

God pulled forth the soiled and yellowing paperwork he had carried for so long and presented them to Fred Zeppelin. Fred took them and gave them a quick once over.

"I see. So you are the creator of the only non-redundant being in Like Everything? Well, everything seems to be in order. Do you have some red tape? Paper clips?"

Jesus reached inside his rotting robes and produced the articles. Fred Zeppelin cut off a length of tape and stuck it haphazardly on the forms them placed paperclips all over the pages seemingly at random. What he was doing made little sense. They did not care.

"So, you want the E.P.A. to declare your creation a wild-life refuge in order to preserve the habitat of this…this…Platypus creature?"

"That's right" said God.

"Well, then I can see no reason why not. After all, its status as the only non-redundant creature in Like Everything is certainly worth preserving. The judgment of the E.P.A. is not your problem." Jesus and God were puzzled. Christ spoke:

"Then, what IS our problem?"

"Your problem is weather or if you know someone."

"Know someone?" asked God.

"What I mean is do you know someone who is an elected official, higher up in the Powers that Be than this lowly agency? All I can do is approve your request…it will take the action of a politician to ratify it through the bureaucracy. Do you understand?"

Gods jaw was visibly clenched. His face turneth red and he leapt forth from his seat.

"AGGHHHH!!" he screamed. Then the Lord cast himself to the floor and threw one hellacious temper tantrum. Jesus was amused, knowing it would be his turn next. After his own tantrum, Christ posed a question.

"Do you happen to have a list of the politicians of the Powers That Be?"

Fred got up from his seat. "Certainly!"

He placed a massive book before Christ.

"This is an up-to-date complete listing. Perhaps if you go over it carefully you will discover that you do, in fact, know someone."

Jesus opened the book as God came to stand behind him looking over his shoulder. Of course, the chances that they would know someone was zero. God and son had, had little to do with the Powers That Be, both being anarchists at heart.

Christ flipped past the table of contents to the first page. The book started with the highest office. Jesus took one look at the page and drew in a deep breath in shock of what he saw printed upon it:

Prime Minister of All, Lord Emperor of Much, Regal Personage of This, Maharaja of That, Sultan of Somewhere, Overlord of Underdogs, Crowned Head of Lots, Prince of Polecats, Monarch of Most, Tyrant of Totality, Shah of Something or Other, The Absolute King of the Hill, Guh Mooga Wump the 2nd.

"What is it, Son?" asked the Lord.

"I think I know him!" replied Christ.

Fred Zeppelin was shocked as well.

"You mean to say you know the Power That Be himself? Of course, you realize that this would practically guarantee that your request will be ratified. You have only to beat the insurmountable odds of actually being granted an audience with him."

"Well…" said God. "Whatever the odds, at least we got a chance!"

"Yeah…" said Christ "all we gotta do is find a bowling alley!"

It is written that the next portion of the God's adventures on Boogus Maximus was facilitated greatly by Fred Zeppelin, who used his transporter to beam the two angels directly inside the planet's largest bowling alley.

The alley was like nothing they had ever seen. There had to be over ten thousand lanes and literally millions of bowling balls. It took a while to sort through them all but after a couple of weeks and with the help of God, Jesus finally found a 13-pound ball with blue and white swirls.

It was another feat of determination and their shear force of will that placed Jesus and his father in a position to see Guh Mooga Wump the 2nd. The Powers That Be had somehow heard a rumor that two human beings, from the domain the king had once called home, had come across the billions of light-years to present him with something he had long since forgotten was once his most cherished of possessions. That was the extent of the rumor. Trouble was, no one seemed to know what the object was, and for the life in him, Guh Mooga Wump could not remember what it might have been himself. This was due largely to his recent brain transplant. At this time, all that was left of his original self was his soul. His former life was like eddies of dust in his most vague memory. Therefore, he was only slightly moved upon meeting the two Gods, who presented him with a 13-pound bowling ball with blue and white swirls. Yet in an astounding demonstration of beating the odds, a tiny portion of Guh Mooga Wump's fresh mind managed to remember his long lost obsession with bowling balls of that description. Then, in another astounding demonstration of the same brand, the gift impressed Guh Mooga Wump enough that he actually saw fit to grant the God's request to have their creation deemed a wild-life refuge.

The news of the new refuge was broadcast throughout Like Everything. One infinitesimal blip, in the billions of blips, broadcast in the daily telling of news concerning the day's events within the Powers That Be. The Powers That Be duly provided the Gods with all the official paperwork they would present to the First Inter-Dimensional Bank to get them off their backs once and for all. This is not to say that the process was fast. By the time it was all over and the two departed from Boogus Maximus they had been on their journey for over 20 years.

Despite the fact that the announcement of God's Domain being officially deemed a wild-life refuge was but a mere blip, those concerned found out about it almost instantly due to the fact that a small army of sailors was employed to listen for stuff like that. When the news hit, the Wierdoes in the fifth dimension dispatched several high ranking delegates to go to the First Inter-Dimensional Bank to verify that it was so.

The bankers had just recently been visited by God himself, and the Weirdoes were shown copies of the official documents showing that it was indeed true.

So, the Weirdoes proceeded directly to Hell for there was going to be hell to pay. The Weirdoes had already warned the Devil of the potential problems Guh Mooga Wump could create for all concerned. After all, Guh Mooga Wump was one of Satan's lost souls, and he was the one who had made this whole major mess possible. Now the worst possible turn of events had occurred after all.

666

Satano was not eager to see the three Weirdoe delegates who had come knocking on his door. They explained everything to him in great detail and apparently everything was all Satano's fault.

"What the heck is a Platypus?" he screamed as he burst into flames. The Weirdoes were not amused.

"That is not important. What matters is that the creature exists on a planet called Earth and so long as it exists we will effectively never be able to buy out God's Domain." The delegates nodded in agreement with themselves.

"Well, then, I'll just go to Earth and kill them. No Platypus, no wild-life refuge! Simple-as-pie!" Satano sat back into his ugly seat and was pleased with his obvious solution.

"We're afraid that it won't be that simple, Sir. Now that God's Domain has been recognized as a wild-life refuge, the forces of the Powers That Be will be out to protect the creature's habitat. We agree that the easiest solution to the problem is to destroy the Platypus but we cannot do so directly. We need to do so covertly some how. If you were to kill the Platypus directly, it is very likely that the Powers That Be will see that the death of the creature was intentionally committed in order to facilitate our well-known intentions to purchase the domain. You would be in deep trouble with them, and there would be no doubt that they would seek to punish us as well.

Satano got out of his chair and began to pace.

"Not to worry, friends. As you know, I have been in the business of destroying God's creation for millions of years. As a matter-of-fact, I have made great progress in the past few decades with instilling evil in the hearts of the clowns who are the dominant species on Earth now, home-world of the Platypus. All I need do to solve our mutual problem is convince the clowns of Earth to destroy themselves in a great and final holocaust which will destroy all life on their world, including the Platypus. It will not be the first time I have gotten a planet full of creatures to do so, and there will be little chance that the Powers That Be will be able to pin the destruction of Earth on us."

The Weirdoes seemed pleased hearing Satano's plan.

"Well, then Sir, that sounds reasonable to us. Tell us what steps will you take on this matter upon our departure?"

The Devil sat back down in his ugly seat and took a deep breath.

"Simple. I will, from this point forward, focus all of my energy on convincing the clowns of Earth to destroy themselves. It is only a matter of time before I succeed."

The Weirdoe delegates were not entirely convinced.

"But, what about God and Jesus? Surely, it will be in their best interests to protect the home-world of the Platypus from this point forward. Their entire plan hinges on the creatures survival."

Satano leaned back in his chair and folded his hands behind his neck.

"I wouldn't worry about them. Their powers are very weak at this time and nothing compared to mine. There will be little or nothing they can do to stop me. Trust me."

The Weirdoes seemed to be convinced.

"Do your worst then, Satano, and keep us posted."

And with that the Weirdoes left Hell on an inter-dimensional wave.

AND SO IT WAS WRITTEN AND SO IT WAS DONE.

Chapter 26
Carnival of Despair

Hear ye all good clowns this day
Your destiny awaits
You can get your tickets
From the Notsees at the gates
Can't you see the midway friend?
The faithful Ferris wheel?
The carnival has come to town
Line up to get your thrills
God has new commandments, brother
Carnival is new
We know you will love it, clowns
Once we baptize you
These are problem times, bozo
There's trouble in the air
Come and get your kicks at the
Carnival of Despair

Tears gently rolled down Nastina's cheeks as she read the advertisement. They were posted on every pole, every lamp-post, and every tree. They were posted in every storefront window, on every public bulletin board, on every mailbox, and every telephone booth. They were posted on every wall in every restaurant, every department store, and every candy shop. They were posted in the keystone stations and the fireclown stations. Smaller versions hung on every doorknob on every funhouse and the streets were littered with flyers. The propaganda could be found in every nook and crannie in Buffoonville.

Nastina had spent a great deal of time in the queer Reality Well created by the mimes imaginations in Buffoonville's sewer system. Their time had a different meaning and function for the place was left out of the space/time continuum. It had taken her a while to figure out how to track time in the well in order to maintain a reasonable schedule outside it on the surface. Living with the mimes had given her ample opportunity to learn how to use the mime power held within her genes. This was how she managed to create the imaginary clock that kept real time for her.

Nastina had kept her job at Slammy's for the three years in real time she had spent dealing with the mimes. She had rejoined her tribe of people. Not only had she learned to fully realize her mime power, but also she had also spent the time there educating the mimes about the serious nature of the Notsee Party.

By working at Slammy's, which was always full of party members, it was easy for her to keep up with the parties movements and report them back to her mime compatriots as she returned to their Realty Well each night.

Another thing she had learned was that mime power didn't always have to be used in a harmless manner. With enough concentration, imaginary things could be manifested for real in clown reality. The trick to it was getting them to imagine things as a large group, which amplified the manifestations greatly. But it was hard to get them to do things in a large group because mimes naturally tend to do things in small troops.

It became necessary for her to completely educate them about the enemy. This bred fear in the troop and by focusing that fear, Nastina managed to teach the mimes to do some really spectacular things. Of course, she also taught them how to recognize the enemy for at the time not all clowns were the enemy. She targeted only those clowns involved in the Notsee Party, specifically the skinheads. Hate was not a natural trait among the innocent mimes but Nastina had found it necessary to teach them this, also. With this knowledge, for the first time, the mimes learned how to hate their common enemy. With their fears and hatreds, the mimes were then able to imagine truly harmful things. Things that she suspected could even kill clowns.

%$#@%

Under the close supervision of Sicko the Clown and with the help of the Supreme Ding-a-ling, the Notsee Party had spread the idea of clown supremacy around the globe. Millions of good clowns indoctrinated themselves into the party once party ideas had been fully integrated with the teachings of the World Circus, which by then had been transformed into the Carnival of Despair. For the life of her, Nastina could not understand how the most holy clown on Earth, the Supreme Ding-a-Ling, could have gotten involved with a hate movement and, furthermore, a hate monger like Sicko the Clown. She could not believe her eyes and ears when she saw his Holiness on television telling of his meeting with God and that it was the Lord himself that had commanded that all mimes must die. She could not imagine that God would use the most righteous creatures on Earth as scapegoats for society's ills. And she could hardly imagine how she could stop the clown supremacists from wiping out the mimes which she had come to love more than her own life.

It all seemed impossible but it was indeed happening. The posters that had so recently sprung up advertising the carnival only reinforced her greatest fears. Now it seemed that the reformation of the World Circus into the Carnival of Despair was complete. Nastina didn't even want to imagine what the carnival would be like. Nevertheless, it became clear to her that she must be prepared to do whatever it took to try and stop this force regardless of how much it degraded her or humiliated her.

%#@%#^

Blinko woke up feeling beat. The crusades and membership drive was a load of work. He had taken up permanent residence in Sicko's bed and breakfast. His twentieth birthday was near and he felt more like a clown than ever. Elvis had just turned twenty-one which mean it was now legal for him to drink. This did not help his already chronic drinking problem. The duo had become heroes to the local townsfolk. Their ability to root out mimes and dispose of them quickly had gotten them a lot of attention from party members the world over. Blinko himself had been given the rank of General in the Sideshow of Doom, a military branch of the Notsee Party. The Sideshow of Doom was composed mostly of clown youth, the most rabid of which usually came from Reform Schools. No surprise there, huh?

Sicko and the Supreme Ding-a-ling had done an excellent job of converting the World Circus into the Carnival of Despair. There were many attractions at the carnival. The most popular attraction along the midway was the Decapitation Booth. Eager clowns lined up to try their hand at the game. The guillotine was set up on a ten-foot stage. At the point of impact was a chute that led to a short alley where a set of bowling pens stood. The idea was to throw a softball at the target which, if struck, would release the blade chopping off the head of the poor mime. The mimes head would then roll down the chute then down the alley to strike the pins. Prizes were given depending on the number of pins left standing. This game alone caused mimes to be in great demand and there was not always enough to go around. But that was okay because there was always plenty of clowns who were traitors or other types of criminals in the eyes of the party that could be put to death in the Decapitation Booth all in the name of God.

Another popular feature was the Baptismal Wading Pool. The wading pool was, of course, filled with Satano's new brand of Obvious, which could be absorbed directly through the skin. Needless-to-say, clowns came out of the pool feeling refreshed and remarkably thoughtful. And don't forget…addicted…which of course was entirely the point.

Loudspeakers loomed high above the midway broadcasting a clever mix of circus rhetoric and party propaganda. Vendors were out in force selling copies of Mime Kampf, candy cigarettes, and toilet seats. The bumper cars had no height restrictions and the cotton candy was always free.

One of the most fascinating attractions at the carnival was the Freak Show. Here, paying clowns could see mimes in various stages of torture and amputation. Some had been force-fed clown food and having no digestive system had blown up like balloons to the delight of the morbidly fascinated goers. Others had been lobotomized and were billed as zombies. The party had a fine selection of evil doctors who performed surgery on the mimes to the delight of the audience who were always amazed to see the empty insides of dissected mimes. The mimes only had two significant organs and they were their brains and their hearts. A mime's heart was three times the size of a clown's. Surgeons took care to cut out the mime's hearts for the inspection of the crowds. The surgeons also liked to sew mimes together creating mimese twins. The Freak Show was always standing room only.

&%#^%$

Despite all the glorious victories and other pomp and circumstance, Blinko still felt that his life was missing something. As of late, he had taken to hanging around Slammy's Playhouse and drinking too much with his old friend Elvis. Presently, both were there having a third one too many.

"Ain't Sicko the most?"

"The most indeed, my brother." Elvis was leaning so far back in his chair he was mere inches from tipping over. This balancing act was a common tendency of clowns like him. Blinko slapped Elvis's knee, an act that brought the clown slamming to the floor on all four legs of his chair.

"Clown, the party takes up all of my time these days." said Blinko.

"These days? The party is all you have ever thought about, fool. Maybe its time you thought about some other things? When was the last time you made whoopi?"

"Not since Reform School with the floosies. Gee, has it been that long? Maybe you're right. Besides I have been feeling a little lonely lately. All work and no play…know what I mean?" Elvis signaled the waitress for another round.

"Look, Blinko, you're a general in the Notsee Party. You can have any suzie you want, especially here at Slammy's. You know these floosies get hot for skinheads. So, why don't ya just sit here get loaded on soda and see if one of these dancers gets you interested?"

Blinko nodded in agreement with his friend.

"Sure, Elvis…what you gonna do tonight anyway?" Elvis stood up and straightened his toilet seat.

"I think I hear a floosie calling me."

Elvis was wearing a huge grin and with that final word he disappeared into the relative darkness of Slammy's. Blinko went for his smokes and took a long look at the floosie on stage.

"Nah!" he thought. It was gonna be a long night.

Meanwhile, and in what would be the first of a long string of incredible coincidences, Nastina was getting ready for her shift a Slammy's. Her plan was simple. She would seek out Blinko, a general of the Notsee Party, and seduce him. She had decided it was time to infiltrate Notsee headquarters in Buffoonville herself to get inside information about the movements and diabolical plans of the party. It made her sick to her stomach thinking about what it would be like to have to touch that monster, to kiss him or…she stopped herself right there…better not to anticipate such humiliations. Little did she know that the young general was sitting at a table, center stage, that very evening just waiting for the right girl to come out. The coincidence was absolutely incredible but such is often the case when worlds collide.

Imagine the moon suddenly striking Earth. The survivors would say *"what are the chances of that happening?"* The chance in fact would be less than zero. Therefore only an "Incredible Coincidence" could be responsible. The Incredible Coincidence is like a type of cosmic event…a circumstance in and of itself. In fact, as you may already know, there is a device in Like Everything designed specifically to notice such things as Incredible Coincidences. For that reason, when Nastina hit the stage at Slammy's, some light-years away, these coincidences were duly recorded by a bald-headed, hunch-backed, female, humanoid on Boogus Maximus, much to her amazement and delight of the throbbing piece of gristle.

Blinko was completely bored by the time Nastina took to the stage for her first dance. He looked at her. She looked at him. At that instant, there was a profound moment of mutual excitement between them. For Nastina the excitement was caused by the fact that the General himself happened to be sitting center stage ready to be tantalized out of his pea-brain by her in the very hour she had chosen to try a seduce him. The only thing that surprised her more than that was the fact that Blinko, on closer inspection, was actually rather handsome with his big muscles and bald head despite the toilet seat around his thick neck. Maybe seducing him wasn't going to be as bad as she had feared. In Blinko's case, it was Nastina's royal blue hair that first caught his attention. Blue was his favorite color after black. The more he looked at her the more he liked her. This wasn't hard to do considering that the suzie was half naked at that moment. Nastina watched as the general raised an eyebrow.

"That's it…" she said to him, "You know you want it."

He sat forward in her direction. Quickly, Nastina gyrated to the heavy throb of the music. Nastina turned around and purred at him.

"How do you like it? You do, don't you? C'mon let's be friends, what do you say?" The general said nothing and grabbed her, throwing her over his shoulder. Nastina was surprised to find herself enjoying this although she was a little afraid.

"Where are you taking me?" she said giggling.

"To your dressing room, which one is it?"

"Number three." Nastina swallowed her fear as the big clown took her inside the little room.

He sat her gently on the bed and immediately began to disrobe. Nastina needed a drink and went to her cabinet for some hard booze. She produced a quart, which she downed in one massive pull. Being a lightweight it messed her up real good. She lost herself to the moment and was ready.

The next morning Nastina was a little ashamed of the things she let herself do with the general of the Sideshow of Doom, stormtroopers of death for the Carnival of Despair. She found it remarkable that she could be so hot for a clown that she knew to be her sworn enemy. But then wasn't that the way it was supposed to be? *...Love thy enemy...*

Blinko thought he had died and gone to heaven. This little blue haired suzie had completely rocked his world last night and he felt better than he had felt in years. It occurred to him then how nice it might be to have a clownette like her around a lot of the time…taking the edge off his responsibilities to the party. He decided that he would take her home with him that very day. His ego made it so that he never thought twice about whither she would want to shack up with him or not. Of course, she would, after all he was literally the top dog around Buffoonville and probably the world for that matter. A suzie would have to be crazy not to go with him.

Nastina did not try to hide her surprise when he invited her to accompany him to party headquarters at Sicko's bed and breakfast. Of course, she hid the fact that her surprise was from realizing that her secret plans to spy on the party, by seducing its general, were going perfectly. She imagined that if Blinko noticed her excitement he would just think of her surprise as some stupid, suzie, Notsee groupie thing.

Privately, she thanked her lucky stars that the clown was good looking and good in bed, at least that would partially make up for all the Notsee rhetoric and hate talk she would no doubt be subjected to all day and all night whenever they weren't making whoopie. She wasn't kidding herself. This clown was the real deal, a killer of mimes, her people. By noon, they were in the cramped backend of a jalop-o-zeen on their way to Sicko's.

$#^%#@

The Supreme Ding-a-ling was angry. It seemed that somewhere along the way in this reformation of the World Circus, he had begun to lose his faith in the Lord. If it hadn't been for the fact that he had actually come face to face with the creator, he would have sworn that all he had done was to contribute to the process of sending the world and everyclown on it to Hell. No matter how he tried, he just wasn't comfortable with all this seriousness. He sat down hard on his ancient golden throne beneath the big top. He could feel his funny bone ache and reached for his syrup blaster. Like everyone else he was addicted to the syrup.

"My God!" he thought in prayer. "There was a time when I would have tickled my funny bone freely in holy brainless devotion to you. I reached the exalted position of Supreme Ding-a-ling in glorious retardation in thy simple minded name. I wielded power over the faithful and performed centuries old rituals of Grand Lunacy, but who's laughing now? Is the threat of the filthy mimes so great that we should abandon our ways in the face of it? Why must we all be so serious? Where is the innocent slapsticking? Where is the pleasure in all that would be comic? Where is the unbridled fun and games? The song and dance? Where are the clowns? Somebody send in the clowns? Amen."

The syrup refreshed his mind instantly. It occurred to him that, that had been the first "one-on-one" prayer he had offered to the Lord in months. He grew fearful that the wrinkled old face would appear before him angry and ready to punish him for questioning his word. But there was no answer. He grew puzzled. Surely, after all he had done to lead the clowns down the new path to salvation, the Lord would answer him. But he knew the Lord worked in mysterious ways. His faith was trickling away and he was unable to stop it. The obvious, that kept him so serious, wasn't helping either.

He had, as of late, turned to educating himself to better understand the task set before him. He had gone into the catacombs beneath the Vatican and retrieved ancient and taboo literature pouring away, lost in the millions of old words and ideas. He had a false hope that somewhere in the library of the forbidden past he would find the answers for today…efforts of a fool.

That's when Satano showed up. The Supreme Ding-a-ling was shocked at the sight of the red skinned Devil there in his chambers deep within the Vatican. The Supreme Ding-a-ling had always wondered when this day would come…the day when he would come face-to-face with the evil Lord of Flies.

"So it is you…Satano… here to test me." The Devil let out a hearty laugh that struck fear in the Supreme Ding-a-ling. "Actually I am here to fire you."

The Supreme Ding-a-ling was clearly puzzled by this announcement which forced the Devil to explain it all to him. Satano told the Supreme Ding-a-ling how he had tricked him into doing his bidding with that phony old man God disguise and explained how the Supreme Ding-a-ling, himself, had led billions of clowns worldwide into damnation. Needless-to say, the Supreme Ding-a-ling was flabbergasted and humiliated and ashamed of what a fool he had been.

"You mean to say that all this time I have been caring out your orders instead of the laws of God?"

"That's what it amounts to. Not to worry though, I have a great spot reserved just for you in Hell." And with that the Supreme Ding-a-ling suddenly burst into flames, dying of spontaneous clown combustion. This was due to the fact that there is such a thing as screwing up so bad that every corner of your being becomes hot with shame which in the case of clowns can sometimes lead to…POOF!

Sicko was pleased to see Satano…especially when the Devil gave him the news about the death of the Supreme Ding-a-ling. Sicko knew exactly who the next Supreme

Ding-a-ling would be. Which clown would take the throne and rule over the Carnival of Despair…him of course…Sicko the Supreme Ding-a-ling. Just days later, Sicko found himself in Rome at the Vatican being ordained by the disciples. The world foolishly celebrated.

7^#%$#

When Elvis arrived at Sicko's bed and breakfast, he found Blinko in a mood like he had never seen before.

"What's the haps?" Elvis clicked his heels as he seig-hieled Blinko.

"Clown, I took your advice and brought her home with me…I can't wait for you to meet her!"

"Whoa, slow down, clown…meet who?"

"My girlfriend!" Blinko got up from the chair in which he was seated and ran to the stair case.

"Honey, honey…come down here…there is someone I want you to meet." Elvis was shocked at Blinko's behavior. He had seen some pretty rough suzie-whippings but this one was looking really bad right from the start. Blinko had a look on his face akin to a baby farting for the first time.

"Blinko, are you nuts? Girlfriend? I only suggested you try and get some yesterday."

Blinko turned towards his friend. His right eye was twitching. Obviously, Elvis had hit a nerve. This made Elvis nervous. He tried to smoothe the waters.

"Hey bro…it's cool… I was just…WOW!"

Elvis clamed up the second he saw her. After all Nastina WAS fine. Blinko turned into jelly right in front of him. It was worse than he thought. Suzie-whippings are bad enough but this was like a suzie impalement. He felt embarrassed and could only watch as Blinko floated to her side like a fairy.

"Darling!" he gushed, "I've missed you so much…"

Blinko was planting little kisses along the length of Nastina's arm which she had held out for him to worship. Elvis felt queasy as he watched the two lovebirds embraced. They were still embracing when "SPY" popped into his head as he looked at her. He didn't know why, but it was just this feeling he had.

"So, what's her name, Blinko?"

Blinko's face twisted up when he realized that he didn't actually know his girlfriends name. All they had done was make whoopie or sleep in the past twenty-four hours. Nastina took the initiative.

"My name's Nastina" she said. Blinko introduced them.

"Nastina, this is Elvis. Elvis, Nastina."

Elvis tried to be polite and offered his hand to the maiden. Blinko slapped it away in a possessive fit.

"Get away from her. You want her, don't you. Go on! Admit it!"

Elvis couldn't believe his own ears.

"He's a goner!" he thought to himself. Elvis said nothing as he turned and left the room. Blinko was so smitten by love that he didn't even take notice of his friend's departure and turned to focus the rest of his wits on Nastina and began to drool.

"My sweet-ums, my lamb-chop, my sugar-pie, my snooky-wooky, my moogy-woogy, my lady, my love, my precious, my tinker-bell, my pretty, my gorgeous, my punkin, my…" Nastina interrupted him.

"Oh, Blinko, you're so good to me, lets go upstairs for a while."

Nastina winked at him and headed up the steps. He followed her in a dream like trance. Later, as the two lay side by side, Blinko drooling, oozing and snoring, Nastina was thinking about what a shock this big stupid clown was in for. He had clearly fallen for her hard and was setting himself up for one heck of a broken heart. But then, that only went to prove what an idiot he was.

$#@%^&

Nastina soon found her will and resolve being put to the test when Blinko asked her to accompany him to the Carnival of Despair. There she would be forced to endure seeing the brutality of the Notsee's crimes against the mimes in person, but she wasn't about to blow her cover. Once the ride to the fairgrounds was complete, General Blinko took her firmly by the hand as he adjusted his golden toilet seat. Nastina used this time to study the clown's mannerisms. The first thing she noticed was how proud the clown was. He marched with his spine straight, shoulders back, chest forward…a true soldier. As the legions came to salute him, he would examine each soldier with an authoritative eye before saluting them back…the Notsee salute. It was a purposeful one. First, the right arm would be thrust straight out at a 45 degree angle. Then, the hand would be brought towards the head until the thumb connected with the clowns honker. Fingers wiggling the clown would then finish the salute by giving a wet raspberry. Nastina noticed that Blinko's enthusiasm during his salutes often left his soldier's faces covered in slobber. General Blinko was popular among the troops so it took them a while to reach the entrance to the Carnival of Despair. Nastina had always loved the World Circus…all the happy clowns, smiling, and dancing, and laughing their way into the brightly colored big top…the loud circus music blaring with its up beat frolicking melodies. But the Carnival of Despair was clearly a totally different animal from the moment she entered the midway. Oh, sure, it was teeming with clowns like the circus but these clowns did not seem to share the slightest shred of humor among themselves. It was nothing short of terrifying to see so many clowns in one place wearing straight faces and upside-down smiles. The clowns all walked around moping. Gone was the usual pep in the step associated with clown festivities. In fact, there seemed to be a great shortage of festivity for every clown she passed looked completely serious, an attitude she had never seen in such abundance before now.

The carnival goers where crowded around the sleazy booths and games. They looked around with suspicious eyes and evidently there was a lot of fist fighting going on. She could see the little scuffles breaking out here and there. She could hear the angry voices and the pitiful cries of clowns beaten or trampled under foot…all of this barely audible over the angry sounding carnival music…a type of demented heavy-metal-polka. As the general escorted her down the midway, the angry sounding music got noticeably louder, growing in volume with each passing step. Then, it became clear to her that she was approaching the source of the sinister tunes. She could see a large sound stage with a live band performing on it. The musicians were all playing instruments she was not familiar with. Hanging behind the band was a gigantic toilet seat with a swastika painted on it several meters across. The musicians where moving about rather violently, and the mass of clowns before them seemed to be running around in a circle, crashing into one another. It was then that she realized what was going on in front of her.

"Those clowns are slam-dancing and that music is punk rock!" she shouted to Blinko, over the noise.

"Indeed!" he said.

"But, I thought that slam-dancing and punk-rock were both outlawed."

Blinko cupped his hand around Nastina's ear and leaned to speak directly in it.

"Well, it was but that was before the reformation of the World Circus. Punk-rock is now the official music of the Carnival of Despair and that, my dear, is the house band. They're called the Toilet Seats."

"Oh." Nastina was endeavoring to get used to being shocked every five seconds.

Blinko led Nastina to a private box where other high ranking party members sat. "I must leave you here for the moment. It's almost time for me to make my speech for the day. I have to make way for the stage."

Nastina took a seat and watched as the general and a small entourage of skinheads took the stage.

Blinko took hold of the microphone and cleared his throat. He was standing before a group of about ten thousand skinhead clowns all of whom were either members of the party or new comers being indoctrinated in it through the rituals of the carnival. Blinko seized the moment…"ALL MIMES MUST DIE!"

The crowd erupted in unison chanting the law of clown supremacy three times before falling silent again. Nastina realized at this juncture just how serious the situation had become. She knew then that the only way she would be able to complete her mission would be to join the party herself and participate in its rituals no matter how offensive they might be. She would have to learn to think like them, be one of them. It would be dangerous and distasteful but she was already sleeping with the enemy and hopefully she could use Blinko to shield her from suspicion. She knew just what to say to him when he returned after his short speech, which had consisted of nothing more than often repeated party rhetoric.

The band had started again. Nastina leaned and shouted into the General's ear:

"Blinko! I want to join the party! I want to join the party now!"

The General looked into Nastina's eyes and felt his heart swell up with pride. He had finally found the perfect suzie. Blinko took her by the hand and moments later they were standing on the stage. Blinko gave a signal and the band stopped playing. He took the microphone and addressed the masses.

"Good clowns of Buffoonville, loyal party members, this here suzie has just asked to join the party and I thought what better way to commence tonight's kick ball game than to indoctrinate her right here on the stage in front of you all. Send for the Poobla and the baptismal vessel!"

Blinko's message could be heard by all and the local poobla began to quickly gather his holy vestments. Nastina was in a quiet state of panic for she had not expected that she would be indoctrinated right there on the spot. She had no idea what they would expect from her and she was not sure she could go through with it. Apparently, the party was so eager to sign up new members that they were prepared to indoctrinate anyone, anywhere, anytime. She suspected then that this was one of the functions of the carnival as it now stood in place of the World Circus.

With Blinko beside her, Nastina stood and watched as a small group of skinheads assembled the Poobla's vestments on stage. A jalop-o-zeen pulled in to the arena shortly and the Poobla got out. He was dressed differently now. Gone was the festive brightly colored clown's suit, now the Poobla was dressed like and evil dictator in a stiff black jacket with knee high boots with white laces. Around his neck was a golden toilet seat emblazoned with a red swastika. Upon his head, in place of the funny hat, was a steel helmet with a little statue of Jesus the Clown strangling a mime to death on top. Behind him came a small troop of Disciples of Utter Desperation, who although were still midgets, were no longer wearing monks robes. Instead, the disciples wore green surgical scrubs complete with shower caps and rubber gloves. The skinheads had unloaded on the stage what looked like a giant birthday present. It was a black box with a big red bow on top. Now the Poobla was on stage followed by the disciples.

"Where is the clown to be baptized?" asked the Poobla.

Blinko nodded his head in the direction of Nastina. The Poobla came in front of her.

"Kneel!" he said. Nastina did as she was instructed and knelt before the clown.

"Good clowns of Buffoonville, this day another of God's children has come to receive the Lord's spirit. She has come to cleanse her soul in the baptismal pool. And before her baptism she will take her solemn oath and profess it to all of us before God. Once this is done, our number will have once again multiplied, for once baptized, she will help to spread the Lord's word and help the lost sinners to find there way to the carnival where they might also find salvation in God's mighty prophecy. We as God's soldiers welcome you, young lady, to your salvation…now into the pool."

The crowd began to chant:

"…THE POOL…THE POOL…THE POOL…"

Nastina swallowed hard and followed the Poobla to the sinister black box. Then the Poobla snapped his fingers and all four sides of the box fell to reveal a gigantic white porcelain toilet.

"The pool!" said the masses.

"The pool!" said the Poobla.

"The pool! said Nastina.

Then the disciples came round and together formed a midget stair case which Nastina was ushered to climb. Now, she sat awkwardly perched on the rim of the bowl. The Poobla spoke:

"Your name?"

"Nastina, Sir."

"Nastina! Nastina, you must take the party oath before you enter the baptismal waters."

"Okay." The Poobla again snapped his fingers and suddenly the toilet seat lit up so brightly it nearly blinded the young clownette. The toilet seat read in giant neon letters…ALL MIMES MUST DIE…

The crowd began to murmur oohs and ahhs among themselves much like bored neighbors do whenever some clown turns on the Christmas lights for the first time. Now, the Poobla was holding a microphone up to her mouth.

"The oath, Nastina…repeat after me…all mimes must die!"

Nastina did as she was instructed. "ALL MIMES MUST DIE!"

She said it and her words were broadcast over the speakers for all to hear. It was then that the Poobla gave her a shove sending her over the edge of the bowl and into its waters. She went in head first. Quickly she kicked her way to the surface. It was difficult because the toilet bowl was filled with some kind of thick syrup. Upon getting her head above the surface, she took in a deep gasp of air and was instantly smitten by a type of mental state the likes of which she had never experienced. This was due to the fact that the toilet bowl was filled with a condensed version of Satano's Obvious. Nastina's mind was blown and she knew then exactly why it had been so easy for the Carnival of Despair to attract so many members to the clown supremacy movement. It also explained all of the long faces there for she definitely was not feeling the least bit funny.

"FLUSH! FLUSH! FLUSH!" screamed the crowd. Suddenly, the syrup in the bowl began to swirl. Nastina was helpless against the current. And then the toilet swallowed and Nastina was carried away down into the plumbing of the bowl. Then just as suddenly she found herself sliding down a pipe which eventually exited into a small wading pool to the side of the giant toilet. She found herself standing to the cheers of the masses before her.

AND SO IT WAS WRITTEN AND SO IT WAS DONE!

Chapter 27
What's the Haps?

As the clowns of Earth woke up the various mornings across the globe, as it turned around to face the sun, it was just another miserable day.

^%#@#^

And, what of Sicko? It is written that Sicko was in tears after being forced to retire his favorite bathrobe. He had worn it for over two decades and it had completely rotted off his soiled body. Reluctantly, he had himself driven to a Roman pajama tailor who fashioned him a new one. After wearing it home to the Vatican, Sicko took it off then urinated on it then vomited thick yellow bile down its sleeves and finally pooped down its back before putting it on again unwashed. The smell went nicely with the stupid hat.

%^$#%^

And, what of Satano? It is written that billions of godzillions of lightyears from the capitol of Like Everything, Satano, Prince of Darkness, eternal ruler of Hell, Inc. having caramel coated eyeballs for desert with his friend Death. Satano had only one thing on his mind and that was his new plans to help the clown's of Earth destroy themselves and the platypus.

%$#^%#

And, what of Jesus? What of God? It is written that half a billion, godzillion lightyears between Boogus Maximus and Heaven, God and his only begotten son were cruising, in the Lowrider-of-the-Gods, on their way back to God's domain. With all of creation now tied up in the legal system of the Powers That Be, it would be only a small eternity before they would be back in Heaven to find out what the haps there was. As terrible as their quest had been to endure at least it was a success. But neither of them was looking forward to all the work it would take to set things right again in the domain for that problem still remained regardless of the status of the Universe dictated by the Environmental Protection Agency.

^%$#^%

And, what of Elvis? It is written that Elvis had lost his best friend to a suzie who he still believed to be a spy. Blinko was spending all his free time with the stupid suzie and Elvis hated the way she wined and moaned and groaned to get her way, not to mention how she used her body to control him.

^%$#^%

And, what of Blinko? It is written that General Blinko, the leader of the Sideshow of Doom, a clown carrying out the will of Sicko, the will of Satano…his life seemed complete. After all, he had power, fame, fortune, good looks, and a girlfriend who was in love with him. All this, and to think for the time being he was also winning the war on mimes.

^%$#^%

And, what of Nastina? It is written that Nastina…fair maiden…secret agent for the Silent Minority…keeper of the Generals heart…a heart she couldn't wait to crush…one squeeze for every mime killed… was pleased with herself. Her mission was working flawlessly, she was getting all the inside information she needed. Soon, she would be in a position to strike, the only question being when.

^%$#^%

And, what of Chesty and Dew Drop? It is written that upon learning of their husbands Laymo and Whammo's release from the funny farm, they packed their few belongings in their stripper bag and split town with an old talking chimpanzee named Sam Simian. The two were never seen or heard from again.

^%$#^%

And, what of Whammo and Laymo? It is written that these two clowns were not having much luck coping with life on the outside. Whammo was consumed with his outrage over catching his son in bed with some clown. It did not take long for Laymo to get sick of Whammo constantly obsessing over the situation. Soon, they got into a major fistfight and were both killed when they accidentally fell out of the tree fort during one of their fights, onto the pavement below fracturing their skulls and bleeding to death.

^%$#^%

And, what of the Platypus? It is written that the Platypus was frolicking in her little swimming pool down under in Australia largely left alone by the few aboriginal clowns living on that continent. The Platypus was also largely unaware of her galactic importance so her primary concern was keeping her little burrow tidy and neat.

^%$#^%

These are the creatures we have come to know and love and this is their story. Did I say that? How cliché. Please excuse me. Anyway, by now I am willing to wager that you are wondering just who it is that has been telling you this tale. Who is this unknown being who seems to know everything there is to know about all these gods and clowns and other people? Well, allow me to introduce myself. It is I, the All Knowing Owl speaking. Surprised? Probably not. You probably figured that out by now. The real question is why? Why am I telling you all this? Well, the answer to that is a simple one as well…ANCIENT CHINESE SECRET…

Chapter 28
Blinko Eats Kahkah

Back in the sewers of Buffoonville, the silent army was once more assembled before their leader Nastina, a clown born unto mimes. Hers was turning into a story the likes of which would make any hero of old envious, for she was the incarnation of the often gestured but never spoken mime prophecy. It was gestured among them that one day, when the poop was really hitting the fan, a clown would come as savior of the silent. The fact that the savior was a suzie did not surprise the silent for their kind held no obvious distinction between the sexes. Theirs was a unisexual culture. However, time has proven that there is nothing more dangerous than a suzie scorned and this was a truth to be sure.

Recently thanks to her single minded ambitions, Nastina had memorized the tactics and movements of the clown supremacists and now the capture of mimes had dwindled to an all time low. Nastina had taught the mimes to utilize their mime powers with precision and purpose. In this way, the mimes had learned to protect themselves while on the surface, simply by imagining themselves to be clowns. This allowed them to move freely without the danger of being caught by the Notsees. The mimes were not limited to imagining themselves to be clowns either. They could become lamp posts or mail boxes or whatever they chose to be to suit their purpose.

Nastina had trained the best dreamers in the well to become a kind of terrorist unit. These were mimes eager to venture to the surface, in disguise, to plant booby-traps and generally raise Hell with the enemy. The Carnival of Despair had effectively absorbed the entire population of the Planet's clowns into the Notsee Party. Nastina had to find a way to organize the mimes in hiding worldwide, and teach them to not only defend themselves but to act as a united group. This was their only hope of turning back the wave of despair created by the fuhrer, Sicko the Clown.

For this goal, Nastina again used the combined powers of the dreamers and they learned how to teleport themselves across great distances with the power of their imaginations. It was in this way that Nastina and the dreamers literally emptied the concentration camps to the utter disbelief of the clown supremacists on guard. Because of Nastinas efforts and the disappearance of the mimes from the camps, it was not long before the suspicious clowns began to suspect one another and blame each other for these events. Soon, entire countries declared war upon each other, and in a few short months, the world was at war for the third time since the original reformation. Nastina herself was extremely upset about these turns of events. It had not been her intention to start a world war. She had only wanted to liberate the mimes from the clown supremacists. She blamed herself and, in a way, it really was all her fault. She knew this. A society that had been functioning as a civilization scapegoating another of their kind, without mimes as scapegoats, had completely turned against themselves.

Nastina had been successful at removing the mimes from the social order of things but had done nothing to solve the social disease of clown supremacy or the Carnival of Despair, and to that cause, she really had no ideas how to help. Therefore, she could only sit and watch in horror of it all. Then things took a turn for the worse. Nastina had taught the mimes to hate clowns in order to teach them how to save themselves. In other words, she had convinced the mimes to go bad. And indeed, the mimes liked it that way and soon hers was not the only silent voice to be gestured in the Reality Wells across the globe. Racist mimes hand- told their new rhetoric of hatred of clowns to the young and old. These were the mimes that took to the street, unseen by clowns, as they planted booby-traps and countless thousands of invisible objects for the clowns to crash into. Life for the clowns soon became total chaos…a double whammy of war among themselves and the war being waged against them by the dreamers and radical mime youth.

Soon, Nastina found she herself being persecuted by these zealots, for no matter how much she had helped them, these neo-mimes could not forgive her for being a clown. Nastina was beginning to wonder if she was really one of them to begin with.

&*^%&*

Sicko's Bed and Breakfast was no place for an attractive and intelligent suzie. That, and the fact she was a spy, made Nastina nervous whenever she was there. There was also the additional problem of being addicted to the Obvious, an addiction she had developed ten minutes after her baptism in the goo at the Carnival of Despair. She was presently right in the middle of shooting up when she realized that maybe her addiction and the sobering effect had been the cause of her trouble relating to the mimes. Was it possible that she had been making big mistakes with them because she had completely lost her sense of humor? Could the Obvious have caused her to be so driven that she had overlooked the obvious?

"Maybe that's how it got its name."

"Did you say something, sweetheart?" Blinko was responding to the sound of her voice.

"Oh, excuse me I was just thinking out loud, that's all."

Blinko didn't even pretend to listen. He was in some seriously deep bozokahkah. He felt like he had had his head buried in paper work for months. Ever since the disappearance of the mimes from the camps, things had really gone crazy. Had he been a foolish clown, things going crazy would not have bothered him, but he had been raised in a strict environment and had spent his entire life helping to regiment the planet.

Now, chaos was the order of the day. He looked over at his beautiful funny looking girlfriend, Nastina, and reached for his syrup shooter. She represented the only thing in his life that he could count on. Nastina had become the source of his mental stability. No matter how bad things got out there he could make it all go away just by spanking her. Suddenly, he lost his temper, slamming his fist down on the desk. Nastina Jumped.

"What!?" she said.

"Oh, nothing, lambchop, guess I was thinking out loud, too."

The cause of his outburst was that Blinko had just remembered last night…last night when he couldn't perform in bed. Sure that could happen to any clown now and then but it wasn't the first time with him. It wasn't even the second. He hadn't been able to perform all month.

"Maybe I'm gay" he thought. There had been those encounters in Reform School. His thoughts turned back to matters at hand…the current crisis…a civil war had broken out in Dimple Plump, an important middle-eastern country. Dimple Plump was

stratigically important as an ally and was the only thing standing in the way of an invasion by the Lint Goblins who wished to control the entire area. To make matters worse, the Frumpy Nuts were already occupying Northern Squambalina and the southern coastland of East Pimplestan.

A memo came up on the teletype. He read it. Dimple Plump had just been over run by guerillas from a radical division of the Sammich Conglomerate, and that meant that nothing now stood in the way of a full scale invasion by the Lint Goblins who were most likely supporting the guerilla faction. This brought to mind the Lump Miesters who were just waiting for the Lint Goblins to take over Dimple Plump because they had been in need of a place to war on the Goblins ever since they had been displaced from Lumpgeria by the Gonads from the Isle of Testicle. With all this political upheaval, Blinko was ready to have a nervous breakdown.

Blinko's thoughts turned to Elvis out of the blue. They had stuck it out together through thick and thin, but somehow and somewhere along the line, Nastina had come between them. He wondered why Elvis couldn't be content to share. He seemed so jealous of her. Of course, the real problem was that Blinko was a genuine knucklehead. That is why he chose to think that Elvis was jealous when the truth was that the clown couldn't stand to see the daily suzie-whipping that Nastina gave his best friend. That, and the fact that he was convinced from the start, that she was a spy. Any fool should have seen trouble in her thinly veiled questions about the party's movements and other stuff like that. But, Blinko was no fool, really. He was a rather serious individual and had rationalized her constant questions as her devotion to the party. Stillm other clues should have tipped him off like the way she never wanted to go to the Carnival or carefully changed the subject whenever Blinko started to talk about the joys of killing mimes. Nope, none of this added up in Blinko's mind because he was in love.

SELF DESTRUCTIVE CIRCUS FREAK!

Nastina sat on the bed looking at Blinko's muscular back. She kinda felt sorry for him. In order to be with him, she had found it necessary to overlook the evil things he did and focus on the good in him. Underneath all that big, bad Notsee bozokahkah was actually a really nice person. She liked him and had feelings for him even if she wasn't about to admit it to herself. The thing of it was, was that her assessment of what a monster Blinko was, was in direct comparison to how perfectly innocent the mimes were.

That was the trouble. The mimes had become almost as bad as the Notsees in their single minded hatred for clowns. Sure, the clowns had asked for it but the fact that the mimes had gone so very bad clouded her opinions of how bad the clown supremacists really were. She suspected that given the chance, the neo-mimes could be as cruel as any clown supremacist. Now, she was totally confuzzled.

"I'm screwed!" she thought. "*Look what I have done. The Obvious slips past me as easily as it slips through my veins.*"

Well, there was no fixing what she had done to the mimes…at least not as long as they had a reason to hate. But, what could she do now? The mimes were mostly liberated and operating on their own. They didn't need her anymore. It was time to focus on sabotaging the party somehow or as best she could. She realized that, in this case, there was little she could do. The Notsee Party and all its trappings had become the religion and the law of the land the world over. She remembered then the fundamental rule of social disruption:….*NEVER UNDERESTIMATE THE POWER OF THE INDIVIDUAL.*

ONE STONE THROWN INTO THE WATERS CREATES A RIPPLE NO MATTER HOW BIG THE OCEAN…

She knew then that her work as a spy in the headquarters of the Sideshow of Doom was finished. Now, she would be as a stone casting herself against the world by taking out a important General of the Notsee Party. The timing was perfect. The party was breaking up into smaller and smaller warring factions…it was consuming itself…but the elite of the party were still holding things together. Here was one of those elite. To kill him? Kill him and he would simply be replaced by Elvis and called a martyr. No, the answer was to crush him. Hit him were it would count the most. She would use his devotion to her as a weapon to bring him to his knees. All she had to do was leave him, simple as that. She would leave him alright…tonight!

^&%$^%

The next morning Blinko woke up with a splitting headache. He got himself out of bed, gritting his teeth, the pain of it was so bad. He stumbled into the bathroom. Upon looking in the mirror he discovered a note. It was stapled to his forehead. He moaned in agony as he pulled it free. Blood ran down into his eyes to mix with the tears as he read it.

Screw You, Blinko,

By the time you read this, I will be long gone. Don't bother trying to find me because even if you do, you will be sorry you did. I never loved you and I don't even like you.

Goodbye forever,
NASTINA

P.S. Elvis was right. I am a spy and I was also the leader of the mime underground resistance. Gotcha!

He stared at the letter…read it over and over but it still said the same thing, every time. His knees went out and on his way down he bashed his chin on the edge of the sink. Bouncing off the sink, his head collided with the toilet.
"Ohh…why…whyyy…? he said, getting up to his feet, feeling what would be nothing compared to how bad he was about to feel. Broken hearted, blood oozing from his forehead and chin, a lump on his head from the toilet, Blinko stumped his toe on the doorframe as he exited the bathroom. He screamed in the agony of it and began to hop on one foot as he held the injured other. Too bad about the roller skate too for he slipped on that, falling on an upright discarded tutti-fruity bottles.
"W*hat else could possibly go wrong now?"* he thought.

^%$#^%

Meanwhile, Sicko the Supreme Ding-a-ling was busy redecorating the Vatican. He hated all the shiny clean surfaces and polished golden ornamentation and had devised a sure fire method of messing the place up real good. Indeed, there was a shortage of mimes but there was no shortage of clown traitors and criminals and other enemies of the state. Sicko ordered that these clowns were to be brought into the various chambers in need of spoiling and he would then have them impaled on giant air nozzles. Then, high-pressure air would be blown into the impaled prisoners causing them to explode and splatter their guts all over the place. It was an efficient process and the remodel was coming along nicely. Best of all, it smelled really bad but still not even the stench of hundreds of gallons of rotting clown guts could compare with Sicko's famous body odor. Suddenly, his nostrils were inundated with a most ghastly odor from unknown origin. Actually, it was just Satano who was wearing freshly soiled clothing from Hell.

"Kneel!" commanded the Devil. Sicko immediately fell to his knees. There were maggots between the Devils toes and Sicko began to slurp them up in an honorary fashion. The Devil was pleased and spoke:

"Ah, Sicko…my old and faithful servant. How are you?"

Sicko answered his master mouth full of squirming larvi. "Imf fime thankmpf youff."

"Shut up!" said the Devil. "Something really awful has happened. I wish I could tell you exactly what has happened but the less you know the better. Someone might get hold of you and make you talk."

Sicko nodded yes.

"Anyway, I have a plan to fix things up but I am going to need your help. Now, remember when I told you that all mimes must die? Of course, you do. Well, I have sort of changed my mind about that."

Sicko's face showed surprise upon hearing the Devils words.

"I know what you're thinking, Sicko, but don't worry there is still going to be plenty of people I want you to kill. It's just that I need to broaden the base a little now. You see, there are others who deserve to die and you're gonna take care of that for me but we must do so with a bit of style, a bit of flash if you will. People will be watching this, of course, so we will need to be convincing. Anyway, I've got a few tricks up my sleeve, actually were sitting on it but nevermind that for now. Yes, the time has come as far as I can tell so lets get started shall we?"

Sicko had raised his had to ask a question.

"A question? Shoot."

"So, who else then? Who else am I supposed to kill?"

Satano looked upwards and placed an evil thumb under his evil chin. "Now, let me see…hmmm…well, as far as my calculations go it looks like….everybody!"

Sicko coughed and gulped.

"Everybody?"

"Everybody!"

Sicko may have been a seriously bad clown but killing everybody seemed a trifle bit drastic. "Is that really necessary?" he asked.

The Devil grew angry over having one of his worthless minions questioning his word. "You think I would joke about wiping clowns off the face of the Earth? Who are you to question me? I am your master. You sold me your soul and don't you forget it!"

Every word that came out of the Devil's mouth did so in the form of flames. Sicko began to cry.

"You're scaring me!"

"Aw, quit your crying, ya big baby. Now, listen, here is what we're gonna do…"

&^$#^$

For a while, Blinko just lay there on his right side agonizing over the loss of his sweetheart, Nastina, and rolling on to this left side to agonize over his homosexual fears. He went on like this, in woe as me fashion, rolling back and forth, until he had cried himself down a bit. Then, his attention was focused underneath his dresser where he could see the lamp cord plugged in.

"I'll kill myself!" he said, thinking of what a number electricity used to do on all those toads he and Elvis used to fry in the little electric chair they had built. Quickly, he got up and shoved the dresser away from the wall. Blinko yanked the cord from the socket and put it into his mouth chewing through it in moments. Then he split the cord in two, separating the positive wire from the ground wire. He placed the two ends on the floor and plugged the cord back in. Now, the wire was hot. All he need do was grab each end in each hand to fry himself like a frog.

Blinko was no chicken. He had the balls to do it. He sat on the floor with the cord ends between his legs. He picked up the ground wire in his left hand, then gritted his teeth, as he reached for the hot wire with his right. The current hit him hard and his hands were instantly stuck to the wires as the voltage surged through him. He shuddered like a vibrator on a desktop. Slobber poured out of his mouth as his glands spasmed. He pooped his pants and his eyes rolled back in his head. His legs kicked out hard hitting the wall sending him flying backwards. This unplugged the cord, saving his life. Blinko lay on the floor unconscious.

While unconscious, Blinko had a vision. In it, he was a little clown again. He was Blinko, the orphan, and he was lost. Being such a small child, he was terrified. It was dark out and the monsters would no doubt gobble him up. Then he saw a porch light come on and he ran for it thinking he could hear the monsters on his trail. Then, a door opened and he could see an old suzie standing in it. Next, he was in her bosom and she was saying:

"Now, now, Blinko, you're safe with Miss Smoochy, baby."

Blinko closed his eyes and felt safe against her warm body. When he opened his eyes, he found himself in her arms only now he was fully grown and laying on the floor in his room at Sicko's Bed and Breakfast. She had his head in her lap. He looked up at her feeling his body ache all over. Her face was surrounded by a glowing white light and behind her he could see fluffy white feathers.

"Wings?" he said.

"All angels have wings, Blinko." Her voice soothed his pain somehow.

"Miss Smoochy?" he said.

"Oh! So, you haven't forgotten me after all." Again, it was like her voice was some kind of painkiller.

"What are you doing here?"

"Why, Blinko, didn't you know? I am your guardian angel. You just about killed yourself, silly boy."

Blinko suddenly remembered all of the pain of the day's events.

"But I'm gay and Nastina left me! She was a spy and our whole relationship was just some kind of sick joke!"

"Well, what did you expect Blinko? You have grown up to be such a rotten young clown."

"What's that supposed to mean?"

Miss Smoochy pushed the clown into a sitting position.

"You're going around killing mimes and following that evil clown, Sicko. You're full of hate. Your karma is totally ruined!"

"So, what goes around comes around, is that it? But, I am only doing God's will!"

"Listen to me, Blinko, you're totally full of kahkah. You have no idea what you're really doing, do you?"

Blinko was confused. "I don't understand." he said, intrigued to hear Miss Smoochy continue:

"Of course, you don't. That's because you have been lied to all your life. Your WHOLE LIFE is just one big lie, Blinko. But never fear, I am here to straighten you out and offer you a chance to redeem yourself."

Blinko was still completely puzzled. "What do you mean my life is one big lie?"

Miss Smoochy stood before him and stretched out her wings. "Blinko, there is something I must ask you to do."

Blinko was now standing as well, before the angel. "What, Miss. Smoochy?"

"I want you to go down into Sicko's basement and find his scrapbooks. There is something very important to you in those scrapbooks."

Blinko protested. "But I can't go into Sicko's basement! Everybody knows that it is off limits. The penalty for going down there is death!"

"Never-the-less, Blinko, you must, it is your destiny. Besides, what have you to live for? You were just trying to off yourself right? What have you to lose?"

Miss Smoochy was right and by now Blinko was curious about the things she was saying. It is written that Blinko agreed to go and seek out the scrapbooks and with that, Miss Smoochy was pleased and bid him farewell, disappearing into a misty white light. Nice touch, that light.

Sicko had been living in the Vatican for several months now and there was little chance that Blinko would get caught going into the basement by Sicko himself. Besides he had seniority at the funhouse and was the only one there, anyway. Carefully, he approached the door to the stairwell going down into the basement. He was finding it difficult to overcome his reluctance to go in. This taboo had been drilled into his brain for many years. Anyway, eventually, he opened the door and was struck hard in the honker by a truly horrible musty smell. It made him wince but after turning on the light, he began to descend the filthy staircase. The floor at the bottom was wet and the smell down there had intensified. Blinko tried not to but he succumbed to the offensive odor because he knew he had to examine the room in search of the scrapbooks.

There was a soiled bed next to a pile of trash and garbage. The air was thick with flies and a layer of vermin and other creatures scurried about in total disregard to his presence. He paid attention to Sicko's altar in front of a tattered Notsee banner. The altar was made of clown bones and what appeared to be skin. Evidently, Sicko enjoyed killing clowns as much as mimes and Blinko began to wonder just how much he didn't know about this clown who had always been his personal hero. The place was chock full of weird stuff. It was like a cross between a garbage dump and a museum.

Then, he took notice of the bookcase. It was mostly full of formerly banned books, all now readily available under the new social codes of the Carnival of Despair, but on the end was a row of scrapbooks. Blinko took down what looked like the most recent one and thumbed through it. The scrapbook was obsessive in the way it was neatly organized and laid out. Apparently, Sicko was rather meticulous about documenting his life. The scrapbook was full of articles related to the Notsee Party and wherever Sicko's name appeared he had highlighted it. Blinko put the scrapbook back in favor of another and slowly but surely worked his way back into Sicko's past life. Eventually, he came to books dated before the Party and Blinko took great interest in them because he could hardly remember a time when there WASN'T a party. The articles he found in these old and tattered scrapbooks were mostly about various crimes that Blinko guessed were committed by Sicko as a young clown. It is written that here he came across the article that would change everything. There was an article describing the murder of two clowns at Buffoonville hospital twenty odd years ago…his parents, Blinko Sr. and Pattycakes! Evidently, Sicko the Clown had killed his parents! Even more shocking was another account of the murder of Sicko's wife and children. Children who were mimes! Sicko's own offspring had been mimes!

Blinko could scarcely believe his eyes. His hero, Sicko the Clown, had killed his parents and was the father of not one, but three mimes. How could this be? Yet, the facts were right there in Sicko's own scrapbooks. Blinko knew then, that all this time, he had been carefully brainwashed by Sicko. Miss Smoochy was right…his whole life really was a lie! All of this totally blew the clowns mind. What a day! He put the scrapbook back on the dusty shelf and sat on Sicko's bed dazed.

"I'll kill him!" he thought, realizing instantly that that was a completely impractical idea. What good would it do, anyway? All that would happen would be him dangling on the end of a rope. This was an entire world that idolized Sicko the Clown Supreme Ding-a-ling, a world that lived by his word as law. Sicko was the next best thing to God in most clowns' minds. Besides nothing would ever begin to make up for all the bad things he himself had done over the years. He didn't know what the truth was but he was starting to feel that he couldn't take for granted all of the things he had been taught to believe. Besides, the pressures on him had been really intense lately and he had secretly been fantasizing about getting out of it all somehow. Now, it looked like he had discovered a legitimate reason. He was having a moment of truth.

His thoughts shifted to Nastina. She had only been gone since last night. He did love her even IF she had only been with him to spy on the party. He recalled that her letter had said that she had been the leader of the mime underground. He realized then that this must have been why he loved her so much. On the surface, she had pretended to a typical, if hot, suzie but underneath she was a powerful leader, his equal only on opposite sides of the track. He wondered, for a moment, how many defeats he had met while with her that was a direct result of her leadership. Regardless of that, this person she was, who he never knew, would be the essential her, the real her, and must have been the thing about her that had captured his heart even if he never knew a thing about it.

Suddenly, he felt that he loved her twice as much as before. She was perfect for him after all, but now she was undoubtedly gone forever.

Then, it struck him. Why was she the defender of mimes? What reason could she have had to choose such a path? With him she could have had it all. In fact, for a time she did have it all but she had turned her back on it now to go off where? All of this saddened him. He looked at Sicko's clock and realized he had been down there brooding for several hours now. He thought to leave.

No sooner had Blinko come to the top of the stairs, than did he find yet another unfortunate turn of events. At the top of the stairs was Elvis looking angry and puzzled and was holding Nastina's note.

"Traitor!" screamed Elvis shoving the note in Blinko's face. You sold us out to that suzie! What are you doing in Sicko's basement? The punishment for that is death!"

Blinko said nothing, for there was nothing he could say, and he simply tried to leave. He didn't want to fight, he just wanted out and away from that place. Seeing Elvis caused it to dawn on him that he wasn't just going to be allowed to walk away from his responsibilities in the party. Now, he would have to try and explain what he was doing to his best friend…a friend that was still as brainwashed as he had been only a few hours ago. Just as he would with all the others including Sicko.

"I knew it all along…your just a mime lover, Blinko, and now your patooty is grass…"

Blinko was deep inside himself. He deserved to hear the truth at least but this only led him to another realization…it occurred to him that all of this was known and would matter only to him. He was on his own because what Sicko had done, he had only done to Blinko personally. Elvis and all the others had nothing against Sicko and probably never would. Of course, there was still the revelation that Sicko's own children had been mimes but who would believe a lone soldier out of the millions with a story like that. Sicko's reputation was beyond reproach. So, Elvis wouldn't care even if he heard the truth. For that matter, neither would the rest of the world….truth is today not yesterday…that's right out of Mime Kampf. That's when a fist slammed into his honker. Elvis wasn't going to give him a chance to explain.

It is written that the fight between Elvis and Blinko did not last long. There were two reasons for this. One was that Blinko was much bigger than Elvis and the other reason was that the first blow to his honker had sent Blinko in to the trance and in that state he was virtually undefeatable. When he came out of it, Elvis, like many others who had tested Blinko, was dead with a broken skull. When he came out of it, Blinko was still holding the bowling pin he had evidently used to kill Elvis. Seeing Elvis dead on the floor with his brains spilling out of his noggin made Blinko hot with remorse. Tears erupted from his eyes and he fell to the floor, at his pal's side, begging to be forgiven by the dead clown. This just wasn't the way he had had things planned. Now, he was totally screwed. His best friend was dead by his own hand…a cold blooded murder of a loyal party member it was. He would hang for that. His girlfriend had left him and was a spy. They would hang him for that one, too. He had ventured in to Sicko's basemen… another hangable offense if they found out. There was only one thing to do. Blinko pulled Elvis's slack body from the floor and threw it down the staircase into Sicko's basement, then shut the door up tight. Now, he would pack his few personal belongings and go on the lam. He figured it would be months before Sicko discovered Elvis's body there at the bed and breakfast, and that other officials would figure that Elvis had disappeared along with General Blinko for the time being. He went upstairs to pack.

AND SO IT WAS WRITTEN AND SO IT WAS DONE!

Chapter 29
Coincidences

The mime had no name, but his identity was gestured to all of the silent in the Reality Well of Buffoonville. He had experienced the worst of tortures, at the hands of the clown supremacists, in a concentration camp. This mime had been given the duty of choosing who would die on extermination days. Yet mimes, in those days, had yet to understand the concept of hatred, so none held it against him. Still, he personally felt much pain and guilt over what the clowns had forced him to do and, because of this, the others felt sorry for him. In a way, his situation had been worse than death and after he was rescued by Nastina and the dreamers, he vowed never to forget or let be forgotten what had happened to him and the others at the hands of the clowns.

Now, he had become very powerful within the mime community in the Well, and thanks to Nastina's unwise decision to teach the mimes to hate clowns, he had become the biggest bigot in the Well and a bit insane to boot. But, who could blame him? Besides the fact that his hatred was more than justified, it was still a form of moral corruption and was no good to anyone, especially he.

It had been several weeks since Nastina had been back to visit the Well and this was unfortunate for her. In those weeks, a lot had happened there and since the Well was out of the time continuum these events had had plenty of moments to take hold in greater mime politics.

The nameless mime survivor of the holocaust had come to believe that the mimes must go on the offensive and wage all out war on the clowns to insure that they would never again be in a position to perpetrate such evils. He wasn't alone in his beliefs, the dreamers were behind him, and so were all of the concentration camp survivors. The nameless one pantomimed his rhetorical speeches to the masses and eventually he had the sympathy of them all. Then his teachings spread from Well to Well until mimes worldwide became united under his cause. For the first time in all their tragic history, the Reality Wells became military states where every mime was drafted into the Legions of Silence.

Nastina arrived in the Reality Well of Buffoonville only to be arrested by guards heavily armed with imagination. The guards escorted her to stand before the nameless one and a heated argument took place, gestured between them. Both participants hand signed melees of symbolics in a blur but in the end Nastina was escorted back to the sewers, exiled from the Well forever, simply because she was a clown. To him, it did not matter that without her he would most likely still be stuck in a concentration camp or be dead even. It did not matter that she was the clown prophesized to be the savior of their race or that, in fact, she had done so. Just like all prophets, she was thrown to the wolves by the very people she had come to save from certain doom. Racism often works that way, which was why it was one of Satan's oldest tricks in the book.

Anyway, the nameless one had pantomimed to her that it was time for the silent to create a new order and one where mimes ruled the earth. It was that statement that told Nastina that her worst fears had come to pass and it was on this point that she pondered as she made her way through the sewers on her way back to the surface. She had tried everything in here arsenal of charades to convince the nameless one otherwise but it was no use. Now she was shunned, exiled, excommunicated not to mention thrown out in a hostile world of clown supremacists. She realized that now that she had left General Blinko of the Sideshow of Doom, she really had nowhere left to go. She had never felt more desperate and alone.

It is written that on this particular day a series of record-breaking coincidences occurred. These coincidences were duly recorded by the bald-headed, hunch-backed, female, humanoid on Boogus Maximus, much to her amazement and delight.

The first coincidence was two clowns, one male, one female, found their entire lives shattered into a godzillion pieces on the same day.

The second was that both had suddenly found themselves outcasts without a friend or country, so to speak. These coincidences are even more coincidental because these coincidences happened to two clowns of the opposite sex that happened to be lovers in the middle of an ugly break-up.

The third incredible coincidence was that these two clowns were presently located within a meter of one another, both having purchased tickets on the same train going to the same destination…San Francisco.

The fourth incredible coincidence was that neither had run into each other in the process of purchasing the tickets, waiting for the train, or boarding the train, and so on.

The fifth incredible coincidence was that both had decided to take the train as the first step in their identical desperate plans to get as far away from Buffoonville as possible.

The sixth incredible coincidence was that the two were seated in the same cabin, neither having recognized the other because Blinko, who had boarded first, was hidden behind a newspaper he was reading when Nastina entered the cabin. Blinko didn't bother to look over his paper until the train was well under way.

The seventh incredible coincidence was that when the clown finally put his paper down and they both realized they were on the same train, in the same cabin, they looked at each other, pointing an accusing finger at one another and saying in unison: "YOUUUUUUUUU…." with ugly faces.

Then they began to laugh because it was all just too incredibly coincidental and created the eighth and final incredible coincidence by reaching for their syrup shooters simultaneously.

It was as if there was some anonymous individual sitting around writing the story of their lives.

"Did you get my letter?" asked Nastina.

Blinko pointed to the little scabs on his forehead. "The staples were a really nice touch."

"I had to leave you Blinko…we just don't have anything in common…and besides the whole relationship was just a big lie anyway."

Blinko leaned forward and put his hand on the suzie's knee. "Are you certain?"

Nastina was slightly annoyed by being touched by him but did not attempt to remove his hand from her knee. "I am not certain about anything anymore." She put her head in her hands.

"You wouldn't believe what happened to me right after I got your letter." Blinko removed his hand from Nastina's knees and stretched his long legs out straight, leaning back.

"Does that have anything to do with why you're on this train?" Nastina stretched out just like the clown in front of her. Their legs were touching now.

"Why are YOU on this train?" asked Blinko.

"You first, Mister." Nastina crossed her arms and waited for Blinko to begin telling her how he ended up on the same train as she. He told her everything starting with waking to find her "Dear John" stapled to his forehead. Nastina freaked out as soon as the skinhead mentioned he had discovered that Miss Smoochy was his guardian angel.

"You mean to say that Miss Smoochy is your guardian angel, too?" She was shaking her head in disbelief.

"What do you mean TOO?"

"Miss Smoochy is MY guardian angel, also Blinko."

Blinko got up and sat next to his former love and was silent in thought for a moment. Then, he told her how he had just learned how he had become an orphan when Sicko the Clown killed his parents and how he had come to live with Miss Smoochy at the Buffoonville Orphanage until she got killed by a jalopy when the driver made a beeline for her bullseye underpants.

Needless-to-say, Nastina was shocked by the incredible coincidence that Blinko had lived at the same orphanage as she at the same time. Eagerly, she told Blinko about how she had been the clown baby born to mime parents who had dropped her off at the orphanage because they could not care for her.

"This is incredible, Blinko…if you had told me this before…gee, it's just too incredible to believe."

Then Nastina talked for a while telling Blinko how she had come to learn that Miss Smoochy was her guardian angel after her own suicide attempt. How she had come to discover that her parents were mimes, which is when she started her mission to save the mimes from the Notsees. She kept right on talking until she had explained everything leading up to her being seated on the train with a General of the Notsee Party. Besides, it felt good to reveal the truth finally and to have someone to talk to about her secret life after all those years. When it came time for Blinko to talk, he finished his story about how he had found out that Sicko was the Clown that murdered his parents. He also told of how Sicko had fathered three mimes and how he had come to realize that his whole life and everything he believed in was a big lie. Blinko eagerly proclaimed to his love that he no longer wanted anything to do with the party. He also spoke of the fact that he had killed his best friend and was forced to go on the lam and that consequently he had decided to get on a train and begin his journey to get as far away from Buffoonville as he could.

They both sort of sat there quietly, neither knowing what to say next. Really? What COULD they say?

The telling of each others life story had answered a lot of questions between them. Soon, the two were talking about how amazing it was that they had both had major moments of truth upon meeting with Miss Smoochy, the angel, after their suicide attempts. Suddenly, it was as though there wasn't anyone in the world but them. On impulse, Blinko stood and pulled Nastina out of her seat and into his muscular tattooed arms.

"I really did love you, Nastina. I know you hated me for the things I did but I've changed…really I have." He held Nastina tightly.

"I know…" Nastina said, as she waited for more. No suzie could resist a good looking clown in the process of schmoozing.

"Now, I am starting to think that we were meant to be together…I mean we have the same guardian angel and despite the odds were both ended up running for our lives."

"I know…." agreed Nastina, again, she waited for more.

"Listen, Nastina, I cleaned out my bank account. I've got three million smack-a-rues in a trunk on this train. We can disappear and be together forever. We can put the past behind us…to Hell with everyone…everyone in the world."

"Oh, Blinko your so cliché!" She kissed Blinko on his honker and nestled down in his strong arms. Later, both shared a candy cigarette and a much needed blast of the Obvious. They felt contemplative after that.

"You ever get the feeling…" pondered Nastina, "…that your whole life is written out for you?"

"You mean that life is just like some kind of fantastic story and there is some clown out there sitting around with a pen and paper just making it all up as he goes along?"

"Yeah, exactly." Nastina said as she kissed him on the cheek.

"Could be" he said.

"So, where do you think this clown is gonna send us now?"

"I don't know, Nastina. I guess we will find out when we get there. And I really like the sound of that."

"Sound of what?" she asked.

"US."

AND THE STEADY PULSE OF THE CHOO-CHOO ROCKED THEM TO SLEEP

Chapter 30
Sicko Messiah

Sicko arrived home at his bed and breakfast to learn of the disappearance of his top General, Blinko, along with discovering that Elvis, formerly thought to have disappeared with General Blinko, was actually lying dead in his basement, which had been broken into and defiled. Got that? Well, he was not happy about this. The timing couldn't have been worse. Not only was his party beginning to crumble but he had been given new orders by Satano to fulfill.

"This freakin' job!" screamed the clown gone bad as he removed his Obvious hose from his mouth. Sicko's veins had collapsed from years of injections and now drinking the goo straight was the only way for him to get serious. Anyway, what was left of his top party members were also extremely upset with the news of Blinko's disappearance and Elvis's death. It was clear that Blinko was the murderer, so Sicko put out some propaganda accusing him of that crime as well as treason and also a death warrant. Now, millions of skinheads would be after the clown. He also declared a week of baptisms in the Obvious which triggered the phenomenon of …WHERE WERE YOU WHEN ELVIS DIED?

Not surprisingly, clowns began to report having contacted the martyred Elvis's spirit during hasty séances or even reported seeing him alive somewhere. Sometimes there is no end to a clown's bozokahkah.

If anything, the events helped to refocus the party for the moment which was good because the skins were getting bored with turning in traitors in the absence of mimes.

But little did Sicko know that all out war against the clowns and the Carnival of Despair was about to erupt, for the Legions of Silence were almost done with their secret plans.

On the ship sailing back to the Vatican, across the sea, Sicko realized that he was actually kinda glad to be rid of Blinko and Elvis, for he never really liked them anyway and they had outlived their usefulness to him a long time ago. For that matter, Sicko really didn't like any clown. Regardless, the trip was uneventful.

Back at the Vatican, Sicko secretly went to his secret elevator and thumbed the secret button that would secretly take him down into the secret catacombs where long forgotten and taboo secret artifacts were secretly stored. The secret artifacts were from pre-reformation days…weird stuff left over from humanity. The last time anyone had ventured into these catacombs was during the Great World War of Morons hundreds of years ago. Back then, the reigning Supreme Ding-a-ling, seeking a solution that could not be found, due to his nearly complete retardation, had sent the smarty-pants into the darkness to bring forth forgotten technology in the form of mighty weapons. The best they had managed to come up with in the end was the Intercontinental Ballistic Cream Puff of Death or the Itsy-bitsy-pods as they were referred to affectionately.

Those old warriors were, of course, complete idiots being devout practitioners of the Doctrines of Grand Lunacy. Sicko, on the other hand, was at this time a total genius. He had been educating himself for thirty something years and had also had his brains rewired in the fashion of a cockroach, a creature that is a lot smarter than the average clown.

Sicko's mission was clear. He was to pour through the forbidden knowledge and from it find the technology to create a Doomsday Device. Satano had not told him when it would be used nor had he explained why he wanted Sicko to make one to kill every clown on Earth, but Sicko didn't care and was actually kinda excited about the whole idea.

"I'll push the button and tape it down!" he said, while reading a thick manual on the subject of nuclear physics.

He had been at it for several weeks now. His plans were coming along nicely. He hadn't had too much trouble finding the information he needed and he had assembled a crack team of smarty-pants to assist him. There were a million details involved and a million working parts to be fabricated. The problem was further complicated by the fact that the technology needed to create all the parts also had to be invented for there were no factories left capable of producing stuff like that. Weeks became months as he worked. He completely lost himself in the project and forgot about the world outside until one day he was bugged by an enlisted skinhead.

"It's war, Sir" said the skinny soldier.

"War? With who?" Sicko's head was buried in a cook book.

"The mimes, Sir."

"The mimes? I thought they had all disappeared ages ago."

"Well, the mimes are back and they're winning, Sir."

Sicko put the book down for this news had gotten his attention.

"You mean to tell me that all of the sudden the mimes are back and that they are winning?"

"That's what it amounts to, Sir."

The enlisted clown was getting nervous because Sicko had turned bright red. If only his Doomsday Device were ready. The soldier took a chance and spoke.

"You better come see for yourself, Sir."

Sicko nodded in agreement and duly followed the clown to the secret elevator.

Eventually, he was seated in his throne room littered of rotting, impaled clowns and brand new television monitors. The place was completely full of flies and news reporters. The reporters were swatting the flies. It made for an interesting sound…all this buzzing and swatting.

Each of the monitors was showing worldwide reports of the war, which had broken out only a few days prior.

Sicko slammed his fist on the armrest of his throne.

"Why wasn't I notified of this earlier?"

A low ranking peon answered.

"We wanted to, Sir, but no clown knew where the secret elevator was. It took us this long to find it."

There was little Sicko could say to that. Sicko focused his attention on the television labeled Buffoonville because that was his home town. It didn't look like much of a war to him. The streets were empty and devoid of pedestrian and vehicular traffic. Where was all the rubble? Where were all the fires? Where were all the dead soldiers and stuff like that? Then a terrified reporters face entered the screen.

"As you can see, this deserted street has been the site of some of the war's heaviest fighting. We have reports of serious casualties all over the city. However, I have just received news that an entire regiment of skinheads is on their way here. Wait! I can hear them coming."

Sicko turned up the volume and could just hear the sound of marching boots. Then, he could see the first of the toilet seat wearing skinheads coming in from the East into the deserted intersection.

"But, where are the mimes?" he thought. The reporter was talking now…

"Here they come folks…, I sure hope they fare better than the last bunch.." Sicko could hear someone shout "CHARGE!" and the whole regiment went running into the intersection yelling their heads off. The result was the lot of them, 45 skinheads, just standing there occupying the space. What happened next was totally unbelievable.

Suddenly 45 anvils fell from the sky landing on each and every skin, smashing them to paste on the pavement. Then, just as suddenly, the anvils began to fade away until they had disappeared all together and the clowns underneath disappeared as well! Now, the intersection was as silent as it was empty. The reporter was talking now…

"You saw it folks…God help us it has been like this all over…all over the world!"

Sicko turned his attention towards other sets and saw the same scene repeated indeed, across the globe.

He screamed, leaping out of the throne. The reporters rushed him holding out microphones at arms length begging the Supreme Ding-a-ling for comments. Sicko would not have it and called his soldiers to clear the room. It took a moment but this was done efficiently enough.

Sicko thought about it and knew that it was hopeless. I mean how do you go about fighting something like that? He began to think about it and moments later realized that all of it was irrelevant. After all, he was right in the middle of creating a Doomsday Device which would kill every clown and mime on Earth anyway! Suddenly, he felt much better and tried to laugh, but he had forgotten how. So, he made his way back to the secret elevator and down into the catacombs to resume his research.

Months went by and the war went on without him. Sometimes though, he checked up on things. Evidently, the mimes had forced the Sideshow of Doom into submission and retreat. The skins were totally unable to defend themselves from the mime's attacks. The mimes had also caused inanimate objects to spring to life to terrorize the civilian populations. It had gotten so bad that the clowns had vacated their cities and towns and villages and hamlets, escaping into the relative safety of the woods and hillsides.

Ironically, these areas were the places the mimes were once forced to inhabit in days of old. As a result, clown civilization on the whole collapsed and there was a complete reversal of fortune, as the victorious mimes took residence in the deserted cities while the helpless clowns began to live barbaric lives in the wilderness. One time Sicko had come out of the lab, sick of living on war rations, in search of food, but the mimes had taken the Vatican over as well. This forced him to abandon his search. He wondered why they didn't notice him and the smarty-pants down there, but didn't trouble himself to find out. He simply forgot about them and went back into the secret chambers and back to work on the Doomsday Device. Besides, there was enough ancient army food to last a life time down there and Satano, of course, kept him supplied with all the Obvious he drink. He had little to worry about.

While the mimes reveled in the total liberation from clown suppression, the clowns themselves had regressed into a pitiful state. Millions upon millions died from withdrawals from the Obvious, laughing themselves to death. With these mass deaths came millions of suicides, as hopeless clowns surrounded by clown corpses decided to off themselves. The clowns that were left tried to get their act together but without the Obvious to keep them serious, their pitiful attempts failed. After all, in their natural state, clowns are perfect idiots and mess up everything. Also there was no longer a social order to keep things going. No circus, no carnival. The clowns had effectively been sent back to the stone age.

All the while Sicko kept working on the Doomsday Device. The mimes completely ignored him, for after destroying the clown's civilization so utterly, they went back to being their pleasant selves and forgot about hating clowns for the most part. What few clowns there were, that were brave enough to enter the city, the mimes mostly thought of and treated like pigeons living on crumbs.

Then, it came to pass that Sicko was forced to leave the comforts of his secret laboratory in the catacombs of the Vatican to seek out special ingredients for the Doomsday Device. To this end, he moved his entire operation onto an old choochoo train and traveled alone for several years around the Eastern Hemisphere collecting the various things he needed. Then one day, after getting together all the stuff he needed to finish the devicer, he loaded it all on an abandoned freighter and set sail for the Western Hemisphere.

Sicko had decided the location for the completion of his Doomsday Device should be Buffoonville. Subsequently, the trip across the ocean was uneventful and Sicko was proud of himself for being such a skilled sailor as well as choo-choo conductor…not to mention, the rather impressive feat of loading all his bozokahkah on the freighter all by himself and a million other seemingly impossible feats that no single clown should ever have managed alone. Yet the clown gone bad triumphed, and to think he still didn't know how to ride a unicycle.

Upon the shores of the Western Hemisphere, Sicko again defied probability and loaded all his stuff onto another abandoned choo-choo and set steam for Buffoonville. A lot of the time he felt like the last clown on Earth, as he passed through the mostly deserted towns. Here and there he saw mimes but even they, for the most part, were hidden from view. He supposed that years of hiding had made them a bit shy. Still, Sicko knew that on judgment day the clowns would come. They would crawl out of the stone age to gather around a familiar, if forgotten, voice.

HIS voice.

They would once again embrace him as their leader. Then, he would push the proverbial button and blow them all to smithereens. He could hardly wait.

777

MEANWHILE IN ANOTHER SECTION OF THE UNIVERSE…

"God, it's good to be home" said Jesus Christ to his Father as their feet hit the heavenly soil.

The trip had been much too long and all those years just sitting there in the low-rider had caused the God's legs to atrophy. Jesus looked down at his skinny limbs.

"I look like some kinda freak!" he said.

"I want to something to eat" replied God.

"Me, too."

Jesus then took notice of a small calamity heading their way.

"Here comes the welcome wagon!"

God looked in the direction of the calamity. He saw a golden chariot driven by Saint Peter and pulled by a team of white horses. There were a dozen centerfolds in the chariot with him. Saint Peter began to rattle off salutations.

"Hey, dudes! What's up? Long time no see! What's happening? Good to see ya! How's it goin'?"

God suspiciously eyeballed the saint.

"What's wrong?" he said.

Saint Peter knew there was no fooling God.

"Aw! I was hoping to keep it a secret from you guys until after you had a chance to relax from your trip."

God sat on the hood of the Low-rider of the Gods.

"Spill it, Pete, we can take it."

"Well…" began the saint, "Positrons have been mighty tight since you guys left twenty years ago. The angels have been complaining about not getting what they were promised and that kinda thing and we have sorta had some female defections…."

"Defections?" asked Jesus coming to sit next to his Father.

"Yeah, you know…when a formerly loyal subject defects to the other side."

"I know what it means, Pete…Who, is what I am asking."

"Not who *was* it Jesus but who *were* it."

"More than a few?" asked God.

"More like a few hundred thousand" replied the saint.

"A few hundred thousand?" said the Gods in unison. God elaborated.

"How could you just sit there and let a few hundred thousand of our women defect?"

Pete kicked at the heavenly soil and shrugged. It was time for him to fess up.

"I didn't just sit there, Jehovah, I actually kinda arranged it!"

"What in creation are you talking about?" God was getting angry.

"Well, you know the Weirdoes have no women and we were out of Positrons to pay the bills and the utilities conglomerate was gonna shut off the power, so I arranged the sale of a few hundred thousand gals to them."

Jesus got up off the hood of the low-rider and came to face his old friend.

"So, you sold a hundred thousand babes to the Weirdoes, is that it?"

"Babes? Heck no, Christ…I sold 'em a bunch of ugly Neanderthals from the stone age. They were glad to go and the stupid, desperate Wierdoes loved them!"

It is written that it was here that the Gods broke out in a fit of hysterics.

"So you paid the bills then…good show old boy!" said God.

"Right on." Saint Peter was relieved. "So, did you guys get some financial advice from the All Knowing Owl?"

Jesus took his turn.

"Better than that, Pete. After talking to the Owl we took his advice and managed to get the whole domain deemed a wildlife refuge thanks to one of Dad's creations, the Platypus being the only non redundant creature in Like Everything."

"That's totally awesome!" Saint Peter gestured with his arm, "C'mon, get in the chariot. Everyone's waiting for you." Jesus and Jehovah got in the chariot and were glad to be standing up for a change. Besides, there were a dozen centerfolds in back with them. The angels were quick to realize that they hadn't made love in ages. There was only one thing to do…

"Take the scenic route will you?" ordered God to Peter as both he and his Son fell into the pile of women who welcomed them. It is written that this was far from unusual.

Soon, they came to the splendid door, which was the doorway into the offices of God, located there in its enormous towers. When they reached the penthouse, in the right tower, they found God's secretary, Marilyn Monroe totally whacked out on happy pills. It was clear that she was glad to see them. Peter was still curious about the Platypus that was supposedly saving the entire universe.

"So, tell me more about this Platypus creature that saved the day."

Jesus let out a massive sigh before answering.

"Well, there is really not that much to tell. The Platypus is this ugly little marsupial that lives on an island continent on the planet Earth. Isn't that ironic, Peter? It's YOUR home-world and where I went and got myself crucified."

The saint suddenly had a painful look on his face.

"Earth? Uh-oh."

God got worried because he had felt all along that all that had happened was too good to be true. He just knew that eventually something would come along and ruin everything.

"What do you mean uh-oh?" he said. The saint was peevish and reluctant to rain on God's parade, so to speak.

"Well, it is just that the situation on Earth has gone critical in your absence. Satano, for some reason, seems to have focused all his attention on Earth lately and he has managed to cause the inhabitants there to war among themselves, which resulted in the complete collapse of the Earth's primary civilization. There is no doubt that he is trying to convince the clowns to destroy themselves. And all the while we, in Heaven, were helpless to do anything about it." God and Jesus fell silent for a few tense moments. Then the Lord spoke.

"It is obvious what is going on. The Weirdoes have plenty of powerful insiders on Boogus Maximus who no doubt informed them of our neat little trick and now they have undoubtedly told Satan of our plans. That is why he is trying to get the clowns to destroy themselves…he is hoping that in the process the Platypus will also be destroyed. Without the Platypus, we are totally screwed! Any fool can see that!"

Jesus got serious.

"Then, there is no time to waste! Let's get down to Earth and try to reverse the evil that Satan has spread there."

God nodded in agreement but had a sad face on.

"Hold on there, Son…we still have one big problem. We're completely broke."

God was right. What little Positrons they possessed, they had just spent on gas during their quest to the Greatest Extreme and Boogus Maximus. God continued sarcastically:

"We don't need much, just enough to ward off Satan's unfathomable evil deeds backed up by all the Weirdoes bottomless resources of Negatrons."

Jesus sat heavily in a chair next to Marilyn who was smacking her gum. "Sapsuckers" said Marilyn.

"Sapsuckers?" questioned Jesus. Marilyn elaborated.

"Yeah, the sapsuckers. Didn't you blow your entire life's savings restoring their world back to a love producing state? It has been over twenty years since you did that. Maybe they're turning a profit in Positrons."

God was visibly relieved.

"Marilyn, you're a genius!" he said. "Where would we be without you? Whose up on them anyway?"

Marilyn was way ahead of the Gods and had already looked up the archangel in charge of the Sapsuckers Planet. After a quick call, she hung up the phone.

"There are several million Positrons at our disposal, thanks to the Sapsuckers." she said. It is written that the Gods embraced, not surprisingly with Marilyn and her big mammerian mcgillicutties in the middle.

"We're saved! I say we clean out the account and book to Earth before it's too late" suggested Jesus.

"I've got a better idea" offered the Lord. "Why, don't we stop by Judas's planet and score some dope before we go so we can deal with things with a good buzz on?"

"Good idea" replied the Nazarene.

AND SO IT WAS WRITTEN AND SO IT WAS DONE.

^%$#^%

It is written that when the Gods arrived at Earth, freshly stoned out of their minds on Draconian Mindwarp, things were actually worse than they could have imagined. Neither had really paid much attention to the planet Earth after Jesus' second coming so it was difficult for them to understand what had happened there. It seemed that some strange off shoot of the dominant species had taken over, living in the cities, while the majority of the beings lived in the wilderness and seemed to have regressed into a kind of stone age.

The primitive clowns wore brightly colored yet filthy loincloths with simple rags tied around their huge feet for shoes. Most of the clowns looked half starved and their faces were devoid of color underneath layers of grime and dirt. The females were topless and many carried around emaciated looking babies. The clowns treated them badly and it looked like the mating ritual had become that of rape and forced servitude. The clown barbarians appeared to live together in loosely organized tribes and seemed to spend most of their time being mean to each other. God and Jesus were shocked to see the clowns in such a sorry state. These were supposed to be some gentle, funny people. The root cause was not clear but it was obvious that Satan had been up to no good there for many years.

As usual, after seeing what their neglect had done the Gods felt guilty.

As the Low-rider of the Gods traveled, in low Earth orbit, they found that the story of the Planet's inhabitants was the same across the globe.

"We better have a look at the Platypus!" said God.

"I agree!" replied Christ who set coordinates in the navigational computer for the island continent of Australia, where the Platypus lived.

God stomped down hard on the accelerator and four minutes later they had arrived in orbit above the land down-under.

"Run a sensor probe of the continent, Son and see if you can locate the little creature." Jesus did as he was asked.

"Aye, Sir…sensors are picking up life signs consistent with the genetic makeup of the Platypus. Setting coordinates for a landing now"

The low-rider responded and soon the Gods had touched down smoothly in a lucky clearing in the jungle. Jesus got out of the vehicle and whipped out his tricorder to get a bearing on the location of the Platypus.

"Getting anything, Son?"

"Life signs, Dad, due East…wait…I am picking up two more patterns…clowns! Two clowns directly between us and the Platypus."

The gods made their way through the thick brush. It was swelteringly hot and the air buzzed with insects. The two had to keep swatting the carnivorous ones, an act which caused God to wonder why he had ever invented such pesky creatures.

"I must have been crazy" remarked God swatting at the back of his neck.

Presently, the angels came upon a little encampment barely holding its own against the constantly encroaching jungle. Two clowns dressed in animal skins were tending to the roasting of some small unknown animal over a campfire. The Gods approached carefully and once within earshot announced themselves...

"Hello, there!" said God waving at the two startled clowns.

The clowns were startled for two reasons. One because it had been several years since they had seen another living soul and two because they had never seen a human being before…much less an angel. They didn't know what to say.

"We come in peace" said Christ with palms out stretched in a very disarming manner. "Perhaps you have heard of me…I used to be very famous here on Earth…my name is Jesus."

Blinko was shocked. What would Jesus be doing in the jungles of Australia… much less particularly in his little bivouac? But. then there could be no doubt that whoever this person was he was definitely NOT a clown. And neither was the old man behind him. Anyway, Blinko was no wimp and was not afraid to speak his mind.

"I have heard the name Jesus to be sure and you would not believe some of the things I have done in his name, but the Jesus I believe in is a clown. Pardon me, pal, but you ain't no clown."

Jesus was slightly amused by the dilemma. Obviously, it would take forever to explain so he opted for the easy way. And with a wonkle, wonkle there stood a grinning, red nosed, white-faced clown with a bald head encircled with bright green hair. Jesus now wore gigantic red shoes over striped sox under plaid pantaloons. He then started dancing a little jig while honking a brass horn with the gloved hand that was not holding the balloons. Then, Jesus the Clown reached down inside his over-sized pantaloons and pulled out his ukulele, which he began to play. In a funny clown's voice he began to sing:

Ah-ding-ding
Ah-ding-ding-Ah-diddle
I play this instead of a fiddle!
And would you like to be my friend?
Ah-biddle-biddle-boodle-baddle-blim!

Ah-diddle-diddle-fiddle-faddel bingo
Ya know I think you're really kinda neato!
And would you like to be my friend?
Ah-biddle-biddle-boodle-baddle-blim!

After this display Blinko was convinced that Jesus was THE Jesus. So was Nastina, who was standing at Blinko's side. It is written that what followed was a rather long conversation between the clowns and the angels about a host of things. For one thing, Blinko had a lot of questions about why God wanted all mimes to die and the shocked angels gladly cleared it all up for the clown. They, of course, had nothing to do with all that bozokahkah and explained that this type of thing was classic devil's work. Blinko was not surprised to learn that he had, unknowingly, spent most of his life serving the devil. He had already gotten used to the fact that his life for the most part had been a lie…he had just never had any other explanation for the way things had happened. Blinko was relieved to finally have some of the answers. So was Nastina, who, for the longest time, had never been able to understand how God could have wanted her people to be slaughtered. God's explanations put her fears to rest, also.

Once all the confusion was cleared up, the clowns suddenly felt incredibly humble for they were, in fact, in the presence of God and Jesus the Clown. Both fell to their knees wringing their hands in awe. Now, the angels were able to get back to their original business.

Jesus and God took turns explaining to the prostrated clowns a short version of their recent journey and eventually got around to the importance of the Platypus. Blinko and Nastina were amazed. They could hardly believe that the fate of the entire Universe literally hinged on that stupid looking, beaked marsupial splashing away like a retard in a near by pond. But it was true. God had said it himself.

Now, they were all standing next to the pond looking at the Platypus frolicking in the water. Jesus was talking.

"Believe me, I can hardly believe it myself. That ugly little animal is the most important thing in the Universe right now. But listen to this. We have come to learn that Satan has stepped up his evil operations here on your planet and we are pretty sure it is because he has learned of the importance of the Platypus. Satan means to cause the clowns to destroy the Earth and in the process this little creature. As a matter-of-fact, we are here to stop the devil if we can. But we cannot be in two places at once. I want to ask your help."

Blinko and Nastina were stupefied. Jesus the Clown was actually standing right there asking THEM for help. At this point, Blinko was speechless. Nastina posed the obvious question.

"What must we do? You wish is our command."

God took over:

"We would appreciate it if you would take it upon yourselves to guard the Platypus with your lives. There is no way to know how the devil will go about bringing destruction to the Platypus, but we would feel better knowing that there is at least someone here to try and protect it." Nastina was puzzled.

"Surely, the best way you can protect the Platypus is to take it with you."

Jesus shook his head to disagree.

"I'm sorry miss but we are about to meet with the devil, head on, in an all out war. The Platypus will be much safer hidden away in this jungle."

"But, why not take the Platypus to another world all together? One that is not on the brink of destruction?"

God spoke:

"I am afraid it is not that simple. This is the only Planet capable of supporting a life form such as the Platypus. I almost never repeat myself with my creations, you see."

Blinko had finally gotten over his lip lock.

"But, how can two mere clowns defend the Platypus from a being as all powerful as Satano?"

"It will not be easy…" said Christ. "You must have a great deal of courage my friend. Here take this." Jesus had his hand out.

"This is a secret weapon for you to use in the event that the devil shows up here himself. You will need to improvise a little to make use of it but it should be sufficient."

Blinko took the secret weapon and stuck it in his pocket.

"Uh…thanks." He said.

"Well then…" said Jehovah. "That pretty much sums it all up. We would like to stay but we really must be going. Got a war to fight."

Jesus nodded in agreement. It is written that the clowns bid God and Son farewell and watched in amazement as they angels flew away in the Low-rider of the Gods.

"Holy smoke, Blinko!" said Nastina.

"I know. It's hard to believe isn't it?"

^%$#%$

While Jehovah and Jesus continued to survey the planet, in order to understand what course of action they might take, Satano was busy with his sinister plans.

Satano was aware of the God's presence near Earth but unfortunately for him they were employing a cloaking device. He wasn't worried about exactly where they were though, because he considered the two to be has-beens anyway. Besides, his powers were tremendous, for he had the backing of the Weirdoes, and therefore felt very sure of himself. Jehovah and Jesus were no threat to him.

Anyway, as fate would have it, it just so happened that this was the very day that he had decided to finalize all his evil plans on Earth. Incredible coincidence? What else?

Satano found Sicko in a field just outside of Buffoonville. The demon manifested himself before the clown gone bad who was in the process of taking the Obvious.

"You like that stuff don't you, Sicko."

The devil had come in his ancient reptilian form. His form was that of a winged, red scaled demon with the eyes of a snake. Sicko spoke to him…

"Master…what brings you here?"

"It is judgment day, Sicko…you have completed the Doomsday Device, haven't you?"

"Yes master…it is finished. Can you not see it?"

Sicko was pointing to what looked like a fair sized mountain.

"Oh, I see. Well, I am pleased. Here, have another swallow of juice."

The devil had forced Sicko back onto his back with one hand while jamming the bottle down the clown's throat forcefully with the other.

"Hmm…it doesn't want to stay put. I'll fix it though."

Sicko could feel the bottle begin to grow inside him, it became impossibly huge which made the clown smile.

"This bottle has a special additive" sneered the devil.

"Thank you, master." And then he passed out.

When he came to, moments later, the first thing he noticed was that he felt much worse than usual and again a smile erupted across his face. Then Sicko noticed that the little lump of coal serving him for a heart had begun to wither until it finally crumpled into dust. The evil syrup had purged the last traces of goodness from his soul.

"How do you like it, Sicko? I have just given you a potion that has made you immortal. Every microbe of good in you has been vanquished into the lonely abyss. You are now pure concentrated evil."

Sicko got up off the table and stretched.

"I really feel bad…I mean I feel just awful."

"That's how your supposed to feel…you like?"

"It's the most!"

Sicko bowed to his master. The devil had some explaining to do.

"You will find, Sicko, that you now possess supernatural powers. You will use these powers to spread my evil across the globe. Now, go into the day and usher in the darkest night your world has ever seen. There are millions of clowns in the wilderness who have lost their way. You will use your powers to bring them here to Buffoonville. You will show them the way back to the Carnival of Despair. Then you will push the button and destroy them one and all. Go now and do your worst!"

Sicko nodded to his master and outstretched his arms in the pose of a crucified man. Then, he began to rise into the air until he was at an altitude sufficient to look down upon the entire town. Sicko let out an insane laugh as all the forces of evil gathered around him. It filled every aspect of his being and ultimately he stood on every corner of the world…he was now omnipotent and capable of being everywhere at once. Then it began.

&%^#^%

The mid day sun was eclipsed by a black disc casting darkness upon the globe. The cries and moans of the dead could be heard as millions of corpses clawed their way to the surface to walk among the living. Birds fell dead from the sky to be eaten by hordes of insects which covered the ground like a thick crawling carpet. The flowers and grass shriveled and died along with even the mightiest of trees. The oceans turned to blood and the earth began to quake. The air was filled with massive swarms of locusts, flies and hornets. It was indeed the beginning of the end of the world.

The clowns of Earth were in a panic. Most had fallen to their knees pleading for God to have mercy on them. This was the moment God and Jesus had been waiting for but unfortunately for them, as well as the inhabitants of Earth, the Gods had chosen that very same moment to park the low-rider behind the moon to get stoned. Therefore the cries and pleas of the millions of frightened clowns went unanswered.

Sicko seized the moment and manifested himself everywhere in the form of a titanic dismembered head, miles across. The floating head bellowed in a voice that could be heard by all. He would deceive the terrified clowns in this moment of their greatest fears and act as their savior…Sicko Messiah.

"I will lead you, my children!" said he.

"Take us, oh ,Lord, to salvation!" said they.

It is written that great and forceful winds came forth and swept the millions of clowns from the surface and into the air. Sicko was using his powers to bring the clowns to Buffoonville. The skies were filled with millions of screaming clowns. Many of them impacted into mountain sides or buildings or trees or any other object set in their path dying horribly. Soon, the multitudes that survived the trip began to arrive at the old fair grounds outside Buffoonville where Sicko had parked his choo-choo train.

&^$#^&

"The Platypus!" shouted Blinko to Nastina over the howling winds. Fortunately, the thick jungle, although quite dead, provided a marked break in the gales. Tree trunks and other debris flew all around the clowns as Nastina jumped into the shallow pond to scoop the frightened platypus up into her arms. Blinko came and held them both with his ape like limbs, protecting them from the mayhemic tornadoes and jungle shrapnel as best he could. He pushed them to the ground using his body as a shield. Here they remained while the storm raged for the next several hours until finally the winds died out and all was calm.

Exhausted, Nastina placed the little marsupial back in its pond. Then, she spoke to her brave clown who was dusting himself off.

"The poop must really be hitting the fan huh?"

"I guess!" said the battered clown.

^&%#$^

A great swarming mass of freaked out clowns blown in by Sicko were assembled in the fields outside Buffoonville before a kind of oddly shaped mountain. The mountain was actually Sicko's freshly whipped doomsday device. The device was composed of a highly radioactive and unstable mixture of plutonium and whipped cream. This mixture in tandem with a very toxic poison meringue had been combined into a nine hundred million cubic foot nuclear creampuff housed in a sHell made from a combination of steel and graham crackers. The doomsday creampuff had been built in such a way that upon detonation it would effectively splatter the entire Planet with a thin layer of deadly radioactive pie filling, killing every living thing in an instant.

How could one clown, in poor physical condition, build such a fantastically huge device?

ANCIENT CHINESE SECRET!

A low hum of prayer was audible as the millions of clowns worshiped the massive floating head that was Sicko Messiah. Sicko Messiah spoke unto the multitudes:
"Judgment day is here!"
His words cracked the sky, thunderbolts crashing to the ground.

777

Meanwhile Jehovah and Jesus were totally fried.
"What time is it, Son?" asked God, lids heavy from the mindwarp. Jesus lifted his arm, in slow motion, to peer at his watch with his bloodshot eyes.
"It's three 'o clock."
"Oh!" God felt like he was missing something. Then he noticed the sun. It wasn't on. "This is it and we're late!"
God stomped the accelerator snapping Jesus hard into his seat as the G-forces hit him. "What?" he said.
"The sun is blacked out! It must be Hell on Earth!"
Jesus looked at the obliterated sun.
"Far out."

$%#@$@

Sicko's voice thundered.
"The time has come my children! It is time for us to be judged by the all mighty God…prepare yourselves and make friends with the dead for they too await judgment!"
The clowns were sent into another panic, finally realizing there were rotting corpses walking among them.
Sicko again began to make more needlessly dramatic statements, which were mostly cliches. Sicko might have been omnipotent but that didn't mean he was a very original speaker.
"Behold my children…"
He began to say but he was interrupted mid-sentence as a giant rubber mallet appeared in the sky above him. Before Sicko could utter another word, he was smashed into oblivion by the Hammer of the Gods. Jehovah and Jesus had used a decent portion of their stash of Positrons to smite Sicko the Immortal.
This bewildered the multitudes of clowns who thought their savior had just been smashed to paste before them. A hush spread across the seemingly infinite crowd who were in awe of the spectacle.

777

God waved his hand and the black disc that was blotting out the sun evaporated.

(More used Positrons.) Soon, the field was illuminated by the light of the sun. Then, the silence was broken by the sound of angels singing, harps twanging and pipe organs, all playing ancient circus music. The music brought comfort and peace to the petrified clowns. Dancing erupted throughout the multitudes as a golden staircase materialized and descended to the earth. (Still more used Positrons.) At the top of the staircase sat an enormous golden throne. Seated in that throne was an equally colossal old clown with a flowing white beard and a truly stupendous white afro. The clowns knew who it was. It had to be God. Jehovah looked down on them from his throne and outstretched his hands palms up.

Then there appeared before the throne a clown, grinning, red nosed, white-faced, with a bald head encircled with bright green hair. The clown wore gigantic red shoes over striped sox under plaid pantaloons.

The clowns could see it was Jesus the Clown who had begun to descend the staircase, his palms outstretched like that of the Lord. When Christ reached the last step, he stopped and addressed the multitude, who had stopped dancing to stand still, stupefied in silence, slack jawed at the events playing out before them. After all they had been through, this was like some kind of dream.

"Clowns of Earth, you have been deceived. Sicko is not you savior! Behold, I am Jesus the Clown!"

The clowns oohed and ahhhed as Jesus began to preach.

"Clowns beware! Satano is here to destroy you all!"

Christ was not prepared for the reaction this statement got from the clowns who suddenly began to scream, all pointing their chubby fingers his direction. Jesus nervously looked over his shoulder. There stood a towering red devil flapping his wings and thrashing his whip like pointed tail.

"Did somebody call my name?" said the devil, who began to laugh.

Jesus and God had not expected Satan to show up in person at that particular moment. The devil intended to take full advantage of this.

God immediately leapt from his throne, shouting out the devil's name.

"Lucifer!"

A mighty white thunderbolt erupted from the pointed index finger of the Lord. Satan laughed and held out his hand catching the weak thunderbolt which turned purple as it ricocheted off the devil's palm to eventually strike God in the chest. God screamed and fell to his knees. The bolt had knocked him senseless. But the devil did not stop there. With a snap of his cruel fingers, a giant guillotine appeared before the throne where God had fallen and with another snap God was positioned in it to be beheaded. Before Jehovah could react, the blade fell, chopping off his head. The clowns screamed. Jesus screamed. Satano laughed.

"God is dead!" said the demon.

But the fight wasn't over. Jesus took a mighty breath and swelled in size until he was equal to that of the hulking devil but it was then that he knew he did not possess enough Positrons to put up much of a fight. Still, he had to try. Satano turned to face him as the clowns watched in horror. Jesus pounced upon the devil but his weak powers were simply no match for Satano's. The devil had Christ in a headlock almost instantly, of which the Nazarene could not break free…try as he might.

"You and your father are fools to try a defeat me in your weakened state. Now God is dead and I have a special surprise for you…behold!"

Jesus was helpless and could only watch as the Earth before him split open to reveal a massive crucifix growing from the ground. Jesus shuddered at the sight of it. Then Satano threw Christ, in a mighty heave, landing him on the cross. Twisted branches erupted from the crucifix capturing the Nazarene. Thorns also came forth to create a crown which bloodied Christ's head. Satano again laughed as huge rusty nails appeared, flying into the wrists and feet of Christ nailing him to the cross. Crucified!

The clowns gasped. God was dead, Jesus was crucified and there stood Satano for all to see. Clearly it was the end of the world.

&^$#%$

The devil eyeballed the multitudes of clowns for a moment, pleased with himself and his easy victory over Jehovah and Jesus Christ. He knew then what he must do. Powers That Be, be dammed, he was going to kill the Platypus and put a quick end to it all. At this moment, he could have chosen to set off the doomsday device but now, he was already involved personally. To Hell with the subterfuge! He would delight in doing it himself. Satano began to flap his wings, which created a great turbulence, knocking over thousands of clowns as well as the dead who stood by them. Now, he was airborne and on his way to the land down-under.

&^$#%$

Blinko and Nastina were just getting over the hurricane and were watching the Platypus as it mindlessly swam in the cool pond. That was when Satano appeared in the sky above them. Blinko was the first to notice the shadow on the ground cast by the flying devil who circled above like a vulture.

"I think it's Satano himself!" said Blinko to Nastina pointing up at the flying demon. Both grew fearful.

The devil landed before them and began to shrink until he stood in equal proportion to the two clowns he had found there in the jungle. Blinko did not hesitate to act.

The skinhead clown ran as fast as he could towards the devil, then threw himself down at the demons feet kissing the cloven hooves.

"Master…oh master…how long I have waited for this moment. I have spent my life in your service and studying the omens. I had a vision that one day you would come to this place to kill the Platypus, and here for many years, I have waited for your arrival! Oh, what a glorious moment this is indeed."

Nastina understood and came beside Blinko to worship the devil with him. Satano was impressed. Regardless of the pressing matter at hand, there was always time for him to bask in the ego boosting presence of devoted slaves. He genuinely lived for stuff like this. Satano reached out and patted Blinko on the head.

"Stand before meo my loyal servanto and tell me your name!"

Blinko stood slowly, head down, unable to make himself make eye contact with the devil.

"Blinko, master…the name's Blinko and this is my wife, Nastina."

The devil reached out his hand.

"Put her there, Blinko…nice to meet 'ya." Blinko reached out timidly with his own, to shake hands with the devil.

Satano could hear a ringing in his ears and screamed looking down at his hand, which he was somehow unable to release from the clowns grasp. His hand was turning porcelain white. Then, the whiteness began to spread evenly across the surface of his red, leather like skin, moving relentlessly up his arm. Soon, it had grown to cover his entire torso as was moving down his legs. Finally, the white spread up his neck and enveloped his head. In the process, the whiteness had transformed him from an ugly demon into a stunningly beautiful angel complete with feathery white wings. Satano's Negatrons had been systematically converted to Positrons and the reason for this was simple. Blinko had shook hands with the devil and in that hand he had wielded the secret weapon given to him by Christ…THE ALL IMPORTANT JOY BUZZER

777

Lucifer smiled at Blinko and Nastina who were amazed by the transformation.

"I feel great!" said the angel. "Thanks! I needed that. I mean I really needed that!"

Blinko bowed in front of the angel.

"My pleasure" he said.

Lucifer looked towards the heavens and smiled. Then, just as his smile reached its zenith, the fresh angel remembered what had happened only moments before back in Buffoonville and realized what he must do.

"You will have to excuse me, friends, but there are matters that I must attend to." And with that Lucifer took flight.

It is written that it was only a matter of moments and a few generous apologies for Lucifer, using his vast recently converted powers, to remove Christ from the cross and heal his wounds. Then, he turned to the decapitated God and closed his eyes. A glow began to emanate from the neck of the Lord and his head reattached itself. The Lord came to his feet reanimated and feeling as alive as he could remember. God looked upon the face of Lucifer standing there and was pleased. He ran down the stairs arms out stretched.

"SON!" he said! Lucifer and the Lord came into each others arms.

"FATHER!" said Lucifer.

"GROUP HUG!" said Jesus and the three embraced.

It is written that a father was finally reunited with his long estranged son. And vice versa. Would you believe that all this bozokahkah was caused by a simple argument thousands of years ago? And an argument over what? God and Lucifer could neither recall what it was about because it had been so long ago. Jesus on the other hand remembered precisely what his brother and father had quarreled about and could only hope that the two would not remember the incident and begin to argue again. After all, the conflict had never been resolved as to whether the toilet paper roll should roll from the top or the bottom. And it had only resulted in Lucifer's banishment, which of course is what started all this trouble in the first place. Such was the pride of a father and the rebelliousness of a son. But that is another story...

SAYETH THE OWL

THE END